Whirligigs in the Backyard

A MEMOIR BY

BEVERLEY JONES

Ark House Press
arkhousepress.com

Cataloguing in Publication Data:
Title: Whirligigs in the Backyard
ISBN: 978-1-7640298-4-1 (pbk)
Subjects: REL012170   RELIGION / Christian Living / Personal Memoirs; REL020000 RELIGION / Cults; REL012030   RELIGION / Christian Living / Family & Relationships.

Design by initiateagency.com

"The past is never dead. It's not even past."

WILLIAM FAULKNER, REQUIEM FOR A NUN.

This book is dedicated to Mike. For it was through his encouragement, support, patience, and unconditional love that I found the courage and energy to reach the end.

Table of Contents

Living in the Sticks

The first time my father told me he named me Beverley after a missionary from his church in Singapore, I was six years old. Too young to wonder if God would one day choose me for a similar high purpose. Instead, feeling vindicated for the effort, sacrifice, and hard work of being the middle child of five, I thrust my chest out towards my siblings, grinning until my cheeks hurt, to let them know I was special. '*I* wanted to call you Sonya,' Mum said, bursting my balloon, as she was inclined to do, before hubris carried me off. 'But your father thought the name had become too common amongst the Asians.' They both nicknamed me Evvy.

I knew about missionaries from Dad. He had told me about the American ones who had travelled to Singapore in the 1920s. 'To introduce the Seventh Day Adventist religion across the East,' he said. 'Americans are the smartest and fairest people in the world.'

'Why?'

'Because they're always inventing things. And they rescued the people of Singapore from the Japanese.'

I guessed those were reasons enough for Dad and his family to join what he said the missionaries called, 'The one true faith.' So, they would be 'assured a place in heaven.' God was paramount in my father's life. And ours.

Mum's revelation about my name did not mean anything to me at the time. Until I was eight and a half years old which was when I began to understand more about my family. It was the beginning of 1963. We had just moved into our brand-new home, out in the flat, fibro-filled waste-lands that sprawled across the Cumberland Plain. It was the only place where immigrants with large families could afford to live. The driest part of Sydney, it lay between the city and the Blue Mountains. Everything was new, in a sterile sort of way. Ancient trees sacrificed for lifeless streets in sparse suburbs. The atmosphere, still and pensive, like a siren was about to go off. Maps named it the Western Suburbs. City people called it the *sticks*.

I had memories from before the move, but it was not until then that I could put meaning to them. Like, why my brothers had unusual names. And why people stared at us. Though I did wonder why my father had nothing good to say about Asia or Asian people. Yet our mum had nothing but fond memories of both. Also, why the religion we practiced seemed to be a touchy subject with Mum. Our parents often had words about it, after which the house would be silent for days.

Dad prayed to God a lot. He taught us to say 'grace' before meals, 'Like Jesus and Saint Paul,' he said. Lips tight, eyes closed, he would wait for absolute silence before commencing. Those times when one of my brothers was fidgeting or talking, I thought I would die of boredom. Sometimes, through a squint, I sneaked a look at his face. Fatigue often showed in his eyes and by the slump of his shoulders. His silky, soft grey hair always looked as if he had just shampooed it. Once I noticed dots beginning to show on his nutty brown skin. *Was our father getting old.* Because he was my favourite person in the world, I never stopped worrying about his health. Had nightmares about losing him forever. He seemed so earnest about this praying thing, I never wanted to upset him. Best close my eyes and bow my head.

Until the move to the *sticks*, I did not know that being a member of the Seventh Day Adventist religion was unusual. Now I was learning that there were not many of us. Adventists, as we followers called ourselves, worshipped on Saturdays when everyone else we met in Australia went to church on Sundays. 'God proclaimed the Sabbath to be the seventh day of the week,' our minister had said. 'He made it holy because he rested on that day after creating the world.'

'So why do other people go to church on Sundays?'

'Because a Roman emperor changed the seventh day from Saturday to Sunday.'

Our Sabbath began at sunset on Friday and finished at sunset on Saturday. Because it was a day of rest, believers refrained from many types of work and activities such as cooking, sewing, cleaning, gardening, and sport. In addition, we were required to prevent intrusions into the holy hours from worldly music, radio, and television programs or by newspapers, books, and magazines.

After dinner on Friday nights Dad encouraged us to read the Bible with him. The next day, at 9:00 a.m. sharp, we attended Sabbath School, which was the equivalent of Sunday School, where everyone else went, followed by Divine Service at 11:00. Dad drove us home for lunch, then we returned for Pathfinders, which was a youth group like Scouts and Girl Guides, but with a greater emphasis on religious development. Everything in our lives revolved around our faith. Our grandmother saw to that. We called her Granny Jones. Dad called her Mama. Mum called her the *old lady*.

The Sabbath was full of things I loved. Like wearing my one good dress, meeting other people, being with my family, and best of all not going to school. Since our mum had started working in an office, a couple of years earlier, our weekdays had been solely devoted to work and school. Both parents were now too busy for anything else. I remember jumping for joy when I heard Mum talking about the farewell party her workmates had given her when we moved. But then she got another job.

Mum used to catch a bus to work before our move. However, there were no buses to her new job, so Dad had to teach her to drive. We only had one car which meant she had to wake up extra early so she could drive him to the factory where he helped to make elevators. If we were awake, he would help us get breakfast before he left. Upon her return, Mum would help us dress, make our lunches, then set us off on the long walk to school. Then she would dress herself and drop Wayne off at a pre-school on her way to the office.

We did not have friends, only relatives. All the members of Dad's family had immigrated with us from Singapore. All together there were two aunts, three uncles, and thirteen cousins in Australia. We only saw Granny Jones, our uncle Terrence, who was Dad's youngest brother, and Cousin Andy whom our mum said was an orphan. Dad's eldest brother, our uncle Bill, his wife Aunty Margie, and their four children had stayed in Western Australia where we had once lived. Though the others lived in Sydney like us, we rarely saw them. So, after a while, they just became people who came in and out of our lives, from time to time.

'More than half are at war with each other,' Mum said about Dad's family. 'We don't talk to those ones. Or they don't talk to us. I've lost track.

They've followed each other around the world. Being close seems to cause them more anxiety than being separated. Your father was once close to his nieces and nephews who were his sister Violet's children. Until the brothers had fights with her.'

'What did they fight about?'

'Ask your father.'

I knew Dad would not tell me anything. Our parents argued a lot about Dad's family. Considering we had immigrated together I wondered what had caused them to fight so much.

My sister Glynis and I wore our best dresses to church, white cotton, stiffened with the starchy water Mum had saved from the rice she cooked each night. Glynis was the eldest. Two years older than me. Both parents had chosen her name, after their 'favourite British film star'. I envied everything about Glynis. Especially her curly hair. Mine was as straight and thin as cotton thread. In preparation to attend our new church, Mum had put it in curlers to make me 'look pretty'. It got so knotted; it stuck to the curlers. I cried so much she had to cut them out, which left uneven patches all over my head. On Monday, Dad had to take me to his barber after school who cut it short, like a boy.

Our brothers Dewey, LeRoy, and Wayne wore neck ties, with elastic that went over their heads because they were too young to wear real ties. Dad put cream on their hair which made it shiny.

'I've got the window seat today,' I yelled; the fly screen door slamming at my heels on the first trip to church from our new home. When you are one of five, you need to keep ahead of the pack. Our black 1947 Ford Prefect had square windows with shiny strips around the edges. A majestic warrior's shield doubled as a solid silver grille at the front. The Prefect led the way on our adventures, like a chariot, albeit a stumpy version.

In the treasured moments alone, before my brothers caught up, I rushed around it, dragged my fingers along its sides, inhaled the heady smell of lubricant from Dad's tinkering under the bonnet. The Prefect always made me feel like we were off on a grand trip to somewhere important. Only one configuration could take all the members of our family for an outing. Four in the back, two up against the straight-backed seat, each by a window and two in the middle, perched forward on the edge. Baby Wayne sat on Mum's knee in the front.

Once Dad had settled us in the back, the swishing sound from Mum's swing dress, told us she was on her way. Dad held her door open as she ducked her head to protect her pillar box hat, then he placed Wayne on her lap.

Mum muttered something when Dad put the key in the ignition. I could not make out what she said but Dewey started giggling. I tapped his arm; shushed him by placing a finger to my lips. The old Prefect had let us down before. But not this time. The sputt, sputt muffled the sigh Mum released, and we were off to the first set of traffic lights.

Sitting high atop a pillow, I spotted the family in the car alongside, craning their necks to stare at us. I lowered my eyes to avoid theirs zeroing in on me.

'Dad. Why are those people staring?' No answer. Just a fiddle with his moustache. 'Dad. Why are those….'

'Because they're curious about where we come from,' Mum responded. 'And don't you dare stick out your tongue at them.'

I pouted and sunk down into the musty scent of the weathered leather seat, wishing I had sat in the middle. I knew I would remember that day for many reasons. Firstly, because it was our last trip in the Prefect. Dad swapped it for a bigger car the next week. Secondly, because I wondered why we lived in a country where we looked different from everyone around us. And, because forever after, I would wish I had stuck out my tongue.

1.1

Winter in the Western suburbs was a dark and scary time for our family. During the first one in our new home, its grip tightened so much, our house became an ice box. The water in the pipes froze. Dad and Mum were too cold to straighten up, so they walked with their backs bent over.

'It's as cold as Leeds.' Dad whispered to Mum one day, but I heard him.

'Where's that?' No response.

The bitter cold triggered Mum's nostalgia for her youth in a country devoid of winters, which in turn reminded her of our arrival in Australia. 'Remember when we came here?' she said to Dad with a twist of her lips. 'It was August. We thought we'd die. Fremantle was so damn cold.'

'Honey, please don't swear in front of the children.'

Mum ignored him and continued, directing her story to us children. 'Your father and his brother Bill lit a bonfire in the garden. I remember the flames leaping to the sky. You children thought it was a magical playground. Running and screaming with joy. But the fire got out of hand and started gobbling up the dry grass.

'The neighbours came running over yelling out. "Hey, you can't do this in Australia mate." They helped us put it out. They said we could have burnt down the damn house. Your father and Uncle Bill came home the next day with two electric heaters. We'd never seen one of those before. Aunty Margie, and I huddled around it the whole day. You children said it made the house feel like it was haunted.'

During summer we outgrew our winter clothes. So, within a week of the start of that terrible winter, Mum arrived home with new overcoats, bonnets, and gloves. Muttering something about Leeds again, Dad insisted we wear them, even in the backyard on some days. I hated them. They made me itch and scratch. Dewey and LeRoy broke out in red rashes.

The worst part about the cold weather for our family was how it increased the asthma attacks that our brothers and Dad had to endure. Mum said they had inherited it from Dad's father. Though they all suffered, the doctors described the severity of Dad and Wayne's as 'chronic and acute'.

Soon, asthma became the boogie man in our house each winter. He did not have the claws, sharp teeth, or wear a black cape and hood, like the 'man from bumpety boo' who Dad had invented for scary stories when we were little. But I imagined this one as the devil, with a shadow that grew longer and darker in winter, lurking around the corners of our house, waiting to pounce.

There was no one to talk to about how I felt. Mum only heightened my fears by confiding her own, 'Asthma plagued your father's family. Leeds is where Andy's mother, Moira, died from an asthma attack. She was your father's younger sister. Only twenty years old.'

Oh no. I wish I hadn't heard that. Dad never talked about Moira; only Mum did. *Dad's got grey hair. He must be going to die soon. I wish I could make him happy.* Poor Mum, with only in-laws in Australia, whom she did not like very much, she had no one to confide in other than us children. But sometimes I think she forgot we were children. Dad did not want to draw attention to his illness in case he lost his job. And so, we never talked about it outside our family. We suffered in silence.

1·2

A restaurant called The Malaya opened in George Street, across the road from Sydney University campus, the same year as we moved. Uncle told us about it. We became loyal patrons from the beginning. Now, whenever Mum said her 'mouth was watering' we piled into the car for the forty-minute drive to the city for a food fix. According to Mum, it was the 'only place in Australia where they serve food like back home.'

The urge would often arrive after Mum had recounted one of her childhood stories about the glorious variety of Asian food she would buy for a few cents from the hawker men. Or the blissful youth with servants to clean and cook. Mum never hid how homesick she felt for her family and her homeland. Poor Dad. He was trying so hard to make life easier and happier for our family. *But why did we come here if Mum seems so unhappy.*

On the long drive to the restaurant, Mum often entertained us with her stories about her never-ending search for Nonya-style food. 'Fish and chips. That's all we could buy when we came to this country. Your father used to drive to the city to search for ingredients and restaurants. We never found any. So, we'd go to the cafeteria at the big department store called Mark Foys for Cornish pasties. *Aiyoh.* I used to mix a little of the yellow curry powder I bought from the corner store. Tasted like it had been on the shelf for a hundred years but I mixed it with water and dipped my pasty into it. Back then, it was the closest thing to a curry puff.'

On another trip, we heard the story of how Mum and Aunty Margie shared in the food misery. 'We bought Heinz spaghetti in tomato sauce because there weren't any noodles. We added Peck's anchovy paste as a substitute for prawn blachan. And fresh chillies from the Italian neighbour's garden. It was the closest thing we could make to Mee Goreng from back home. But it never tasted like it.'

The owner of The Malaya was a man of Chinese origin. When Mum first told him where she was born, his eyes lit up. His travels throughout South East Asia had inspired him to create the restaurant. Despite the scarcity of suitable ingredients, he had managed to recreate some of the Nonya-style recipes to satisfy the increasing demand from immigrants from the region flowing into Australia.

The waiters' faces would light up when they saw us at the door, their squinty eyes almost disappearing. I remember the day one of them raced to let us in, ushering us past the small, laminated tables, towards a huge round one, with a sort of turning thing in the centre which made it look like a giant version of the record player in our new stereogram, which Mum had bought from the company where she worked. Hands clutched together like he was praying as if to contain himself, the waiter leaned in so we could all hear, then whispered, 'The boss is *sooo* happy to see you children eat our spicy food. He installed it just for you.'

My parents no longer needed to look at the menu, they had their usuals. Dad ordered the Special Chicken Curry and Mum the Char Kway Teoh. Now that I was almost ten years old, I grabbed a menu to order my own. I liked to mimic the way the Chinese waiters ran two or three words into one for the Malay dishes they had difficulty pronouncing. Unlike Dad, who insisted on saying each word individually.

In his pukka English accent, he ordered, 'Mee ... Goreng. Special ... Chicken ... Curry. Char ... Kway ... Teoh.' I giggled at the sight of his eyelids shuttering up and down as the waiter read back the order, 'Meegren, Chicorry, Qwaydu.' Thank goodness the dishes we ordered included plain boiled white rice, which the waiter called Wye-rye, or we might have died of starvation waiting for Dad to finish.

On the trip home, I slumped against the door in the crowded back seat of our silver Valiant station wagon, a fitting replacement for the old black Prefect. Belly full, satiated, and sleepy, I drifted off hearing Dad say to Mum, 'Char Kway Teoh is pronounced with three words, Honey, not one.'

1.3

The chaotic activity of our move had taken my mind off the start of another school year. Then, even the fun of running around our new back-yard could not quieten the butterflies gnawing at the insides of my tummy. This would be my fifth new school in four years. Standing at the bottom of the steps to the principal's office with my siblings, waiting to be enrolled, I reflected on the welcoming message I had received at the age of six from my third new teacher. 'Don't expect special treatment. You're no different to the other children.'

I did not know what my teacher meant by those words, but I had wondered why everyone stared at my siblings and me. It had made me feel stupid. Like a bird had pooped on my hair. Or I had spots on me or something. I reckon Miss *Strongarm*, the nickname I had assigned to that teacher after watching wide-eyed as she lifted a boy in my class high above his desk with a single grab of his upper arm, had a book of warnings for new children. I was thankful she had never hit me across the fingers with her wooden ruler like she had some of the other kids. I would have hit her back. Like I hit my brothers when we had fights.

The remainder of my infant school years had been an endless procession of other types of pain. Nurses jabbing me with vaccine needles. Health officers running paper straws through my hair to sift for lice. Dentists pry-ing in my mouth. I could not escape the creepy feeling in my hair, or the screams from children getting needles, but the dentists never got a chance to drill my teeth. I took the permission notes from my bag, ripped them into tiny pieces, then tossed them in the garbage bin on the walk home. Dad's promise that this would be our last school had come too late. So many moves meant I had no friends to anticipate seeing at the beginning of each year. I preferred my siblings anyway. We had learnt to occupy ourselves after our mum had started working.

'You both look so grown up in your new uniforms,' Mum said, bringing me back from my daydreaming.

'At least I'm old enough now to dress like the others,' I whispered to Glynis, proud of our forest green tunics over crisp white blouses. 'Maybe now the other children will think we look like them.'

Once inside the principal's office, Mum sat in a big chair across from him. We gathered around her, like bodyguards. Glynis on one side, me on the other, each resting a hand on her shoulder. Dewey sat cross legged on the carpet at her feet. LeRoy on her knee. Wayne was at pre-school.

'The boys have unusual names,' the principal snorted as he cast an eye over each one of us before staring back at Mum.

'They were named after Americans who helped rebuild Singapore after the war.'

'Yes. I see from the paperwork the children were born there. Does the family speak English at home?' A deathly silence filled the room. I shot a look at Mum. *Oh no. I hope his question doesn't upset her.*

'Of course,' Mum said, forever even-tempered. 'It's the first language of Singapore you know.'

'No. I didn't know that.'

Mum made me feel so proud. Does every child think their mum is beautiful? Dad called ours Honey. Said it was because she was so sweet. I had become accustomed to seeing our mum dress up in pretty dresses for Sabbath and the office where she worked. For the interview she had chosen her rose-coloured dress made from a crinkly sort of material. Mum said it was the latest for working women because it could be washed instead of dry-cleaned. Compared to other mothers, ours seemed more delicate, soft. Her eyes, almond shaped, deep brown, almost black like her hair. Skin, crisp, moist, and eggshell white, like the inside of a pear. Nose, tiny and flared. Cheekbones, so high they jutted out from her face. Lots of people stared at our mum.

'The children are English,' Mum said with a smile. 'Like their father.'

'That must be where the Jones comes from. Is their father dark skinned?'

'Yes.'

Lots of people asked about the colour of Dad's skin when he was not with us. I guessed it was because we all had brown skin like him whilst Mum's was so fair. *I get upset when they ask. Dad would be horrified.*

'I am Eurasian,' Mum said.

She happily told everyone this. Though no one ever knew what it meant.

'It is a mix of Asian and English. My father was also Eurasian. His father travelled from England to Malaya where he married my grandmother.'

I loved how proud Mum was to be Eurasian. I wanted to be proud too, but Dad did not like hearing anything with the word Asian in it.

'What religious denomination are the children?'

When Mum said we were Seventh Day Adventist, my body tingled with delight at the memory of Dad's words about our family being assessed for the government home loan as 'house proud, hard-working, and Christian.'

'Well, there's no one from that religion in this school. They'll join the Anglican scripture classes.'

That night, as Mum prepared dinner, I caught the twitch in Dad's face when she recounted the story of the meeting with the principal.

'Fancy asking if we speak English at home,' she laughed.

Oh no. Dad's pinching the top of his long, fleshy nose with his thumb and forefinger. Next, he'll run them down the length of it. When he reaches the base of his nostrils, he's going to spread his fingers on each side of his bushy moustache. I think it's how he controls his temper. A sort of calm before the storm. I love the way it parts into two wings and drapes over the top of his mouth. Mum says it disguises his thin lips.

Dad's eyes met mine across the table. 'They know so little about the British Empire and her Colonies. I thought Australians would know more. I am English and so are you children. Your grandfather was born in Barnstaple. It's a town on the River Taw in Devon, on the Southwest coast of England. Just across the water from Wales where his family came from.'

Most people did not think Dad looked like the son of an Englishman, despite him telling them so. 'Not with that nutty brown skin,' some said. 'Or those deep-set, chocolate-brown eyes.' Nonetheless, he was identical in every other way to the old Englishman in the photo frame labelled *Papa*.

Dad had proudly told us that his papa was Walter Jones. He had joined the Army as a Boy Soldier in the last years of the nineteenth century where he had trained as an artificer. 'That is what the Army called a mechanic in those days.' Like many members of the British Army, Walter had served in India at some point during colonial rule.

My teacher had told the class about colonial rule in social studies. It was what the British Empire had established in Australia in 1788, then in India in 1858 where they called it the Raj. That was how Papa Jones came to be there about forty years later. Dad said he was based at the fort in Madras as a Driver in the Supply and Transport Corps which was where he had met and married Dad's Mama.

I was glad Mum did not tell Dad she had told the principal she was Eurasian. I had witnessed him go into one of his moustache-fiddling routines just upon hearing that word. I wondered why it was so important. Especially when it did not seem to matter what we said, because most people just made up their minds based on how we looked.

Dad's words had always confused me. But not as much as Miss *Strongarm's*. When I told her about the funny words my mum used and how they made me giggle, she said, 'Well dear. You are not Asian. You do not have yellow skin.'

'Daddy says we are English.'

'Poppycock,' she said throwing her head back. 'You're not English. Your skin is not white. Your eyes are not blue.'

Our mother's skin was whiter than most of the people I had seen in Australia. Even my new teacher had a sort of pinky-coloured face. Some people had orange spots all over theirs. I decided I would look out for some different coloured people the next time the circus came to town. For now, I wondered why we did not live in a country where we looked like everyone else.

Our mum was good at changing the subject when she knew Dad was reaching the point where he might choke on his dinner. 'The principal said Dewey will be attending a different school because the education system has assessed him as being retarded.'

Glynis and I knew our brother had suffered an illness called meningitis when he was a toddler which had caused permanent damage to parts of his brain. Mum and Dad had hoped he would improve with time. However, our new principal had been advised about his problems from the previous school. After a thorough assessment it had been determined that his inability to retain information meant a *normal* school could no longer accommodate his needs.

'They're sending him to a special school in Strathfield,' Mum said through the tiny crystals I saw appearing in her eyes. 'They have their own bus to collect him each morning and bring him home. The principal said he can sit next to you Evvy, until someone comes to make the official transfer. Sometime next week.'

'He's not retarded,' Dad said, his shoulders slumping. 'He could develop normally with patience.' He pushed his chair back noisily. 'I'm going to help the boys get ready for bed.'

Dewey was not silly. He just could not concentrate on things. If we were trying to play a game, he would tease us or take the ball or bat, or whatever toys we were playing with and run away. We would have to chase him to get it back. He acted a lot younger than his age. For that reason, Mum and Dad treated Glynis and me as the two eldest. But Dewey was still their second child and first son. And my big brother by a year. We were close. My siblings and I only had each other. One of the benefits of being part of a big family was having ready-made playmates at any time. My tummy churned with fear at the thought of someone taking Dewey away from me.

My lips would not stop quivering when the lady from the special school arrived to take him. Watching Dewey place his hand into that of a stranger, forced me to grip his other so hard my knuckles hurt, reminding me of all the years we had kept each other safe. Then it slipped away. Though I knew I would see him that night, watching my brother being led away by a stranger seemed unnatural, eerie. I was angry with this new school for separating me from him.

Some summer days, it was so hot and dry, I thought I would perish. Like my teacher said the famous explorers had when they tried to walk across Australia. Both Mum and Dad were concerned about us walking through the sparse streets, so Dad drilled us to stick together. 'Like Jacob's sheep,' he said, quoting the bible. 'You must never deviate from the straightest route. And never speak to strangers. Glynis is in charge until your mother, or I come home from work.'

After Wayne started Kindergarten, Glynis chaperoned us to and from school. When the home bell rang, the four of us would meet under a big gum tree midway between the infant and primary schools. I tried hard to push away the thought of how responsible Glynis had become. And how much I resented her for it. I hated how she snitched on me for not heeding her warnings like staying on the same side of the road as her or not crossing until she gave me the nod. Dad should not have made her the boss of me. Who was ever going to listen to their big sister?

Whenever we came across people standing outside their houses, they would stare at us. The same way some women stopped Mum in the street to say, 'Oh my, look at their beautiful black eyes. Their silky brown skin.' Anyone would think the five of us looked the same. Apart from our eyes, our features were different from each other. Skin, varying shades of brown. Noses, different shapes. Some of us were tall, others short. Why must they stare? What's the big deal? Even if it was because they were curious as Mum said, it annoyed me. Dad said we were amongst the first immigrants from Singapore to come to Australia. Though more were coming, we were most certainly the only ones in our suburb. Nevertheless, I tired of hearing the women clucking.

Midday at school was horrible. The teachers forced us to eat lunch under the scorching skies, which was at odds with the weather out there in the west. It did not make sense to me. We sat on low-slung benches under a lone gum; our spit-polished, black shoes tap dancing amongst its dusty, mottled shadows.

'Schools in Malaya close at lunchtime because of the heat,' Mum said when I pouted about it. 'We used to walk home for lunch. When my family moved to Singapore, we'd buy Char Kway Teow from the noodle man's cart at the convent for two cents.'

Mum never quite got the hang of making lunches like the other kids brought to school. I remember the first time she decided to cook one of her Malay-style omelettes to put in our sandwiches. I missed the end of a dream because of it. Awoken by the smells and sounds emanating from our kitchen. Onions sizzling in globs of browning butter. The tap-tap-tap of eggs being beaten then blistering into a hot frying pan. The rustle of cellophane coming from the packet of crunchy beansprouts bought from the Chinese greengrocer near the city. I stumbled sleepy-eyed to see Mum sprinkling the black dots of salty soya sauce on top, then the omelette being sandwiched between two slices of buttered, milky-white bread.

'Peugh-ee, what's that smell?' The kids sitting either side of me said pinching their noses. Though Dad said he loved Mum's omelette sandwiches, we children complained. However, Mum continued to make them, sighing that she had 'no idea' what else to put in them. Soon we came to expect the same reaction despite how many times the familiar smell seeped out of our lunch boxes.

One morning, recognising the telltale cooking smells and sounds, I steeled myself for the inevitable taunts. But wait, that day something tasted nicer, sweeter, yummier. 'Hey,' I yelled out to my friends. 'I've got tomato sauce on them today.'

With no desire to trade their Vegemite, honey, or peanut butter sandwiches for a pongy one, the boys took off as soon as the bell rang. Doubling over from his loud, belly laugh, one of them stopped to poke his finger at the girl sitting at the end of my bench. Her lunch box had sprung open spilling something that looked like noodles swimming in a red sauce onto her tunic.

'Smelly garlic muncher,' he yelled.

Though I felt sorry for her, I lowered my head in silence, relieved it had not been me whom he had called a *wog, dago*, or even a *New Australian*, like lots of people called the immigrants from Italy, Greece, or just about anywhere. My throat tightened at the memory of what the owner of The Malaya had said about more Eurasians coming to Australia, wondering what awful name would be dreamt up for people like me. Better tell Mum not to give me the omelette sandwich for school any more, even though I've grown to love them.

Our journey home from school was long for little legs, during the thirsty summer months. The hot, compressed air hung heavy, like weighty curtains, ruffled only when the dusty pollen from the desert dry plains crawled into my nose, eyes, and ears, like the spindly legs of frenzied worker ants. 'My friends in Singapore warned me Australia was like a desert,' Mum said whenever I complained. Then, in the special way she had of brightening my day, she would remind me of one of my favourite stories. The one about her family catching the launch from her aunt's house in Prai to Penang Island, which always made me feel like my family was meant to live by the sea. Like it was in my blood.

2

Memory Keeper

Mum was our memory keeper. Deep in the suburbs of Australia, she kept us connected to our birth country by sharing the stories of her life in Malaya and Singapore. I listened closely, noticing the changes in her emotions whenever she recounted them. Her voice, full of joy when she teased us with tantalizing tales of glorious sounding food, softening when she spoke of her family, whimpering as she reached the end of those stories. Then, her face turning ashen as she spooked us with the spine-chilling experiences of living through the Japanese invasion of her homeland during the Second World War.

'My father was a railway driver in Malaya and Singapore. We lived a good life because Daddy always had a good job. That was before the war. Then the Japanese secret police, the Kempeitai, arrested him. They took him to work on the Burma Railway. He suffered there. They beat him and starved him. Did I tell you he helped a lot of Australian soldiers?'

I only knew this grandfather, whom Mum said the locals called Sonny, as the man in an old black and white photo dressed in a khaki uniform, boots, and white pith helmet. 'That's what he wore every day to work at the nearby station in Taiping. Except for special outings and church. Then he wore a white suit, white shirt, and tie. It was the European custom in Malaya.'

I felt sad knowing I would never see Grandpa Sonny when Mum said he had died within weeks of us immigrating to Australia. 'He carried you and your brothers and sister on the dock before our ship left for Australia. Glynis was four years old, Dewey three, you two, and LeRoy, only five months.'

I much preferred the fun stories of Mum's childhood, which she interspersed with choppy-sounding Malay words including a few profanities. Longing for the tastes of Asia, she would tell us endless stories about food. 'The tick-tock noodle man. That's the sound he makes by tapping his chopsticks on the side of his wooden cooking cart. The ching-a-ling, ching-a-ling of bicycle bells told us the satay man, or the ice man was nearby.'

'Please tell us my favourite Mum?'

Drooling from the memories, Mum would roll her eyes. Then as if she was telling us a secret she would whisper, 'Close your eyes. Imagine a man pulling up at our front door with a wooden cart full of heavenly, bite-sized snacks, called *kueh*. They're steamed so they're wobbly and sticky. But they don't look or taste anything like the cakes or puddings in Australia. They come in the colours of a rainbow. They make hot pink ones, frog green, yellow, orange. When you bite into them, the sugary coconut filling crunches between your teeth. I loved the purpley-blue ones. They're called *ondé-ondé*. The old Nonya women make them at daybreak, ready for the hawkers to sell for breakfast.'

After telling us that one, Mum would often stare into space with the hint of a smile on her lips as she added, 'I used to run out the front of our house with my brothers and sisters to buy one, for just one cent. They make the dough from a special sort of flour after they've coloured it with blue butterfly pea powder. They roll the dough into balls like walnuts, then fill the centres with a pinch of coffee-coloured *gula melaka*. The little balls are steamed over huge pots of boiling water. Then rolled in freshly grated coconut.'

Mum's eyes would grow into the size of saucers when she said, '*Aiyoh*,' as she emphasised the rise of the first syllable, 'When you bite into the centre, the sugar which comes from the sap of the flower buds of a coconut palm, we call it *gula melaka*, bursts in your mouth, crunching between your teeth. Sooo tasty *lah*.'

Mum's *lahs* sounded the same as the la-sound in the doe-re-me song. I loved seeing her happy face when she described biting into a piece of Nonya *ondé-ondé*. The mere mention of something as wonderful sounding as blue butterfly pea powder was enough to make me long to go back to the magical land where it came from. How had Mum coped with leaving such an enchanted life behind? I sensed her funny words were able to transport her back. I loved hearing them. They made me feel like we still belonged 'back home' as she continued to refer to Malaya and Singapore.

'What's a Nonya woman, Mum?'

'It's the Malay word for a Chinese woman born in the Malacca Straits.'

'Where's that?'

'On the west coast of Malaya where my mother was born.'

'How come you lived in both countries?'

'Well, the two countries were once joined at the hip when they were both part of British Malaya. After the war we moved to Singapore for my father's work.' Mum paused, then added, 'When we came to Australia, it was still called British Malaya. They've changed its name now, to Malaysia.' Despite the change, Mum continued to refer to her birthplace as Malaya.

Hearing about our other grandmother, whom we referred to as Granny Ware, made me want to go back home even more. 'What is your mother like, Mum?'

'Mummy was a very traditional woman. Very careful with money. She would save so she could buy each of us two new sets of underwear, socks, and Bata shoes every Christmas. She chose them from a catalogue from England. Mummy followed the rules of Queen Victoria. She was so darn strict. She whipped us with the bamboo cane if we got a bad report card. Rubbed raw chilli on our lips if we answered back.'

Oh gosh. She sounds like a tyrant,' Glynis said.

'She was a terror.'

'Tell us another story Mum.'

Through Mum's *tellings* I became intoxicated with the East of yesteryear, wondering if I would ever have similar exotic experiences or meet such enchanting people. I often giggled and copied her funny words. Forever dropping an *aiyoh* here, or a drawn out *lah* at the end of a sentence like Mum said the people back home did. I had hoped to draw Dad into revealing more about his life before we came to Australia. My actions just irritated him. To the point he would plead, 'Why ever would you want to speak that way?' Then he would admonish Mum, 'Honey, why do you encourage the children?'

'But what about before we came here?' I pleaded.

'What do you mean?'

'If not for Mum's stories, how would we know about where we came from?'

'Australia is your new country.'

'But it's not where we come from. Even some of the furniture we brought with us from Singapore is different,' I said pointing to the black teak coffee table and lamp stand. 'What about the stone pounder Mum uses to prepare the onions and chillies for Laksa? And they're nothing compared to what you and Mum brought inside you. That's part of us. Without those we're empty. Like castaways.'

'But you children are not Asian or Eurasian just because you were born in Singapore. I am English like my father. And you are English because of me.'

'We're not Australian Dad. And we don't even look English. We don't eat the same food. We don't sound the same. Why can't we be Eurasian like Mum?'

'You will have a better life in Australia if you forget about the past. It's why we came while you children are still young. The Asians are cruel people. No respect for human lives.'

I could not understand why Dad wanted us to leave Asia behind. However, I did not want to argue with him in case it brought on an asthma attack. They were becoming more frequent since the change in season.

2.1

Towards the end of the second year at our new school, the principal made an announcement in assembly one morning. 'The government has grave concerns that Australian children are still suffering vitamin deficiencies despite the milk scheme being in operation for some years. Starting tomorrow it will be mandatory for students to receive a daily dose of calcium. You will each drink a 1/3 pint, paid for by the government.'

The next morning, I watched in horror as the milkman stashed crates of small bottles into the brick bunkers which had been built near the front gates of the school.

'I'm not going in,' I said to Glynis as I turned and started walking home.

'You must. You're not allowed to go home on your own.'

'But they never forced us before. I hate this school.'

'I can't drink it either. But we can't go home.'

Sullen, sulky, and sick from the knot growing in my belly, I made my way to the classroom to await the drama I was certain would unfold at recess. The clink of bottles being delivered outside our classroom window by the newly appointed milk monitors, other children forced into making the delivery, made it impossible to concentrate in class.

'But I can't drink milk,' I cried to the teacher, my eyes squinting as the first drops touched my lips.

'You will grow to like it,' she scolded as I vomited it up.

After weeks of tears and vomit, the principal agreed to excuse us. But only if we brought a note every day from our mum. After making breakfasts and lunches, dressing us for school, driving Dad to the factory and returning to prepare herself for work, there was no time left to write silly school notes.

Dad's response to the milk fiasco came as a shock to us all, especially me, when he proclaimed, 'The children must have dairy products to grow strong and tall, like a European.' *Oh no. The pantomime of puke is about to play out at home as well as school.*

When the weekend arrived, he coaxed us to drink a glass of cold milk by adding two heaped teaspoons of a pale, yellow-coloured powder called malt. We all gagged and cried. The next Sunday, he tried cocoa powder with sugar. We gagged again.

'For goodness' sake, stop forcing the children,' Mum yelled from the bedroom at the continuous hullaballoo bouncing off the walls of our house. 'We only ever drank coconut milk back home.'

Determined we could 'learn to love it', Dad tried again the next weekend by whisking some of the milk with a raw egg and a few drops of vanilla essence into what he called an egg flip.

'It's delicious,' he said. 'And good for you.'

'Make sure they drink it in the bathroom,' yelled Mum.

I reckon our mum was smart. Because before getting to the bottom of half a glassful of the disgusting drink, each of us vomited in the sink, in the toilet, then all over the bathroom floor. Dad remained silent, despite wearing the disappointment on his face. I got the feeling he blamed Mum for not encouraging us to drink milk after she had finished breast feeding. He never forced us again, though he continued to extol the virtues of dairy products. Despite his disapproval, I was never going to drink milk. It was sour and smelly. It made me retch. On the days Mum forgot the note, we all vomited. Oh Dad, can't you see we're never going to look like Europeans. But did you know, I'm one of the tallest girls in my class.

3

Grandmother is Dutch Though She Was Not Born in Holland

The closest I came to hearing hints about our father's past life, occurred whenever Granny Jones paid a visit to our house. Except for the time Dad took Glynis and me, without our brothers because he said they were 'too hard to handle,' to visit her in the red brick cottage in the Sydney suburb of West Ryde where she lived. Mum assured me I had been to the house years earlier. Yet even as I stood on the front porch, I had no memory of it.

The little metal bell let out a strangled ring when Dad twisted it. I spun around towards the street, half expecting to see one of my brothers' bicycles come skidding around the corner. I recalled the vision of the vigorous nodding of Mum's head as we had jumped into Dad's car, 'We lived there for a while when we moved to Sydney. All seven of us crammed into one room. Till the argument and the old lady threw us into the street.'

I turned towards the street and wondered. Did Granny really throw her grandchildren out there? How old was I? Wayne must have been just a few months old. Is that why Mum did not come with us today? Does this grandmother not love us? So many questions but a rumbling belly and the sting from the mosquitoes feasting on my ankles fuelled an urgent desire to get off the dank concrete porch.

'Shush. Here they come,' Glynis said at the sight of two shadows growing bigger as they approached the frosted panes of the front door. Glynis was so good. Always behaving.

'There's Uncle Terrence and Granny,' she said as the latch clicked, twisted, and woosh we were swept in through a cloud of citrusy cologne.

I cupped one hand over my mouth and whispered, 'Oranges and lemons say the bells of St. Clements.'

'Mama,' I heard Dad say as he kissed Granny on the forehead.

'Hello Butch,' Uncle said shaking Dad's hand. That was what Dad's brother called him. It was a nickname. Like *mate*, which the neighbours called Dad and all the other men in the street.

Granny smiled at the sight of Glynis and me. 'Did you go to church this morning girls?'

'Yes,' Glynis replied as we filed through the dim passageway, towards the light at the back of the house.

We had come bearing gifts. 'Papaya is Granny Jones' favourite fruit,' Dad said placing two plump ones on the dining table. Granny swayed her hand, inviting the three of us to sit. Her arms revealed dusky coloured skin, like mine. We each pulled up a wooden chair. I sat across from her. Granny's hair was grey, braided into two plaits which looped together at the back, into a low-slung bun. I could not tell the colour of her face because she had covered it in white powder. She wore no lipstick or eye makeup. She looked fat compared to our skinny mum. She had massive breasts. The floral frock she wore made her look dressed up, as if for a special occasion. I guessed she had gone to church.

The table looked like Christmas. Granny had been busy baking. There were pastries and cakes. My eyes landed on a big plate, overflowing with misshapen, sugary, sandy-coloured caramels. I had seen them before but did not know it was this person who made them. Granny nodded towards the plate, 'They are made with jaggery. It comes from the sap of a toddy palm.'

I greedily grabbed the biggest piece. Stuffed it into my mouth. The sugar-water melted on my tongue. Some collected in my cheeks causing me to splutter, 'What's a toddy palm?' Nobody responded.

While we sucked on the crunchy caramels, I watched Granny peel the papaya then cut it into tiny pieces. She must have sensed me looking at her, for she lifted her head. Our eyes met. Hers, as dark as mine, glistened from a single shard of sunlight forcing its way through the lacy white curtains. They matched the crochet doilies on her table. Dad had been right about the papaya. He and Granny chatted away about all sorts of things.

I liked to hear them talking. The members of Dad's family only spoke English. Granny pronounced some of her words differently to Dad, but I would not have called it a strong accent. Not like some of the *new Australians* I had heard speaking at the shopping centre. Not like Peggy and her husband Con at the corner store. Not even like some of the Aussie kids at school. Granny Jones spoke English like what my friends called posh, the same as Dad. I wondered about her family.

Dad mentioned his work at the factory. I remembered how Mum had said he and his brothers had worked as supervisors of projects rebuilding Singapore after the war. I did not know what that meant but it sounded more important than what he did now. Then I thought about Papa Jones being in the Army when Granny met him. I wondered if she had ever worked like our Mum.

Their conversation moved onto other topics. I heard school, food, and cars mentioned. Also, the names of people whom I recognised as members of Dad's family. Hearing their names reminded me of our thirteen cousins in Australia who were little more than strangers to me. Even the ones in Sydney. Maybe Granny Jones had thrown them into the street too. I stared at my grandmother, wondering if she would ever teach me how to make her special jaggery caramels.

Dad interrupted my thoughts, 'Where is Andy today, Mama?'

We children loved Andy. He was our favourite cousin. Twenty years old and so cool. *Yes, where is he today?* Mum had told us the sad story of how he had become an orphan, at the age of two, when his mother died. It was why he lived with Granny and Uncle. Granny shrugged in response to Dad's question. Dad's eyes flickered and he dropped his head. He worried about Andy as much as he worried about us.

Sitting in Granny's dining room, eating caramels, exchanging smiles, made me happy. I thought about how my school friends said they loved to visit their grandparents. We did not have any grandfathers, but I wondered why we did not see Granny more often. Maybe if our mum liked her more, we could be like the other children at school who had lots of fun stories about their relatives. Dad woke me again from my daydreaming, 'We are going to take your grandmother for a drive to the city.'

Glynis sat in the front. Granny and I sat alongside each other in the back. I snuck peeks at her through the corner of my eye. She stared out the window at the hustle and bustle of busy streets, pausing every now and then to ask me a question. 'Do you like school? Do you study hard? Granny did not wait for my response before turning back to her window. There was not much for us to talk about. We hardly knew each other.

Whenever the car stopped, Granny waived her handkerchief around. Like I had seen the Queen of England do on television. Granny had tied a knot in one of the corners of hers then doused it with cologne. I wondered if she had learnt it from the queen. Each wave filled our car with her scent. When we stopped at the traffic lights near Central station, I watched her staring at two young women crossing the road in front of us. Her eyes followed them, until they reached her window. With a slow bend of her elbow and without taking her eyes off the passers-by, she raised the knot to her nose, took a deep sniff then muttered, 'Creatures.' I learnt that was what Granny called women. Especially the ones who wore lipstick.

On the long drive home after returning Granny to her house, I asked Dad questions about some of the things that intrigued me about his mama.

'Was Granny Jones born in Singapore like us?'

'My mother is a Dutch Burgher.'

'Is that a hamburger from Holland?' I giggled.

Annoyed I had made fun of his mother, Dad's response was stern. 'No, it is a person from Ceylon who has Dutch blood. 'My mother was born in a country called Ceylon.'

'Then why is she Dutch?'

'Because that country used to be Dutch. My mother's ancestors came from Amsterdam. The Dutch took it from the Portuguese. Then they gave it to the British.'

The new information stopped me in my tracks. I had heard the word Portuguese from Mum, but it was the first time I had heard of the country called Ceylon. I begged for more. 'Who owned the country before the Portuguese? Why did the Dutch take it from them? When did the British arrive?

'Stop asking questions. The country doesn't exist anymore.'

I had become aware of those times when our dad refused to answer questions about his life in Asia. His mood would change. It was as if he had pulled a veil over his head to conceal his face. Then his eyes would fill with those crystals, like our mum.

4

Tank

After Dad had almost died from an asthma attack in the car park at the local shopping centre, the emergency doctors at the hospital recommended the use of oxygen therapy at home. They hoped by combining it with his other medications, the formula could prevent his attacks from escalating.

The frightening looking cylinder arrived by truck. It was mostly black with patches of peeling white paint at the top. LeRoy and I nicknamed it Tank. A knot grew in my belly as I watched a man wheel it into a corner of Mum and Dad's bedroom. Instead of feeling relieved at the sight of something capable of fighting the boogie man, a feeling of dread washed over me. Tank's arrival had confirmed Mum's concern about Dad's asthma getting worse. *Was life going to be sad and dreary now? Would Dad still play with us in the garden, tell us funny stories at night?*

Whilst Dad let the delivery man out, we children gathered around the sinister looking intruder. Standing taller than Wayne, it looked like it had been treated roughly. We ran our hands along the scars and scratches. Tank scared me. I wondered whose homes it had been in before ours. And if someone had died to make this one available.

I became obsessed with what it might feel like to struggle for such an automatic thing as breathing. Slipping out the back door, I sat on the back step which Dad had recently painted green. Closing my eyes, I breathed in as much air as I could, then held it till the inside of my chest felt like it was on fire. Was that what an asthma attack felt like for Dad and my brothers? It did not feel as painful as they had often looked. I emptied my lungs, bent over, and blew out even more air, then held my breath again. Within seconds my head was spinning; my breathing got out of whack. If I had not opened my eyes and breathed normally, I reckon I would have fallen off the step.

The first time Dad turned on the oxygen, it made a hissing sound. A new scent filled the air. Despite the doctors saying there would be no smell from the oxygen, the addition of medicine made our house smell like a hospital. When he strapped on the see-through plastic mask, Dad looked like a creature from the space show we had begun watching on television. But I did not laugh. None of us did.

That winter, just about anything triggered an attack in Dad. Particles from dust, smoke, or pollen, or the odour from chemicals and certain foods. Most of those things also affected my brothers, but Dad's reactions were faster and more severe. A cool change could be enough to send him to hospital.

'Dear God,' I prayed. 'I'm going to hate winter in Australia forever.'

Mum started nagging. 'The smell from that glue you use is going to bring on an attack. Too much of that ice-cream will start you wheezing.' I guessed Mum was feeling scared for Dad. We all were. Dad ignored the warnings. Mum said it was because he had a stubborn streak. But I felt sad because I was sure he was trying to make his life as normal as possible. *Don't worry Dad, I'll take care of you.*

'Come inside. You're going to end up in hospital,' was our mum's most common plea, after Dad had spent a day in the garden. Which is what happened one chilly afternoon when the darkness came early. We children had begun eating dinner, but Dad had not yet come inside. Through the window behind my chair, I saw him dragging himself towards the back door. *It's going to be pitch black in a minute. Why doesn't he hurry?*

Mum must have sensed something was wrong because she stopped what she was doing and raced out of the kitchen. I caught whiffs of the hospital-like smell. Tank's eerie hissing filled the house. 'Glynis, call an ambulance,' Mum screamed. 'Dial 000.'

My brothers and I snuck along the hallway, saw Dad sitting on the edge of a chair, hands on his knees, no bend in his elbows, his back hunched. A mask covered his face. His shirt lay on the ground. The neckline of his white singlet, which he wore to keep his chest warm, hung loose. It was not the first time he had ripped at his clothes, gasping for air.

When he saw us at the door, Dad removed the oxygen mask for a few seconds, not to smile at us, just to lick his lips. I raced to get him water. When I returned, the mask was back on. He had become restless, was standing up then sitting down; his eyes bulging from their sockets. I felt scared and sorry for him, at the same time. Through the mask, I could see his mouth open. I wanted so much to rescue him. We all did.

'Is Daddy going to die?' LeRoy asked.

Dad began flailing his arms in the air. His eyes darted around the room. Then in a sort of crazed way, he ripped the mask from his face, letting it hang by the side of Tank. With nostrils flared, his breathing became noisier. Desperation now etched onto his face. My eyes welled at the rattling sound of his breathing. His face had lost all colour, was turning grey. He looked like he might explode.

Breathlessly, he said, 'Take me to the hospital, Honey. Don't wait for the ambulance.'

Glynis and I helped put Dad's arm around Mum's neck then helped her walk him to the car. He gasped all the way, like he was suffocating.

'My legs won't stop shaking,' Mum cried out as she jumped behind the wheel.

'Thank God,' Glynis and I both whispered when the car started first go.

The five of us stood on the verandah watching the car pull out slowly. It had hardly passed a few houses when the passenger door opened, and we watched as the top half of Dad's body dropped towards the road. Mum jumped out, ran around to help him back into his seat, then drove off again. Halfway down our street, he did it again. At the sound of the commotion in our otherwise quiet cul-de-sac, some of the neighbour's lights came on.

We heard the siren of the ambulance rounding the corner just as Mum reached the end of our street. Glynis ushered us inside, locking the front door behind us. None of us were interested in finishing our dinner, so she cleaned the dishes then we all went to bed. I wondered if it would be the last time we saw our dad. Sometime during the night, Glynis leaned over me to say, 'Mum just rang. The doctor said we almost lost Dad tonight. He's staying in the hospital. She's on her way home.'

5

Being Different

Neither of our parents visited the school after our enrolment, regardless of the importance. So, open days became the bane of my existence. I guessed it was because they were too busy surviving in the new country to take much interest in our education. And in general, schools did not encourage parents to get involved, other than on the days set aside for them to attend a function. My siblings and I were achieving good grades so perhaps Mum and Dad did not think they needed to interfere.

Education week was one such opportunity for children to demonstrate what they had been learning throughout the year. Students would perform a play or musical item. Fathers rarely attended because of their work. Mothers with younger children and often grandparents would gaze lovingly at their protégés before gathering in the lunch area under the big gum tree to eat the picnic lunch they had brought to share. I remember how hard I laboured towards those special days. The thought of abandoning lessons to accompany Mum around the school, showing off my achievements, excited me.

My teacher let out a deep sigh when I said our mum could not attend. I got the feeling she did not care that our mum worked until five in the evening every week day. They expected her to attend school events regardless. Mum's employers made it difficult for her to take time off. She saved her sick days or leave for our illnesses or hospital appointments. A family of five children was unusual. We were the only ones with more than three in our street. Most had two.

One year, after begging for weeks, Mum promised she would come to an open day. Glynis had already gone to high school, so LeRoy, Wayne, and I sat on a seat in the playground and waited until the toll of the home bell signalled the end of the day; time to walk home. Perhaps something came up at the office and Mum had no choice in the matter, but my disappointment was gut wrenching. I made a pact with myself never to ask her again.

My fourth-grade teacher, Mrs Templeton, introduced me to the lunchtime library club. I will be forever indebted to her for being such a wonderful teacher and caring person. She taught me how to escape into a book, to imagine, to create, and to write stories. When I was not escaping with the Famous Five, I dreamt about how and when I would be old enough to flee to Singapore.

However, that glorious year had not prepared me for the next when an unhinged *new Australian* teacher became my fifth-grade teacher. There were many occasions on which his behaviour had been aggressive for no apparent reason, so it was hard to say what had caused him to explode on the day that he caned every member of the class, except for one girl, with a bamboo cane, for not achieving 100% in an arithmetic test.

As he moved down the line whacking and raging like what looked to me like a madman, some children cried, some shook uncontrollably, some wet their pants. No one came to our rescue. His reek of rage reached me, long before his body did. Then, eye-level with his chest, the sewer seeping from it made my throat burn. And my eyes itched at the sight of the mass of black hair bursting from the collar of his shirt. Confused by his behaviour, I stared into his coal black eyes, which he took as insubordination, so I am certain, whacked me extra hard.

LeRoy had upset me with his stories of being beaten with a similar cane for silly things like talking in class or not drinking the milk. Before that year, I had never seen a cane, believing it was not something girls had to fear. I felt such shame, I never told my parents or siblings. It was something I would keep inside me forever.

The mere thought of teachers caning children made my palms sweaty, my tummy churn. Doubling as the deputy to the principal, my sixth-grade teacher was responsible for caning boys sent to him by the female teachers. A former military man, he believed caning was the best form of punishment for boys. So, I spent my final primary school year trembling whenever boys, including my brothers, arrived for 'six cuts of the best'. The male teachers caned offenders in their own classrooms.

During that same year, I became a proficient high jumper. Despite being elected by the team as their captain, a mean sports teacher prevented me from competing in the trials because I had left my sports bloomers at home. Not competing resulted in automatic dismissal from the finals. Our team lost. I never jumped again.

5.1

Going to church had been my favourite family time for as long as I could remember. It had made me feel warm all over, safe. After turning twelve years old, I did not feel the same. Those new feelings frustrated me. When my friends talked about their weekends, I would lean in to hear more about their activities like playing team sports, going to the beach, being spoilt by grandparents, or meeting each other to see a movie where they had munched on hot popcorn and swigged cans of Coca Cola. Sounded like they were having a lot more fun than me. I envied them.

I loved my brothers, but I no longer wanted to don the red Annie Oakley outfit, which had been my Christmas present the year before, to play cowboys and Indians with them. Pretending to be American soldiers in our war games was not the same after Dad used the mound of sand, which we had loved rolling down, to build the new carport. Glynis and I did not play together because she thought I was such a baby. Her cowgirl outfit had never been worn. She had safely tucked it away in her glory box.

Basketball and soccer matches were held on Saturdays. As were ballet lessons, sporting events and just about every other social event, including school fetes. So, my siblings and I were not permitted to participate. A year or so earlier, I had happily told my friends I could not attend those events, feeling proud that I would be at church, worshipping the Lord. Now, when they said, 'You're weird. Church is on Sunday. That's why it's called Sunday school.' I secretly wished God would switch our Sabbath to Sundays like that Roman Pope had.

After another of the Sabbaths when our mum had not come to church with us, Glynis and I whispered about it before we fell asleep. 'The Adventists come from another century,' Glynis said. 'It's impossible for

Mum and Dad to keep the Sabbath from sunset-to-sunset when they both have to work full time.'

'And Dad would lose his job if he had to leave before knock-off time every Friday afternoon,' I added.

Since Mum had commenced working for a company which imported the latest household goods, she had slowly added many modern conveniences to our home. We now had a fully automatic washing machine to replace the old copper boiler, a huge refrigerator with a massive freezer drawer at the bottom, a stereogram, and numerous small appliances. Mum loved the advantage of being able to buy the equipment at a reduced price.

Though it was a good job, Mum often complained about the office being situated in an out of the way industrial suburb around thirty minutes from our home and even further from the shopping centres. Banks closed at three o'clock and were not open on weekends. Post offices and supermarkets closed at the same time as most offices and at midday on Saturdays.

Mum had no choice but to do the weekly shop at a corner store on her way to and from work. The shop she located was run by a woman called Peggy. She, and her husband, Con, were immigrants from Greece. They took pity on Mum having to work with so many children to look after. To help, they offered to pick and pack the groceries from a list Mum could drop off on Friday mornings, ready for collection on her way home in the evening. It was an offer too good to refuse. Peggy and Con were such nice people. They never failed to put a chocolate Wagon Wheel full of marshmallow and jam or a crispy chocolate Kit Kat amongst the groceries for each of us children.

By the time she reached our front door juggling numerous bags of groceries needing to be sorted and put away, and with a flock of hungry children chirping at her hip, our mum had well and truly lost her race with

Friday's setting sun. She joined us less and less at church. Instead, spending the precious Sabbath cooking and cleaning. Dad helped with everything in our home throughout the weekend, except the cooking.

Because the Sabbath consumed our Saturdays, Sundays became my favourite. The hustle and bustle of weekday mornings was replaced by sleepy slumber and breakfast banter. On a cold or wet afternoon, Dad made pancakes because it was the only dish he could cook. He ate his with sugar, but I had started to prefer Vegemite on mine.

Our family never went on holidays. We could not afford them. 'Not with five children,' Mum would say. Instead, we watched our neighbours pack up their caravans, drive off to faraway beaches and camping grounds, then skite about it on their return. Other than our visits to the Malaya restaurant, attending church, and school, we went to a nearby adventure playground, or we spent our holidays at home.

Dad did many things to keep us entertained. One weekend he built a swing and see saw set. The next, a pair of stilts for each of us. A pair of stilts consists of two upright poles with supports or ledges for the feet to enable the user to walk at a distance above the ground. Dad said he and his siblings had them when they were children but, other than us, I never heard of anyone having their own. The ledges on ours were about two feet off the ground but we were soon racing each other up and down the backyard. At the sight of us having so much fun, Mum said, 'You know I used to climb the coconut trees in our garden in Malaya' which made us all giggle.

Though Mum and Dad insisted we remained indoors when they were at work, we were permitted to play with the other children in the street on Sundays. After breakfast, if the weather was fine, we would stand at our letterbox, signalling to our friends we could come out to play. Dad had painted the letterbox the colour of a forest, the same colour he had painted the concrete verandah, the steps leading to it, and the back steps. He built the carport because the cars were fading. We now had two. The grape vine he planted to cover up the steel structure grew into a jungle, so we sat under there on the hottest days. Soon our house colour-matched the name of our suburb, Greenacre.

When our friends joined us, we would head off to the final vacant lot in the street, where we climbed trees, performed pantomimes on the stage we had built from scrap wood and branches, and concocted schemes so important we believed the survival of the world depended on them. All the while we ate purple mulberries which our parents had banned us from doing. Sometimes we ate so many our bellies ached.

We played until our mates ran off yelling, 'Our Mum's calling us for tea.' I saw their mothers at the door with aprons on their hips. Some wore them all day. Within minutes Dad would be calling us to dinner. Knees and elbows scratched and bleeding, cuts on our heads, covered in bluey-red stains, sweaty and smelly, we ran home.

Mum often cooked up a storm of Asian dishes on Sundays. When she made the extra smelly Prawn Laksa, she ran around the house shutting the bedroom doors so our clothes in the wardrobes would not smell. Dad would spray air freshener everywhere to prevent the neighbours from smelling it. It did not make any difference because our friends pinched their noses as they ran past our house yelling, 'What's that stink.' Each time that happened I thought of the immigrant children, who other children made fun of when they ate, what Australian's called, wog food.

Mum said her family had a kitchy girl who cooked their food in an outdoor kitchen when she was growing up in Malaya. The smell never worried me at home because the food was delicious and most days our home smelt like a garden which came from the grassy fragrance wafting from the pan of boiling rice on the stove.

'It's the pandan leaf,' Mum said to Glynis and me as she ran the long, thin, dark-green leaf between her thumb and forefinger. 'My mother taught me to add one to the rice pot, tied in a knot like this,' she said, twisting it between her fingers. The aroma of pandan in boiling rice became a constant in my life. It permeated throughout our home, seeping into the crevices of my childhood, luring me towards my birth country.

On the Sunday I invited my school friend, Anne home for lunch for the first time, Mum cooked extra rice. She served it with a bright yellow curry made from beef tripe, and a side dish of shiny purple eggplant, atop a mound of the fragrant rice.

'What's this?' Anne asked with her forehead crinkled into multiple furrows. She had picked out a strip of tripe and was waving it at me.

'It's tripe. It comes from the lining of a cow's stomach you know,' I proudly declared. When I looked up again, she had swirled her meal into a technicolour kaleidoscope. Mum acted quickly and brought each of us a cheese and tomato sandwich.

Dad spent most Sunday's improving our new house. Inside, he painted the walls white then added French doors to the lounge room before painting just about everything outside forest green including our play equipment. At the end of the day, the seven of us would sit together on our new lounge suite with the dancing maple leaf pattern and pine wood arms, to watch a favourite program on our brand-new television which Mum had bought at a bargain price from work.

The show was about a man and woman in America, who had traded their swanky Manhattan apartment for a tumble-down house in a sleepy rural town. We would sway from side to side, gurgling and giggling, as we sang the opening song, 'Green Acres is the place to be. Green Acres we are there.' I loved having so many siblings.

It was during those happy times at Greenacre that I began to accept that our family had moved to Australia forever. However, it did not diminish my desire to return *home* one day which was how I had begun thinking of Singapore. A decade had passed since Mum had seen her mother and siblings. Her eyes still filled with sparkles whenever she mentioned them. I could never imagine not seeing my family. Dad said that buying a home, feeding and clothing a family of seven, and building a good life in Australia meant there had been no money for a trip home. Mum agreed but added that she was planning one to see her elderly mother as soon as possible.

6

No Turning Back

'We were all born on the equator you know,' Mum reminded us in the middle of another harsh winter. She delivered this softly spoken token whilst staring into thin air. Like it was a fragile memory capable of becoming one of the fairytales she would read to us before she started working.

'I used to catch tadpoles in the streams with my brothers and sisters,' she continued. 'The Japs were all around, but we went anyway. After the war when my family moved to Singapore, I used to eat dinner with my friends from work in the outdoor restaurants by the harbour. The weather was glorious. Years later, when I told people we were immigrating, one of them said Australia was a wilderness compared to Singapore. He said I'd never be happy here. He'd been to Western Australia. Said it was as barren as the face of the moon. Though he did say it would be good for children because the houses had huge back gardens.' Mum smiled at the memory of her friend's comment. 'And he said that each one has a giant whirligig in it that rotates around and around in the wind to dry all the clothes.'

'We've got a huge backyard now,' LeRoy said. 'As well as our very own whirligig.'

Mum opened her mouth to say something, then closed it. Responding instead with a slow nod. I was old enough to read the signs when our mum was missing her family and home. *Is she as unhappy as her friend said she would be?*

I turned to Dad. 'Mum said it was always hot in Singapore. So why did we leave?' I watched him purse his lips, take a deep breath through his nose, exhale, then sigh before repeating his usual phrase about forgetting about the past. I sensed something different, the slightest pause, his eyes blinking. I held my breath to force myself to remain still and silent. Only a few seconds passed before Dad began to speak.

'Because, after the Japs surrendered, the place was a mess.'

'What do you mean? I thought the war finished ten years before we left.'

'Everyone hoped things would get better when the British came back. But after the Japs left, different races started fighting against each other. The Malay communists were burning people's houses, attacking trains, rubber plantations, and police stations. They were mostly young people. Then, all hell broke loose when three Chinese men killed three Europeans in the State of Perak in Malaya where your mother was born. Killing a European was the final straw. The British called the situation an Emergency. But it was really another war.'

Mum piped in, 'The people were angrier than ever. They started fighting each other. Chinese communists, Malay Muslims, Christian Europeans. We thought we were safe in Singapore. Until the fighting spread there. We were living in a bungalow in a place called Serangoon Gardens. It was on a housing estate the British Army had built for their officers. The streets had British names. A lot of our neighbours were European. We all became targets for the rioters and kidnappers.

'The year you were born, Evvy, Chinese students clashed with police. They burnt homes and buildings, attacked and killed innocent people. Two years later, when LeRoy was born, the riots got worse. Gangsters from Chinese secret societies were rioting and attacking anyone with British or European blood. Kidnapping, assaulting, murdering.

'Everyone in our estate became suspicious of Chinese people. They were whispering to each other about what the Chinese would do to hurt us. "Don't buy food from the hawker man," they said. "He'll put ground up glass in the noodles. And if they kidnap our children, we'll never see them again." Your father stopped our Chinese amah cooking for us. And he wouldn't let me leave any of you with her. He was sure there would be no peace for people with European blood in Asia.'

Dad got annoyed at Mum's statement. 'Honey, they're mad over there. You know that. The fighting went on long after we left. There were race riots in Singapore, years after we came to Australia. And after we left the boat in Fremantle, it took Australian soldiers to Singapore to continue fighting the Emergency. Some of them lost their lives there.'

Dad stood up to leave the room. Smoothing his moustache, he turned towards me. 'When the politicians started arguing about Singapore joining up with Malaysia, well that was when we made up our minds. We were never giving up our British Passports. There's no turning back. I told you. Forget about the past.'

7

Race and Religion

Mum's lack of attendance at church happened gradually. Before we knew it, she was not coming at all. I did not know if it was due to a single event or if a multitude of incidents, unknown to me, had contributed to her decision. I just remember it coinciding with the increased visits from Granny Jones.

Other than Granny and Uncle, we did not have many visitors. So, the sound of a car turning at the top of our street, was enough for me to rush to the lounge room window for a peek through the white venetian slats. If I saw the old boneshaker, which is what Dad called Uncle's white Zephyr, pull up out front, I would yell out to alert the family.

I used to think Uncle was Granny's chauffeur because she only ever sat on the left-hand side of the backseat. There were two scenarios to their visits. If there had been a recent argument about the old lady, Dad would race out to chat to his mother through the car window. One time I walked with him to see them. Eyes beaming, Uncle jumped out to embrace his brother.

They seemed close. Like our family. Perhaps we were the only people they had to visit. Uncle smiled at me, patting me on my shoulder.

As Dad leaned into the open window to kiss Granny, I heard her ask whether we had been to church. Hearing it made me angry. In a lightning reaction I shot a look up at the sky, hoping to hide my face from Dad in case my twisted lips revealed what I was thinking, which was that one day I would hear him say, 'No, Mama. They didn't go today.'

A faint 'hello' reached me, forcing me to look at Granny. She had a sweet smile which lit up her eyes. I heard her say something about me getting taller. Then her voice grew faint, along with Dad's and Uncle's. I had stopped listening. I was peeved. My thoughts had stuck on her annoying question.

Scanning the interior of the car, I saw what looked like several editions of the daily newspapers, scattered across the faded red leather seats. A steel thermos lay on its side, a dinner plate and cutlery beside it, smeared with the remnants of a meal. Granny wore a simple dress, no hat, or gloves. Uncle, a casual shirt, no suit, or tie. Where had they been? And what church did they go to? Until then, such thoughts had never crossed my mind. Now they overwhelmed me, chipping away at my feelings about this granny. Why must she make our dad walk all the way to the car just to ask that question? She knows he is not well.

Lost in a labyrinth of negative thoughts, I failed to realise the visit was over. Until I heard Dad say, 'Wave goodbye to your grandmother.' Together, we watched Uncle's car move away from the kerb, meander down the street as we began walking towards our front door.

Unable to hold my tongue any longer, I blurted out, 'Where has Granny Jones been today?'

'Your uncle takes her on drives to places she finds peaceful.'

'Where do they go?'

'Lots of places. Centennial Park near the city. Or Bondi Beach. We've taken Granny to those places too.'

I recalled the trip to the city. The one where I had sat next to Granny in the back seat and heard her call women 'creatures'. To delay my final question, I grabbed hold of Dad's hand. We smiled at each other. But it did not work. Since hearing Granny ask about us going to church, I had been gritting my teeth, clenching my lips. Now, like our new puppy freeing himself from the leash, the question circled twice in my head, bounded over my tongue, then escaped through lips no longer able to contain it.

'Why does Granny Jones ask if we've gone to church when she doesn't go?'

The innocent sounding question sliced through the air before hanging within the confines of our front verandah. Dad's silence coalesced with the stillness of the chilly Sabbath afternoon. He let go of my hand to open the front door. I followed him inside. My question remained at the threshold. Dad's silence started me wondering why Granny did not go to church. It seemed like her visits to us were not to say hello or see how we were going. They were simply to ensure we had fulfilled some desire of hers. *What's going on with this granny? What's it got to do with her whether we go to church or not?*

When enough time had passed since one of Mum's outbursts about the old lady, we could anticipate the second scenario to a visit from Granny and Uncle. The ones where they would come inside, often bearing what Granny said was 'the food your Daddy likes to eat.' If I was quick enough, after hearing that comment, I could catch Mum sucking in her lips to avoid blurting out what could cause another row. Regardless of which scenario took place, their visits always left a feeling of tension in the air between my parents. I began to dread their arrival.

Except when Andy accompanied them. Now I was close to becoming a teenager, I imagined Andy akin to the picture of the dashing James Dean movie star whom Glynis and I had drooled over in a magazine. Glynis had wanted to join her school friends to see his movie, but Dad would not let her. It was cool to have a cousin who wore stovepipe pants, slicked his hair back in a duck-tail rockabilly style, and whom we had seen jive and rock-'n-roll.

Andy had inherited the porcelain skin of his English father, in stark contrast to the ebony hair and eyes he had inherited from his mother. Mum, rather than Dad, had revealed more over the years about Moira who had died in Leeds in England. 'She married a drunkard. He was cruel to her. Your father helped her to leave her husband during the war. She died in your father's arms. Poor Andy was only two years old.' *How did they get to England?*

Since Glynis had become a teenager, Dad had started saying stuff like, 'You should marry an Englishman. They make good husbands. And he should be an Adventist because he won't drink alcohol or smoke cigarettes.' When I reached my teens, he started on me. Now I knew about his sister Moira's husband, I wondered why Dad said we should marry Englishmen when our mum said they were all drunkards.

'Mum, didn't you say Andy's father was English?'

'Yes. Your father doesn't want you or Glynis to marry an Asian.'

My siblings and I relished the times spent with Andy. Dad would allow us to stay up late to play board games with him, often until the wee hours of a Saturday night. Monopoly was our favourite. We would trick and tease Andy by passing cards under the table with our toes, giggling our hearts out. I imagined him to be an older brother whom we all adored. Perhaps he saw us as the siblings he never had. At the very least he was a cool cousin. We never saw the others. Despite those fun times, Andy never seemed happy. His chronic asthma kept him gaunt and fragile, like Dad. I often saw him pull a face if he was asked to do something by Granny, his surrogate mother. I could not imagine ever letting her tell me what to do.

The visits when Granny came inside never lasted long. The one I remember the most was the shortest. I was too old now to be interested in every car turning at the top of our cul-de-sac. So, we did not know we had visitors until Granny and Uncle were knocking on the front door. Before settling, Granny insisted that Uncle fetch something from the car. When he returned, the sweet smell of cinnamon and cardamom trailed from the cardboard box he carried to our dining table.

Granny snapped orders, 'Put the box on the table. Take the big saucepan out first. Make sure you don't spill anything.'

My mouth opened in shock to hear Granny speak this way to Uncle as if he were a child. It snapped shut, in unison with her turning her head towards me. She chuckled with a hint of embarrassment, then continued the instructions. Uncle obeyed, lifting each saucepan by the double knot tied at the top of the faded floral tea towel wrapped around them. The first parcel unleashed its spicy, piquant aroma throughout our house. From the second, I recognised the fragrant nuttiness of basmati rice.

'Mum cooked a lamb curry for you Butch,' Uncle cried out like an excited child. 'There's rice too. Eat them while they're still warm.'

My brothers leaned forward as Uncle placed a brown paper bag on the table in front of them. 'These are for the children.'

Dad pursed his lips in response to his brother's announcements. Either he did not have time for chatter, or he was impatient to get the visit over and done with. I held my breath when I saw Mum come into the room.

Without delay, Granny said, 'Did you go to church today?' Oh no. Granny is going to upset our mother. She must know Mum's not going to church anymore.

'Boys, go outside and play,' Dad said. His sigh echoed in the silence as Mum left the room with Glynis and me in her wake.

In her bedroom, Mum whispered some swear words about the 'bloody old lady', blew her nose, wiped her tears. Glynis sat on the edge of the bed with her arm around Mum's shoulder. I was standing at the door feeling helpless when Mum turned to me, 'Please go and help your father.'

Dad was seated at the dining table eating, not paying much attention to Uncle's chattering, 'How's work? How's your asthma?'

As soon as he had finished, Dad started transferring the remaining food into our Tupperware bowls for storage before going to sit with his mama. 'I'll eat more later, Mama. Thank you for cooking.'

I was angry that Granny had upset my mum. But I also felt sad for Dad. I knew Mum did not like being asked about church. Even I had tired of Granny checking up on us children and was close to screaming. But I wondered what else had made Mum dislike the old lady so much. Dad chatted with his mama for no more than a few minutes. It was obvious the visit was over when he stood up and began helping her to the front door by taking hold of her arm at the elbow.

Uncle picked up the box with the empty saucepans. 'Sorry Butch. Mama went to a lot of trouble.'

Neither Mum nor Glynis came back out of the bedroom.

I said a strained 'Bye'. There were no grandmotherly cuddles, no kisses. I walked to the venetian blinds. Saw my brothers race around the side of the house to see them off at the front gate. A washing machine of emotions churned in my tummy at the sight of Dad kissing his mama on the forehead, then helping her into the car. He shook Uncle's outstretched hand. *Dad's a polite man. Always has such good manners.* These two people were the only relatives who visited us on a regular basis. So, why did every encounter have to end this way. I watched Uncle's car pull away from the kerb. *He really is Granny's chauffeur.*

An almighty clanging and banging from the kitchen forced me to spin around, so fast the sharp edge of one of the slats sprang back and sliced across the tip of my finger. I sucked on it as I raced to the kitchen. The metallic tang sat heavy on my tongue. I saw Mum hovering over the garbage bin, sobbing as she scraped away the last of the lamb curry. She flung the bowls into the sink with such force I was thankful they were made of plastic.

'That wicked old woman. Hides behind her religion. Calls herself a good Christian. Doesn't even care about you children.'

It was not the first time Granny had come bearing food for Dad. Nor the first time I had watched Mum throw it all in the bin. Feeling helpless, I glanced around the room. Smiled when I spotted the brown paper bag on the dining table. My brothers had rescued it. Saved a caramel for Glynis and one for me. I closed my eyes as I sucked on mine. Felt the sugar water start gathering. Knew I would remember Granny's crumbly, misshapen caramels forever. Though after that day, I never saw one again.

7.1

For a woman who always spoke softly, even when she was disciplining us children, we began seeing a new side to our mum, in response to Dad's attempts to persuade her to come to church. 'Don't talk to me about religion, she started snapping at him. 'I'm sick to death of hearing about it.'

When Mum spoke these words, I saw such a fierceness in her eyes. Until then, our parents had kept their discussions to the privacy of their bedroom. We children only heard their whispers. Things had changed. Mum no longer cared if we overheard her yell or cry. There were times when she yelled so loud, I felt embarrassed that the neighbours must have heard.

Mum's outbursts about Granny came primarily after a visit. One Sabbath visit, she overheard Granny ask Dad, 'Did your wife go to church?' Waiting until after Granny and Uncle had left, Mum let go a tirade of anger like I had never heard from her. 'Tell the old lady to stop preaching to me,' she screamed. After which she sobbed and went to bed without eating the dinner she had cooked. It seemed rude to me that Granny never called Mum by her name. It was always 'your mother' to us children or 'your wife' to Dad. *I hate how Granny makes our mum cry.*

Those arguments were not much fun for us children. However, it was often after one that I learnt something new about our family. There were times my anticipation of uncovering new information during an argument between Mum and Dad made me feel guilty. Sometimes they spoke in such a whisper, I had to strain to hear them. One time, I bit down so hard on my bottom lip to concentrate, it bled. But if I was going to continue learning stuff about my heritage, I had to press on.

Like the time I persisted with my question about why Granny did not go to church. After repeating it numerous times over the ensuing months, Dad had finally responded, 'Your never-ending questions. It's because she lost her eldest son, her youngest daughter, and our father because of the war.'

'Does she blame God?'

'She's broken hearted. Now no more questions. Forget about the past.'

I missed Mum coming to church with us. We all did. And I felt sorry for her whenever Granny made her cry. But I was also feeling angry, and worried. Our religion had kept our family close, united. Mum's behaviour was creating problems. Was she causing our family to fall apart? Why did Dad have to go and marry a Catholic anyway? And why did Mum convert to Adventism if she was not going to stick to it? Was that the reason Dad had begun his push to encourage Glynis and me to marry an Adventist? He never said it to the boys.

I did not have to wait long for answers. Glynis and I were in our beds, listening to Mum and Dad talking following another heated visit from Granny and Uncle.

'The old lady thinks she's a good Christian,' Mum said. 'That her religion is the only one.' Dad did not respond, which Mum took as an opening to continue. 'What about when you told her we were getting married in the Catholic church? Remember how she punched your chest with her fists. Screamed that your wife might as well be the daughter of the Antichrist.'

Mum's voice faltered, 'My father was a devout Catholic. I broke his heart.'

Glynis and I did not say a word to each other. We fell asleep. The next Saturday, Dad said he would collect us after Sabbath School as he was not coming to Divine Service. Granny did not visit for a few weeks.

Mum's disclosure that she and Dad had married in a Catholic church was like a bombshell exploding in the face of everything I had grown up with. I had believed Dad about ours being the one true faith to follow. Our teacher at Sabbath School had told us stories about how Catholics had tortured people for being Protestant during the 1500s in Europe. Everything we were being taught was against the Catholic religion. How their statues and crosses were against God's will. How they did not worship on the right day. How they had proclaimed their Pope as God's representative on earth.

I recalled one of the stories Mum had revealed about her father. 'Just weeks after we arrived in Australia, I received a telegram. My father had died. I can still see him standing at the dock. He didn't stop waving till our ship was out of sight. I broke his heart.' Because of this story, I had assumed Mum had broken his heart by leaving Singapore. Now I had heard it was because she had renounced her family's faith. I knew Mum had been raised Catholic, but I never thought of her as one. Not anymore. She just could never be.

The revelation played on my mind for weeks, but I was afraid to raise it with Mum. In case it caused another argument about religion. We all disliked those. They were so tedious. Until one day when Dad had taken the boys to look at cars along Auto Alley, one of his favourite pastimes. With just us three girls alone, Mum got out her wedding gown to show us. It was still intact though the satin and lace embroidery had yellowed with age. Glynis and I oohed and aahed.

'Oh Mum, it's heavenly,' Glynis said. 'Can I try it on?'

'Mum, you must have been tiny,' I said.

'You must have looked beautiful,' Glynis said.

'We were in the papers for our wedding. My friend was a photographer for the Singapore newspapers where I worked. And we were getting married in one of the best churches in Singapore. The Cathedral of the Good Shepherd,' Mum said with pride as if it was something stupendous. 'It's the Mother Church of the Roman Catholic Archdiocese of Singapore.'

My mind did somersaults upon hearing Mum's proclamation. I could not talk, feeling relieved when Glynis found the courage to ask the question I had been holding onto for weeks.

'How come you got married in a Catholic church Mum?'

'Because your father agreed to it.'

'Why?'

Silence.

'Does Granny Jones hate you?' I piped in.

'She thought I wasn't good enough for your father to marry because my mother has Portuguese blood. And is Catholic. Your grandmother is too proud for her own good. Many of the Dutch Burghers are the same. The Dutch despised the Portuguese. Asia was full of wars over race and religion. Most of them started after the Europeans came. The Dutch were protestants. When they took over Ceylon, they wouldn't even employ the Portuguese because they were Catholic. They treated them like second class citizens. Anyway, I don't want to talk about it anymore. Your father will be angry.'

Words like Roman Catholic, Cathedral, and Archdiocese sounded so powerful they scared me. I compared them to the image of the tiny, wooden chapel, painted white by the members of the congregation, where we worshipped each Sabbath. Now that Mum no longer came to church, I hoped she was not considering going back to being a Catholic. My heart pumped double time at the thought of what might happen to us children if she did. *Could we be locked out of the gates of heaven?*

It filled me with joy that Dad and Mum had loved each other so much they were not prepared to let anything, or anyone, stop them from being together. But I could not come to terms with the thought that Dad had contemplated crossing over to the Catholic side. Not after being baptised into the Adventist religion and accepting it as the one true faith. And I could never imagine his mama letting him become Catholic.

If the icy relationship between Dad's mama and ours had come to pass because Dad loved our mum more than the faith his mama had chosen for him, then I reckon Granny must have missed the Bible lesson which teaches that God considers love superior to hate. Because, despite Dad's strict faith, no amount of praying, evangelizing, or proselytizing had restrained him from true love.

Mum's words about Granny not caring for us came flooding back. How could it be that a grandmother found it hard to love her grandchildren because their mother was a different religion? Or maybe it was because ours had Portuguese blood. Granny did not seem like a cold person to me. She was never overtly mean to us. But come to think of it, she had never kissed nor cuddled us. In fact, I do not remember her ever touching me.

I did not need to know the history of Ceylon to realise Granny had not left the past behind as Dad had encouraged us to do. Instead, despite it dating back 500 years, she had brought the baggage of her Dutch ancestors with her to Australia. And she was still making her son pay for the aeons of hatred that swirled within her. Why else would she feel compelled to persecute Dad for his transgression against the faith she had chosen for her children, when he had chosen to marry a Catholic of Portuguese descent?

No wonder Dad did not want to talk about the past. It made me feel guilty that I still wanted to pursue it. But he could not have been right because I was learning that the past never stayed buried forever. And it was all we had. Maybe Granny and her family should have dumped all their religious and racial baggage overboard on their voyage to Australia. The revelation about Dad marrying our mum in a Catholic church should have made me angry at him. Instead, I took my anger out on the old lady. And Mum, whom I blamed for introducing all this Catholic stuff into our lives.

8

High School

If there had ever been a time when I had sat on a mat and enjoyed having stories read to me, like other young children, by the end of my primary school years, I no longer remembered them. Instead, my school memories were of throwing myself on the pedestrian crossing outside the front of school rather than spending another day with Miss Strongarm, being forced to eat lunch under the scorching sun on the edge of the western plains, walking home from school at the height of horrendous summers and the depths of deplorable winters, being barred from competing in the high jump team for forgetting my sports bloomers, being hit with a bamboo stick by a madman whom we were made to address as Sir, and spending my final year cringing at the cracking sound of a bamboo cane on the hands of young boys. Through it all, I had to endure the never-ending drama of being forced to drink something sour and smelly because the government said so. Then being totally miffed at my father for agreeing with the practice because he believed it would make me 'grow strong and tall like a European'.

There were some fond memories of school. I loved mathematics and English, had enjoyed spending my lunch breaks in the library club, was proud when chosen to be in the choir representing the school at the annual Choral Concert at the Sydney Town Hall, was elated that I could high jump, had learnt to play a mean game of marbles with the boys, and had made friends with some genuinely kind girls. As for the teachers, how could it be, from the age of five to twelve, I had only found two out of eight to be nice, happy, and encouraging?

Obeying Dad's wishes to forget about the Asian part of our race and heritage had become more challenging. Looking into the bathroom mirror to brush my teeth was a daily reminder I had come from another country. Everyone I met still struggled with my race, regardless of whether I said I was English, Asian, Eurasian, or Eskimo.

The safe and peaceful life, which Dad had sought for us, had resulted in a lacklustre childhood, compared to Mum's which had been fraught with risk and adventure. Dad's involuntary references to exotic places like India and Ceylon, Wales, and England, fuelled my desire to get out of the sticks.

Our home life had started to change as well. Mum and I were now clashing on a regular basis. We could not seem to agree on anything like clothing, hair, or food. I still loved to eat hot, spicy Asian food which Mum now only cooked on weekends and holidays when she had time for the lengthy preparation. Instead, she began experimenting with the latest food fads being introduced from America which had been created with the working mother in mind. And so, it become quite the norm for us to eat a variety of the easy-to-prepare meals for weekday dinners.

For breakfast we ate cereal out of box instead of eggs or leftovers. Using a variety of western style packaged and frozen foods, Mum could get a hot meal on the dinner table for the seven of us within thirty minutes of arriving home from the office. There was packaged flavoured rice, frozen peas, corn, beans, and carrots, frozen pieces of fish covered in breadcrumbs, and powdered potato which created a creamy mash with the simple addition of boiling water. Some days Mum bought hamburgers or fish and chips at the milk bar on her way home. Potato scallops were my favourite.

Some of the quick-cook meals were okay, but I detested others. Dad would not let me complain no matter how much I moaned and cried. 'I can't eat those green beans. That packet curry sauce is disgusting. It's got bits of red stuff in it. The fish fingers make me feel sick.'

'Don't you dare be rude to your mother,' Dad would say, showing no sympathy for me.

'But I can't eat it.'

'No buts. Your mother has worked hard all day. You will eat it and not complain. Or go to bed hungry.'

The more Dad berated me for complaining about the food our mum cooked, the more I refused to eat it. Evenings became intolerable. If Mum was going to cause my father to be mean to me, I wanted nothing to do with her. After all, she was the reason our family no longer went to church together. Even Glynis had stopped attending the afternoon groups saying, 'They're just for kids.' And although Dad had not always come to the earlier sessions, he had often returned alone for the hour of Divine Service. Now, he refused to come at all without our mum. We children went alone. After dropping us off, he would return at lunch time, simply to collect us. I feared Dad was going to become like Granny Jones. Forcing us to go even though he no longer attended.

Dad and Mum had made so many sacrifices to give us a good, safe life in Australia. Maybe I was turning into an ungrateful brat. Mum and I were disagreeing on so many things. But she could not dislike me. I was her daughter. Getting into trouble from Dad, because of Mum, made me resent her more. I became totally frustrated by not being able to say anything against her in his presence.

Some of Mum's criticisms made me cry because they hurt so much. Sometimes I had to squeeze my lips together hard, to stop myself from bursting into tears. Like when she said I looked like Granny Jones because we had similar features, that my hair was so thin she could not do anything with it, and that I was always moody and sulky. The final straw came when I spotted a pile of photos she was preparing to mail to her family in Singapore. On the back of the one of me she had written in bold black ink, 'She is as stubborn as an ox'. *When did Mum and I grow apart? Could it be because I had not supported her about the Catholic thing?*

Dad was not aware that Glynis and I knew about him marrying Mum in a Catholic church. Neither of us had revealed it. How could I find the words to convey my feelings of betrayal. Even though it happened before my siblings and I were born, I still could not believe Dad had considered crossing over. I quashed such an implausible thought because I knew I could not maintain any anger towards Dad. I loved him too much. He was the one who always took time to listen to me. The one who took me shopping when Mum said she did not have the patience with my indecisions. He was the soft, kind one. He was the one who could have died from numerous attacks of asthma.

Yet, the unexpected sadness I felt at the thought of Mum having to change religions after the grand Catholic wedding caused tears to well in my eyes. Especially because doing so had broken her father's heart. There would be time enough to seek information about what had changed after the wedding. For now, I felt an overwhelming desire to be still and let the relief sink in that our mum had converted, rather than be on the side with the torturers.

Coinciding with Dad's diminishing attendance at church, our pastor began visiting our home to instruct Glynis in the religious teachings necessary for her to be baptised into the faith. Adventists practice full immersion baptism which takes place when a person has accepted Christ and the Seventh Day Adventist religion as the one true faith. The event is both a solemn and joyful part of the usual Sabbath service. We attended Glynis's special day as a united, happy family which included Mum.

Dad bought Glynis a cream-coloured, leather-bound Bible and Hymnal set as a gift to mark the occasion. As if he had been offered two for the price of one, he bought me a set too, except that the shop had sold out of the cream version so mine had to be black leather like his. He gave it to me that Christmas, which for a while made me feel like I had already been baptised without the pomp and ceremony. Rather than feeling happy at being given the gift early, it caused me to worry about how much I would get to use it. Now that Mum did not want to come to church, and Dad was coming less and less, I imagined our whole family might stop attending. And so, I was delighted when our pastor approached me the next Sabbath to say, 'We'll start baptismal lessons with you Beverley, closer to your fifteenth birthday. Okay?'

'Yes.' I beamed, feeling like my feet were lifting me off the ground. I could not wait to be baptised. It was a way of letting God know I was a true Adventist. Along with my sins, he might wash away the stain on my family that my parents had married in a Catholic church.

8.1

High School felt like freedom – something about the energy soaring from more than 200 new girls. I stood tall amongst the murmuring mass of pigtails and ponytails at the first open-air assembly for the class of 1967, which consisted of more people than I had seen in one place throughout my whole life.

Under the searing January heat, my knotted hands sweated behind my back. The stiff seams on my egg-yolk coloured blouse scratched at the tender flesh under my arms. My new royal blue tunic tickled my knee-caps. The teaching staff strutted around us. I thought of the peacocks I had seen at Taronga Park Zoo last summer when Dad drove us to what seemed like the other side of the world, but which turned out to be just the northern foreshore of Sydney Harbour. Some teachers smiled and nodded a welcome. When one asked a girl in my line to stop talking, a voice from the crowd muttered, 'Better stay away from that one.' We all giggled. The teacher smiled and walked off.

A handful of the senior students stood on the dais with the teachers. One of the girls in my line whispered that her sister was a senior. 'She drives a car to school,' she said. Some of the girls oohed and aahed. I fixated on the one introduced as the School Captain who looked similar in age to some of the teachers. She wore a different uniform from the rest of us. A skirt and blouse rather than a tunic, flesh toned nylon stockings and black court shoes with mini heels. Unlike the opaque black tights and Bata blacks the rest of us would be made to wear that winter. Wavy black hair hung loose over her shoulders. Even from a distance I spotted the shiny black eyeliner and *lipsticked* lips.

The seniors that year were amongst the first cohort of students across New South Wales to commence Sixth Form as part of a new education system to prepare them for university. The rules had been relaxed to encourage them to stay the extra year. As part of the leniency, they enjoyed a common room which was out of bounds to other students. Within the confines of their room, they were permitted to play music, cook food, and smoke cigarettes. I was in awe of their freedom. They were godlike to me. I sighed at the thought of waiting six years to become one of them. It seemed a lifetime away.

At the end of the induction formalities, the whole student body applauded and screeched loud hoorahs towards us new girls. A high voltage shiver, both peculiar and pleasant, zinged up my spine, one vertebra at a time. Apprehension churned in my tummy. Bobby socks covered my feet. But I no longer felt like a child.

Not everyone I knew from primary had enrolled in the same high school as me. Some had opted for schools closer to where they lived, or Catholic colleges. Dad had floated the idea of sending me to the Seventh Day Adventist College a few suburbs away, but Mum said they could not afford it. So, I went to the local high school as Glynis had before she had left to start working whilst she studied accounting at night. My smile must have lit up the bus on my first journey which was also the first time I had ever been anywhere on my own. No parents, nor siblings.

Bronwyn was one of the few friends I had kept from primary. Though she lived two streets away from me her house was on a different bus route. Only one bus in the morning and one in the afternoon passed close to our house. Bronwyn had represented our area in basketball, so she knew a lot of the locals. It was another reminder of how observing the Sabbath had prevented me from joining friends for Saturday sports, spending the weekend at their houses, seeing a movie together, or meeting up at the local shopping centre. Not being able to participate in those activities during the 1960s boarded on anti-cultural for a teenager. It left me feeling like the gap between our religion and the Australian culture was growing as wide as the Great Dividing Range separating the east coast of Australia from the outback.

Rather than melding into a country free of discrimination and war, as Dad had hoped, or fulfilling Mum's desire to play hockey or basketball, like she had as a young girl, our religion continued to set us apart from others. We already looked different. Now we could not do many of the things other teenagers were doing.

I began following Dad around the house, out in the garden, in the car — begging him to allow me to participate in more activities with my friends. After much coaxing from Mum, he consented to my going to the school dance with Bronwyn. Surprisingly, he said I could get dressed for it at her house. But what would I wear? My one Sabbath outfit had become old fashioned and childlike.

Now that Glynis had begun working, she was able to buy trendy clothes and makeup. Surely, she would not notice if I borrowed one of her dresses. I could stuff it into my bag, wear it to the dance, then sneak it back into her wardrobe when she left for work. I chose one of the newer ones. The woollen shift in cobalt blue, styled with a neck tie of swirling paisley in pinks and blues that hung halfway down the front, was the trendiest dress I had ever seen.

Bronwyn and I were full of joy preparing for our first ever dance. Until her mother walked into the room and said to me, 'Your mother rang to say you're not to wear all that makeup tonight.'

I glared, stone-faced at this woman, speechless. When she left the room, I whispered my thoughts to Bronwyn, 'There's no way my mum would ever do that to me. And no way she would relay a message through someone else. Though we never talked about it, Mum had not stopped me wearing eye makeup which I bought with the few dollars that she had started paying LeRoy and me for pocket money. With Bronwyn's mother out of the way, I looked into the mirror and painted an extra thick line of black across my eyelids.

Dad's leniency stopped at permission to dress at Bronwyn's and attending the dance. 'Forget about it,' he said. 'You're not going,' when he overheard me telling Mum that I had met a boy there who was a senior at the nearby Catholic college. I had given him my telephone number and we had made plans to meet after school one day. It was the most embarrassing day of my life having to tell him I could not come, when he rang to arrange the get together.

By the commencement of third term, I had abandoned my primary school friends, including Bronwyn, to hang out with a group of popular girls who were pretty and smart. I liked how they talked about hair, makeup, and boys. I wished I could have talked about those things with Glynis, but we were not close. The memory of her controlling behaviour over previous years still lingered. She no longer had to walk us home after leaving primary school, but she had continued to mind us through the school holidays until she commenced work. How tedious those days were for my brothers and me. Glynis probably felt the same and would have preferred to be with her friends rather than taking care of her pesky, hard to handle siblings. But she had become such a bossy-pants.

Being cooped up for nine hours a day for weeks on end could result in a disastrous outcome for anyone. Add five children to the mix and it was anyone's guess as to what horrors we could plot and execute. There were times our frantic telephone calls to our mum's work had forced her to race home. Some days, it was in reaction to a serious situation such as 'LeRoy had a fall. His head is bleeding.' Or 'Dewey found a box of matches and he's started a fire in the laundry.' On occasion, our fights escalated to physical violence. 'Dewey's gouged my face with his fingernails.' Most of the time, we rang out of boredom, which would prompt Mum to drive all the way home to appease us with a pie or sausage roll from the canteen at work or ice creams from Peggy's shop.

My refusal to obey Glynis's orders during my final year at primary school had taken its toll on our relationship. Like the era when she started experimenting with cooking. One time she used up Dad's milk by mixing it with green cordial. After refusing her ultimatum to drink it, she locked my brothers and me outside, agreeing only to let us in if we drank her lime-coloured concoction. She excused Wayne because of his age. Despite my persuading, LeRoy gave in. Only Dewey and I remained outside. I yelled out, warning Glynis of the trouble she would be in when Dad arrived home. Luckily for her, and me, it began raining, and she unlocked the door to let us in. Then destroyed the evidence of the green disaster by throwing it down the outside drain. But it was too late. We were on a warpath, exacerbated by the screams echoing throughout our house on a regular basis, 'Mum, she's used my makeup. Mum, she's worn one of my best dresses.' Soon battle lines were drawn up by a piece of string signifying the centre of the bedroom we shared which I was forced to step over to get out.

My new friends were cool. They thought I was 'unusually pretty' so chose me to represent our form in the Spring Beauty Pageant – a grand production staged by senior students. The same selection committee quickly dropped me in preference for a buxom classmate, after our first swimming lesson, when they saw that at almost thirteen years old, I was still flat-chested in a swimsuit. Though we all got along well, they also thought going to church on Saturday was weird. I dared not admit to them that whilst they were playing basketball, or meeting for a hamburger at the new shopping centre, I was singing hymns.

Many of the girls in my year had started going to the cinema in the city to see the latest movies. One Saturday I remained in my Sabbath clothes after Dad had collected us from church. My outfit was a lemon and white paisley shift dress which I paired with baby pink ribbed stockings. The outfit made me feel so grown up, I was certain Dad would let me go to a movie. After all I was now in high school.

'My friends are catching a train to a cinema for one of their birthdays,' I said. 'They've invited me.'

'Absolutely not.'

'Why? Because it's Sabbath?'

'Yes. But that's not the only reason.'

Stamping my foot on the ground, I yelled, 'Then why?'

'Because the Bible says Satan built the cinema houses. To further detrude the moral state of the world.'

'What does detrude even mean? Please can I go? My friends will think I'm a baby. I'll feel stupid telling them I can't.'

'Satan uses the cinema to thrust people into hell. You shouldn't have told your friends you could go.'

My anger was surpassed only by my total embarrassment at having to telephone the friend who had invited me. 'But everyone's going,' she said. 'We were going to sit together.' A flush of heat burned across my cheeks. I was thankful she could not see me. I swallowed and lied, 'My parents don't want me to catch the train to the city.' I hung up the phone, rushed out the front door, slamming it behind me. Still wearing my paisley dress and pink stockings, I protested by standing at the letterbox for over an hour.

There were seven levels at our school for First Form, which is called Year 7 today, A to G. My new friends were in B, one level lower than me for mathematics and a few other subjects. So, in my mind, being in the B class was where all the hip girls were. One day, I snuck into their mathematics class to be with them, managing to hide there for weeks. Until the day my teacher, who was absent, was replaced by the maths master.

'What are you doing in this class, Beverley? You made it in to the A class.'

'I don't want to be with the oddballs,' I said, rather than sounding weak and saying that I did it to be with my friends.

'Oddballs?' He sniggered. 'You're an ace at mathematics. Your grades show you've got a mathematical brain.' *What would my cane-happy fifth-grade teacher think of that?* Despite my protests he ordered me back to the A class and prohibited me from swapping classes for the rest of the year.

I embraced most of the changes demanded by high school. Like adjusting to different teachers and rooms for each subject, being in an all-girl environment except for a few male teachers, and the newfound freedom of catching a bus on my own. But I still felt constrained. Whilst I was at church listening to our minister preach about sinning, my friends were out having fun. Each Monday they talked about winning at sports, shopping for new clothes, or the movies they had seen together. Some of them had boyfriends so would talk about kissing them. When we sat together in a group at lunchtimes my mind would race in search of answers to their questions about which boys I liked, what I had done on the weekend, and did I want a cigarette after school.

The many times I had nothing to add to their conversations, I would stare down at the ground when they talked. Part of me wanted to be like them, part of me did not. Sometimes they were horrible to other girls, making fun of them for not being 'hip'. I would just nod in agreement to avoid attention. I did not want to commit a sin. But I wanted to have fun like my friends. Could having fun even be a sin? Was everything they did a sin? It seemed like normal stuff to me. If wanting to do some of the things they were doing was being sinful, maybe I had no choice but to become a sinner.

But that was my secret. One I dared not say aloud. I had stopped sharing my thoughts and dreams with Mum and Dad. I feared they might kill Dad from one of his asthma attacks. Afraid Mum would not even listen.

Since Mum had stopped coming to church, the two of us had become even more distant, clashing more often. I still had the feeling that she did not like me nor have time for me. I still blamed her for causing our family to grow apart by not coming to church. And I had stopped listening to anything she had to say. Until one evening, when she said through the crystals in her eyes, 'My mother is coming to Australia for a holiday.'

9

This Granny is Portuguese Though She Was Not Born in Portugal

My lips tingled from the memory of the gift Mum's mother had sent me two years earlier. The event of receiving something addressed to me personally for the first time in my life, would be burnt into my brain forever. 'Evvy,' Dad had called out. 'I collected a parcel for you from the post office.'

The solitary cylindrical shape had been wrapped in brown paper. I picked it up from the dining table. Turquoise, mustard, and white coloured postage stamps had been pasted across its front. A red and white label, slapped around it, attested to its fragility. I coddled it like a new-born kitten. Amongst the official clutter I saw my name and address. On the back, hidden beneath a bold purple stamp revealing its country of origin, was the name and address of my maternal grandmother in Singapore.

'Be careful,' Dad said. 'That sticker means it's made of glass. Maybe you should wait till your mother gets home?'

Ignoring Dad, I peeled away the thick wrapping. Each layer released a musty cardboard smell, until the final cloak, a green and white-checked tea towel, starched stiff for the journey, fell away on its own.

The afternoon sun from the kitchen window zeroed in on the mysterious arrival, a screw top jar, the size of a small biscuit barrel. Suspended inside an oily red liquid that looked potent enough to glow in the dark, I saw bits and pieces of fruit. What looked like tiny lemon halves, vied for space amongst slivers of something dark brown. And a pale-yellow version of the hundreds and thousands that children have on fairy bread at birthday parties, floated throughout. Catching sight of a juicy looking green chilli, twisting its way through the bottle, I smiled. Yum, this is going to be hot and tasty.

'My mother is famous for her lime achar,' Mum said when she arrived home from the office. 'That's what we call pickles.' Tears leaked at the sight of something that had travelled all the way from her mother's kitchen bench to ours. 'She sells them to her neighbours. To earn a little cash. It's different to most because it's from her secret recipe.' Wiping a runny nose, she added, 'Can't buy it like that.'

'Why not?'

'Because the Portuguese in Asia are a dying race.'

Portuguese Granny, as I called this grandmother after receiving the parcel, had sent the gift in response to a letter from Mum, saying I had taken a liking to hot, spicy food. Her secret recipe contained a fruit called blingbling. 'That's what the people in Malaya call it,' Mum said. 'Fresh, they're bright green and crunchy. When they're preserved, they turn dark brown. Like the ones in the achar.'

That night, the teaspoon I added to the corner of my plate brought my dinner to life. At first my lips stung from the effects of the spicy green chilli. I shared it with the family but only Mum, Glynis, and I could tolerate the heat. With each serving, my lips burnt less. Within a week, I could eat it without a glass of water nearby. The bling-bling turned out to be my favourite ingredient. Eye-squintingly sour, it had hooked me after the first piece. Saliva pooled at the sight of them, forcing me to ferret them out until only lime halves and the yellow hundreds and thousands, which Mum explained were called mustard seeds, remained. Within two weeks the jar was empty.

I wrote a letter to Portuguese Granny thanking her for the 'delicious achar'. She responded with a little card with a pink rose on the front. Inside she had written, in ink-blue shaky words, "Be a good girl for Mummy".

Portuguese Granny's achar burnt more than my lips. It rekindled the links to my birth country. And now the maker of it was coming to Australia for a visit. Mum had sacrificed a holiday back home to enable her mother to visit us in Australia. I was so happy about that because if Mum had gone to Singapore, I may never have had the chance to touch the hands of the woman who had lovingly wrapped the green and white-checked tea towel around a bottle, walked it to the post office, and paid express postage to ensure it reached me intact.

Planning for Portuguese Granny's visit offered a welcomed distraction from school. I begged Mum and Dad to let me take the day off to accompany them to the international airport. I simply had to be the first of my siblings to greet the woman whom I knew only through Mum's childhood stories. They would have taken Glynis had she not commenced working. And so, Mum, Dad, and I joined the small group crowding the frosted double doors that separated us from the passengers in the arrival hall. Each time they swung open we craned our necks like swans, hoping for a glimpse of our loved ones.

At the release of a stranger, we smiled at those around us. Many of those waiting had faces revealing they had hailed from foreign origins, like us. It helped unite us in excitement, but also anxiety about our loved ones being scrutinised in immigration and customs. Mum's friends at the office had told her about the foreigners being arrested on a regular basis for smuggling things into Australia. 'Did you hear about the Italian woman who tried to hide jewellery in her bra? You know the Chinese people try to smuggle herbs they can't get here.' I wondered if Portuguese Granny had brought a bottle of her lime achar. When the doors slammed shut, we sighed, returning to our family groups, me with visions of my grandmother being arrested because of a bling-bling plant being found tucked inside her blouse.

Mum had told us that her mother was born in Malacca, which lies on the west coast of Malaysia, between the monsoon winds of the South China Sea in the east and the Indian Ocean in the west. And how her ancestors dated back to the early Casados, Portuguese men who were living in Malacca from 1509. The King of Portugal had promised to release them from servitude to him and exemption from crown taxes if they married a local woman. So, when this grandmother's female ancestor married a Portuguese man, their offspring became known throughout the East as Portuguese Eurasians.

Knowing this grandmother's racial mix, made it difficult to imagine what she might look like in the flesh. I had only ever seen a black and white photo of her, sitting on a shiny, teak pew in a cathedral, wearing a white dress, with matching netted pillbox hat. Just as I began conjuring an image of a woman born in Malacca, of Portuguese descent, arriving in Australia dressed in her Sunday best, Mum screamed, 'There she is.' Then burst into tears.

I recognised Granny immediately from my imaginings, rather than the photo. Splendid in a cotton suit of vivid ochre, russet and brown batik that danced with mysterious ornate patterns, she was beautiful, but her hair was grey. 'Poor Granny,' I said to Mum. 'She hasn't seen us since we were babies.

We will be as foreign to her as she is to us.' Despite this. I felt we loved each other instantly.

Mum had cried over a decade's worth of tears in the days leading up to Granny's arrival. Now her wailing reached new heights, either from my comment or the sight of Granny, or both. The same way she cried whenever one of those flimsy sky-blue aerogrammes arrived in the mail. She pushed through the crowd to reach her mother. They embraced. Then leaned back, cupped each other's face with their hands, traced each other's features with their eyes, then embraced again, tears streaming.

After a hug for Dad, Granny turned towards me, touched my face with the tips of her fingers, ran them down from the skin on the edge of my eyebrow to my chin. Through a thin-lipped smile she said, 'Hello girl. No school today?'

Though I ached to get close to this grandmother, I was wary from Mum's childhood stories. Some had been enchanting. Others scary. My sister and I had learnt much about Granny's fiery temper and code of conduct for girls. Whenever Mum spouted the poignant witticisms ingrained from her mother, they related mostly to Granny's opinion on the three Ms: morality, money, and men.

I took Mum's place in the front seat so the two of them could sit together in the back. My feelings were conflicting. Everything about this granny seemed familiar, yet foreign. She even had her own smell, a mix of bath soap and moth balls. Soon the whole car smelt of her. Mum held onto her mother's hand from the time of her arrival until we drove into our driveway. At first, there was little talking between them. Except when Mum enquired about her brothers and sisters. Or when she explained things about Australia. 'We live far from the airport. Back home the same drive would take you to another country.' We all giggled.

Granny's first language was Malay. She also spoke English, albeit in a sort of choppy way because her sentences often missed the articles like *the* or *a*. As the chatting increased in the back seat, Mum's voice started to sound more and more like her mother's. Not at all like when she used the longer drawn-out vowels to speak to the neighbours. Between the two of them I think I heard a thousand *Aiyohs* and *lahs*, and a bunch of the Malay words she often used at home.

When Dad turned the key in the lock of our front door, it swung back to release a gush of pent-up aromas from Mum's cooking. She had been at it for days. When the smell of smoky fried chicken laced its way to Granny's nose, she said, '*Aiyoh*, Ayam Goreng' recognizing one of her favourite dishes. Mum smiled through smudges of runny eyeliner and rouge.

Dad led the way inside, carrying the small suitcase. The second we entered, Granny became shrouded under a cone of sunlight, so brilliant it blinded me. All I could make out was her shape. She dazzled like a saint. The ones I had seen in my bible study pamphlets. Then it struck me. The reason I found this old woman so intoxicating was because she embodied what we had left behind. The world from where we came. She was my first tangible link. Everything until now had been stories.

I saw it in the colour of her skin, oiled, nut-brown, and creased. Her lips, sealed, solemn, and sober. Her eyes, deep, dark, and mysterious. As Mum led her mother down the hall towards the bedrooms, the shaft of light disappeared, as quickly as it had come. I realised it had been the setting sun, piercing through the lounge room windows, which ran across the west wall of our house.

The clip-clap from luggage latches echoed up the passageway. I raced to the bedroom. Dad had set up a bed for Granny alongside Glynis's and mine. The smell of mothballs and soap had permeated our house since the arrival of Granny and her suitcase. Now that it engulfed our bedroom, I was not going to miss the opportunity to sticky beak at its source.

Amongst the crisp, clean-pressed garments, mostly in pink, were gifts for us children. My jaw dropped when Granny handed me a string of black pearls sent from Uncle Freddy, one of Mum's four brothers. There was one for Glynis when she got home from work. Granny knew her the most because she was the eldest. She was overjoyed to greet her in the same way as me. There were gifts for my brothers who had arrived home from school during Granny's unpacking. They were talkative, excited to have a visitor in our home, even though it seemed to be an awkward introduction. We had been so young when we left Singapore. Wayne had not been born.

Our dining table only seated six, which was why our mum rarely ate with us. For our first meal with Granny, she fed Dewey and Wayne their dinner early. She was often so tired during the week after cooking our dinner, Mum would need to lie on the bed before eating her own. Sometimes, I wondered if she did not like being with us. Or was it just me. Had I complained too much about the fish fingers and curry sauce? Was it because she said I was stubborn? Maybe all those things had contributed to her not wanting to do fun things with me.

I wished this granny lived here. Despite her stern face, she seemed warm, much more touchable than our other grandmother. Even my brothers had behaved. I tried extra hard not to stare at Granny across the table, but I wanted so much to hold her, caress her, breathe in her scent. If she lived in Australia, we would have a grandmother who loved us. I made a promise to myself that I would visit her all the time.

Mum beamed as she served her banquet. The chicken, charred brown from coriander, cumin, and brown sugar, sat piled high on her best serving plate. Its aroma filled the room. Alongside it, a mountain of rice, coloured canary yellow from the threads of saffron lacing through it. The salad, crisp chunks of cucumber and pineapple, decorated with pounded dried prawns, red chillies, and purple onion, moistened with a vinegar and sugar dressing.

Mum sat on Dad's right; Portuguese Granny next to her. I watched Granny's face, as Dad served from his seat. Her smile did not offer any clues as to whether she approved or not. Mum had acquainted us well with stories about Granny's fussiness around cooking. How she prohibited the substitution of a single ingredient in a recipe. Better wait 'til she thaws a little before trying to guess her thoughts.

The clanging of a saucepan lid prompted everyone at the table to turn towards the sink where Mum had gone to start cleaning up. It was an accident but because of her response I guessed she must have anticipated the flinch I saw come from Granny. 'Mummy,' she said. 'Remember how you used to whack us with the bamboo cane. One for each sound we made with the washing up.' Then, rounding the table with possum-like eyes she added, 'Children, your grandmother used to whack us for just about any-thing. Getting a bad report card, carrying mud into the house on our shoes, playing in the tadpole infested ponds. Most of our friends got the same from their parents. I didn't get into as much trouble as my brothers and sisters. Because I was so scared of that cane.'

Back at the sink, Mum kept talking, 'Remember how I used to go to the market to buy vegetables and meat for you, Mummy?'

'Yes. You were good girl. But you never bring home meat.'

From my seat, I caught the twist in Mum's lips. I felt sure she did not find Granny's comment funny. She stopped and turned towards the table, directing her response more towards us children than her mother. 'Well, that's because we had to buy our meat at a place called a wet market. Sometimes the men killed chickens and goats in front of me. They cut up the meat then laid it out on tables. There was blood dripping everywhere. It stunk.' She shrugged her shoulders, 'Urgh, I wasn't going to touch it. Not even when they offered to wrap it up.'

Changing the subject, Mum squinted towards me. 'Your grandmother rubbed raw chilli on our lips for answering back.' She turned towards her mother, 'Times have changed Mum. 'Nowadays the children answer back all the time.'

Portuguese Granny blushed. I wondered if it was from embarrassment about the forms of punishment she had administered to her children. Or could it have been pride? Either way, heat rushed through my body like my blood was boiling at the anger I had felt towards Mum lately. It was bad enough she no longer came to church with us. Now she was telling her mother bad things about me. By the time Mum sat back at the dining table, the light-hearted conversation had taken on a serious note.

'They were very different times children. There were all sorts of diseases around and parents were frightened their children would catch something and die. Like the time the whole town caught smallpox. Remember, Mummy? We were the only family who didn't catch it. You and Daddy wouldn't let any of us leave the house. Then when Malaya had a cholera outbreak during the war, we were all forced to line up for hours in the hot sun. The Japanese guards jabbed us. Mummy, you must have been frightened for us?'

'Yes.'

Portuguese Granny's answer was succinct. It made me wonder if Mum was rehashing memories this grandmother preferred not to remember.

'During the war, the curfew ruled our lives,' Mum said. 'It was your strictest rule. Ah Mummy? We had to be home by six o'clock at night. That's when you let the dog off the chain.'

Mum had told us many stories about her mother's superstitious nature. How she believed that everything in life was at the command of either God or the Devil. That an angel or a demon lurked around every corner waiting to reward or punish. That evil spirits took over from the day at sunset. Hearing the stories told in front of the perpetrator added a new layer of intensity, bringing them to life.

Portuguese Granny smiled, muttering something about 'spirits' then said no more. Gosh, she's the opposite of our other granny who doesn't fear anything.

'If we girls missed the curfew,' Mum said looking at Glynis, 'Mummy whipped us with the bamboo cane till it stung and left thick red welts on our arms and legs. Then looking at LeRoy, she added, 'My poor brothers got it worse.' Her voice trailed off. The words left hanging in the air.

My eyes expanded to the size of saucers at the thought that Mum might raise more horrifying stories. She must have read my mind because she stopped talking.

Nodding slowly, Granny responded to Mum's accusations. 'In my day, must have obedience from children. Sometimes save life.'

As if to defend her mother, Mum said, 'When the Japanese arrested my father during the war, your grandmother had to look after us on her own. We lived in fear of the soldiers because they were so cruel. They were dangerous times. Weren't they, Mummy?'

I looked across at my grandmother's face, trying to contemplate what horrors she might have seen during those long years and how she had survived.

'I had nine children during war. No husband. Japanese take him. Like Queen Victoria. I must be strict when so many children.'

Dad weighed into the conversation, 'The British believed that discipline was part of living a civilized life. Apparently, the queen made her husband tie the children's hands together before he whipped them with a cane for being disobedient.'

Sounded cruel to me but I was not going to say that in front of Portuguese Granny. My thoughts rushed to the single cut of the cane I had received from the crazy grade five teacher and how much it had humiliated me. Poor Mum and her siblings. Thank goodness I had not grown up in that era. Lucky for us, Mum never hit us no matter how naughty we were. Though I remembered those times when she had pinched a lump of skin on our arms or thighs, twisting it until we squealed. Often to stop us complaining or wriggling while she was trying to watch something on television.

I wanted so much to hear some of the stories from Portuguese Granny's lips. But it did not seem right to soil the air with sad memories. Instead, I asked if it was true that she believed the most important skill for girls was to learn how to cook and clean. She nodded once. And again, when I asked if it were true that she had forbidden Mum and her sisters from whistling because she considered it unladylike. Or, learning the violin because the teacher was a man. So, I was confused when Granny then told us how well she could play the accordion and loved singing.

It was hard to go to school whilst Portuguese Granny was visiting. I did not want to lose a moment of time with her or miss something of interest that she might say. I dared not even think about her leaving, though I knew the time would arrive when we would have to say goodbye to the only relative who had ever shown such love and warmth to us children apart from our parents.

During her visit, Granny made sure she imparted some of her gems relating to the three Ms to Glynis and me. One morning, she leaned across the breakfast table to whisper, 'If girl get pregnant before marriage, she broken pot. No man marry her. Keep your legs together.' Over a Sunday lunch she said, 'When money trouble fly in one window, love fly out other.'

Granny's most unrivalled words of wisdom during her visit were, 'Men are like itchified dogs.' Funny that she didn't have any of those gems for my brothers.

When Granny cooked for us, Glynis and I watched with trepidation as she imparted metronome-like instructions for cooking rice the Asian way. 'Must wash at least three times or rice dirty. Add lots salt and cold water. Water only come here,' she said, pointing to the first joint of her middle finger with her thumb, before placing it on top of the rice. 'Add pandan leaf from your Mummy's plant then put to boil.'

Granny put the lid on the saucepan with one side of it tilted. Rather than using a timer, she stood by the stove watching the pot until the water bubbled, frothy and white. Just before it spilt over, she turned down the 'fire' as she called the element on the stove, to a simmer. We had an electric stove, but neither Glynis nor I felt game enough to correct her.

'Now you must watch and check grains,' she said as she stared at the pot for what seemed like an eternity but was in fact about ten minutes. We watched with interest as she scooped out a few grains with a spoon. Splitting one of them between her fingers, she pointed out the white dot in the centre. 'When you see tiny dot, turn off fire. Must take off fire quickly and scrape top with fork so steam come out. Or rice be sticky. Then put back on stove. Lid tight. Not open.'

Granny made it clear that a pot of perfectly cooked white rice was one of many Asian emblems. And, that a woman who could not deliver one, had failed in life. I knew in my heart that the image of Granny resting the top of her finger on the rice to measure the water level would be imprinted in my memory. Also, that although it comes pre-washed in Australia, the urge to wash it in copious amounts of water, in addition to conducting a meticulous search for tiny stones, bugs, or bits of dirt would stay with me for ever.

I sobbed when Portuguese Granny went home, feeling like she was taking a piece of my heart with her. I worried about her travelling on her own. She was skinny, frail. Months later, when Mum told us her mother had applied to immigrate to Australia, I squealed with joy. Recalling her disappointment at not being able to make her special lime achar whilst in Australia, I smiled at the memory of her promise, 'Next time Granny make for you.'

Knowing there really was going to be a next time, Mum searched different vegetable and grocery stores in Chinatown for bling-bling. When nothing turned up, she bought various brands of lime pickle. None of them tasted anything like the one which Portuguese Granny had sent from her kitchen in Singapore. Nor did any of them contain the sour tasting fruit.

After her visit, I was certain Portuguese Granny had begun channelling through our mum. Already a perfectionist when it came to Asian recipes, Mum now became even more fastidious about authenticity, which she conveyed on a regular basis to Glynis and me. 'You shouldn't cut the lemongrass. Just knock it to soften. This rice is raw. Don't put cumin powder with beef.' Or was it coriander powder? I had forgotten. Even the wait staff at the Malaya Restaurant received her reprimands, 'Please tell the cook not to put fish sauce in the Kway Teow.'

I thought a lot about the differences between our two grannies. Both seemed bossy, but the old lady exerted more control over our lives. No doubt because she lived in Australia, but every one of her visits had brought tension into our home. Portuguese Granny had been kind and loving towards us. We had not had that sort of affection from other relatives. Granny Jones' crumbly caramels may have been special, but she had never cuddled my siblings or me. I did not ask Dad why. I did not want to make him sad.

My heart had been filled with expectations of a meeting between the two grannies, imagining they would have had so many things to talk about. Like the old Singapore they both knew so well; whether it had changed and if so, how. I had imagined a big happy family get-together. The kind my siblings and I had missed all our lives. But that did not happen. They did not see each other. No one told me why.

Mum usually ended her scary stories about how her family had suffered through the Japanese occupation, by saying, 'My mother prays to holy Mary as well as many other saints. Her prayers saved our lives during the war.' So, I had expected Portuguese Granny to preach to my siblings and me about Catholicism. However, apart from making a few slips of the tongue when she let out a 'Mother Mary' or an 'Oh Deus', expressions we had often heard Mum use when she was annoyed or worried about something, this grandmother had not mentioned religion.

When I asked Mum why she had not taken her mother to a Catholic church on at least one of her Sundays in Australia, she twisted her lips to one side. 'Your father would never let me do that. And my mother is not like the old lady. She would never talk about religion in this house.'

And so, Portuguese Granny never tried to convert us. I loved that about her. I wished we still lived in Singapore. I wished the two grandmothers could swap places. But that would make Dad sad. Portuguese Granny's visit had unsettled me, forcing me to think more about travelling to Singapore. But how would I get there?

The failure of Portuguese Granny to mention religion like Granny Jones did on a regular basis, caused me to wonder about the argument I had overheard between Mum and Dad about getting married in a Catholic church.

Since then, I had learnt in Bible Study that Protestant religions came into existence in Europe in retaliation to the persecution of Christians by the Catholic Church in the 1500s.

Our church pastor knew Mum had once been Catholic. He was an Australian who had preached the Adventist religion in Singapore and Malaya where he had baptised Protestants escaping Ceylon. On one of his visits to our house to encourage Dad to return to church, he talked about his experiences as a minister in South East Asia. I guessed he had been trying to get closer to our family by revealing that he had studied a lot about the history of how the Dutch rulers had introduced Protestantism to Ceylon through the Dutch Reformed Church.

'My mother's family were members of that church,' Dad said.

'Yes, most Protestants from that country were. Before that time, the Portuguese explorers controlled the country. They introduced Catholicism to the heavily Buddhist country. But after a hundred years of their rule, the local people rejected the harsh practices of Catholicism. They rebelled and supported the Dutch to seize control.'

Dad took in a deep breath then sighed, trying to change the topic by offering the pastor a glass of water, knowing he most likely did not drink either tea of coffee because many Adventists did not drink caffeinated drinks. He declined the offer and continued talking, boasting about his international experience. I remembered how Adventists prided themselves on being humble, but I was itching to hear what he had to say.

He repeated some of what Mum had told me about the Dutch and the Portuguese when he added, 'The Dutch were obsessed with keeping their blood as pure as possible. When there were none of their own women to marry, they encouraged Dutchmen to marry the indigenous Singhalese women, like your ancestors, in preference to the Portuguese. Despite an extra deep sigh from Dad on hearing this, the pastor continued, 'New settlers married the children of those unions, again in preference to the Portuguese. The new rulers treated Portuguese Catholics and their descendants as lower class. They wouldn't grant them land or permit them to work in the new trading company. They could only enlist in the military.'

Upon seeing Mum shuffle in her seat, the pastor stood up. 'Time to go,' he said, extending his hand to each of us. 'The congregation would be delighted to see you more often,' he said when he reached Dad. The steely-eyed look making it difficult for Dad to look away.

After he had left, Dad admitted his surprise about our pastor having preached in Singapore and Malaya and how much he knew about the country of Ceylon. The opportunity to press Dad for more information about his family was too good to miss. 'Remember how you said Granny Jones was a Dutch Burgher. Well, did you hear what the pastor said about them being powerful people? Was your family powerful too?'

'My grandfather was a circuit judge in the Ceylon Law Courts. And my grandmother's father was a pastor in the Baptist church. Her grandfather was a Colonel in the Dutch Army. The family lived on their coconut plantation on the west coast near the country's capital city of Colombo. Even though by the time my mother was born, the country had been under British control for over a hundred years, the Burghers still held great power and respect.'

'Did your grandparents go to Singapore with the rest of the family?'

'My grandmother did. My grandfather's plantation was burnt to the ground by the rebels.'

'What were they rebelling about?'

'The British.'

Hearing some of the history of Ceylon from our pastor, combined with Dad's information about his mother's family, forced me to reconsider the reasons behind Granny Jones' behaviours. Being raised in a racist and conflicting religious era must have affected her prejudices and attitudes. The more I learnt about her, the more each one of her characteristics rang out like a pair of brass bell clappers. With each reverberation I heard her voice, saw her face, felt her pride, smelt her fear. Though I did not condone them, I understood for the first time, this granny's obsession with race and her contempt for the Catholic religion. My sympathy for her peculiarities, however, only lasted until her next visit.

Dad had not long been home from work one day, when I spotted Uncle's car arriving. I watched him hop out and walk around to help his mama from the backseat. I raced out the front door, raising my hand like a stop sign. 'You can't come in,' I said. 'Dad's lying down because he's not feeling well.'

Uncle glared at me. 'What a rude child,' he said. 'I'll be telling your father about this.'

The look of confusion on Granny Jones' face made me think she had not heard me, prompting me to quickly add, 'I don't mean to be rude, but you can't come in.'

Without another word, Uncle got back behind the wheel and drove off.

When Mum arrived home from work, she sounded pleased to hear what had happened. 'Good. Your father won't be happy. But good.' Oddly, I never heard anything from Dad despite it being the first time one of us had been rude to his mama. I wondered if Granny or Uncle ever told him. And what would happen the next time I saw them. I do not remember when that was. I only remember that by the time the hot, north-westerly winds of a dry December, fluttered shut the monochrome pages of my first year at high school, I had been complaining out aloud about how much I was dreading the long, six-week, end-of-year holidays.

I had been trying hard to be good at school to keep my promise to Portuguese Granny, but I was really struggling. I loved learning new things in maths, English, and art. The cooking classes were fun with a lovely teacher coincidentally named Miss Ovens. However, if I had ever wished to be capable of making my own clothes in sewing classes as Glynis had, the bunch of scrawny older teachers who tottered around the rooms, carrying a sewing basket in one hand whilst tinkering a teacup and saucer in the other, lost me on day one. 'I do hope you're going to take a leaf out of your sister's book,' the head of the department had said, pinching her lips to savour her sip of tea. Fat chance I was going to be like anyone. Let alone my big sister.

In response to my increased whining about not being able to see my friends on Saturdays, Dad reacted by allowing me to join a group of friends who had planned to meet at one of their homes over the holidays. They were all a lot worldlier than me. A few of them smoked cigarettes, used a lot of swear words, and talked about having sex with boys. I had mixed feelings about their actions. I did not want to seem like a baby, but I also did not want to commit the sins our pastor had preached about. I did not go again. I did not need to. I had found a new outlet. The social and music revolution, which had been wending its way throughout much of the western world, had found me. Christened as a 'counterculture', the movement turned my world into a kaleidoscope. So much so, that from the dawn of my second year, everything I did, or did not do, caused controversy.

10

War

Billions of transistor radios were manufactured during the 1960s. I got one of them for my fourteenth birthday. Until then, my only access to music had been through whatever Dad played on the radio or whatever records were being played on the family stereogram. For Glynis, it was her collection of Motown music and other disco records. Dad played Pennies from Heaven by Bing Crosby. Mum swooned over Johnny O'Keefe as he screamed You Know You Make Me Wanna Shout.

Music changed everything in my life. With unlimited access to whatever I wanted to hear, I lay awake some nights, often until the early hours of the next day, listening to bluesy folk and rock music from around the world. The Young Rascals sang about *"Groovin' on a Sunday afternoon."* For the Beach Boys it was about cosmic energy, colourful clothes, and sunlight or feel-good music about Californian beaches.

Australia had not experienced the same level of social conflicts as America surrounding equality, justice, and protests for the war in Vietnam, but the lyrics that emerged from the music in support of those ideals, lit a fuse inside me. Songs from America and England addressing sexual freedom, women's rights, and modes of authority, called attention to the fact I was living a million miles from where I ached to be. Listening to lyrics urging young people like me to demonstrate, meditate, take psychoactive drugs, and to explore who we were and who we wanted to be soon became the only way for me to connect with the outside world. The more I listened, the more isolated I felt living out in the sticks in addition to belonging to a cult-like religion.

When my transistor belted out Bob Dylan's anthem for change, about young people being beyond authority because the times were *"a-changin"* I cried for days, yanking at my hair with frustration. But I was too young to join the bohemians who sought the freedom to do whatever they wanted. And so, I interpreted that freedom the only way I could. By dressing how I liked, listening to the music of my choice, pursuing my own social beliefs, and determining how I should be educated. I no longer wanted to conform. The term "dropping out" became popular around the same time and I learnt that young people all over the world were abandoning conventional education and work to live as hippies – members of a countercultural movement rejecting mainstream society and traditional values. I considered doing the same but when I mentioned it to my parents, Dad went berserk, refusing to talk about it. I do not recall Mum's reaction.

Everybody seemed to be talking about the Vietnam War. It was difficult for me to relate because I did not know anyone who had joined up or been conscripted. However, the nightly news, the lyrics of much of the music I heard, and the front page of Dad's daily newspaper kept me informed about the devastation, loss of young lives, and political chaos it was causing. Then one night, Dad brought the reality of the war home to us when he started talking about it after watching the news.

'When the North Vietnamese made their biggest attack against the allies,' he said. 'They did it at dawn. Just like the Japs in Singapore.'

Dad was referring to the Tet Offensive which had happened a few months earlier when North Vietnamese and Viet Cong forces launched sweeping attacks on more than a hundred hamlets and towns in South Vietnam. He had been leaking experiences from his past in recent months. Did he think he was going to die because of that last asthma attack? Was this a sort of unveiling? Or was it because he finally felt safe now that we had lived in Australia for a decade. Had he feared we would be sent back to Singapore at some point before now.

Dad began comparing the similarities of the Tet Offensive with the dawn air raid on Singapore by the Imperial Japanese Navy on the 8 December 1941. Coinciding with their landing in Malaya, which Mum had told us about many times, he said, 'The Japs dispatched aircraft to bomb Singapore.' A flash thought reminded me that Mum had been a twelve-year-old child in Malaya and Dad, a twenty-year-old man in Singapore, at the time of the Japanese invasion.

'They did it just to let us know they were on their way,' Dad said with eyes so wide they were pushing the skin on his forehead into furrows. 'The authorities told us not to worry. "Singapore is an impregnable fortress," they said. 'But the Japs surprised everyone. Especially the British.'

'Why?' LeRoy asked.

'Because we thought they'd come by sea. That's why the guns on the coast were pointed south and east. But they came from the north. Up in the jungle. Their soldiers marched and rode bicycles through that jungle, you know. That jungle wasn't fit for humans.'

Dad repeated the word 'jungle' so many times, it sounded to me like he was still trying to convince himself, more than a quarter of a century later, that the Japanese really had managed the Herculean task of penetrating the dense tropical growth, on foot and bicycles.

'By Jove, none of us expected it. The Brits said that even the Japs were surprised they'd pulled it off. We assumed British reinforcements would arrive at any minute to save us. We thought they'd never risk losing Singapore. Not their Jewel in the Far East.'

Prompted by Mum, who sat on his right, Dad took a break to eat some of his meal. Dewey and Wayne were not interested in the story, so left the table as soon as they had finished their dinner. Glynis, LeRoy, and I stayed put. Our eyes glued to Dad, keen to hear every word of his story.

'There were whispers of an attack, but no one seemed worried. It was a typical weekend. My family went to eat a meal at a food stall.'

As he recounted the events of the invasion, every so often Dad would shake his head from side to side and purse his lips. Rather than chide the British for wrongly preparing for an attack by sea, he seemed to find it incredulous that the Japanese, 'of all people' had managed to penetrate the fortress of Singapore by tricking the British.

'That was the first time my papa started to question if Singapore really was impregnable. But when the bombing stopped, so did the worry. People just went back to their daily lives. We all wanted to believe what the British said. The night after the bombing they held the regular dance at Raffles Hotel. Until the air raid sirens started again. They turned out to be a false alarm and nothing more happened for the next three weeks. So, we all thought that was the end of it. That all the rumours about the people being abandoned were false. Until the beginning of January when the attacks started again. This time a lot heavier.

'At first, their planes mostly attacked the dockyards and airfields. But every now and then they flew over the city to bomb the streets. That caused complete chaos. They bombed all day for a month. In between, and without warning, everything would go quiet. Sometimes it stopped for hours. Sometimes a whole day.'

I watched Dad's face twitch. Was it fear? As if trying to steady his response, he began his moustache flattening routine. Then he drew in a deep breath, began a slow shake of his head from side to side, and sighed, 'Every time they stopped, we thought they'd given up and gone home. Until it started again. We found out later they did the stop-start routine deliberately. To keep the British occupied, while they were making their way down to Singapore, through the jungle.'

Dad sounded annoyed. 'Even with all that commotion, the civil authorities didn't start their evacuation plans until the end of January. They said it was because they didn't want to create panic. They broadcast over the radio that it wasn't compulsory or urgent to evacuate. So, even at that late stage, like a lot of other people, we didn't know that the fare for evacuation was free. Right up till the end we didn't even think the threat was serious.'

'Not serious?' I cried out. 'Mum said the British knew the Japs had landed in the north, weeks earlier.'

'Anyway,' he continued. 'A lot of the British people had escaped from Malaya to Singapore. The authorities were only allowing European women and children to evacuate. Then, the old and sick men.'

'That makes me so angry,' Glynis piped up. 'How did you get out?'

'Because we had papers. British papers.'

'But you had an English grandfather,' I said turning to Mum. 'How come you didn't get out?'

Mum had remained silent throughout Dad's story until my question. When she responded, I heard the sarcasm in her voice. 'We didn't have a choice in Malaya,' she said. 'Only the British ran.'

Dad shrugged his shoulders then continued, 'We had to get travel warrants because we didn't have passports in those days. The bloody bureaucrats made everything twice as hard. They wanted so much darn paperwork.' Dad cast his eyes downwards. I assumed it was because he had used a swearword in front of us.

'What kind of paperwork?' I asked.

He turned to face me. I saw the lightning-fast ripple turning up a corner of his moustache as he answered, 'Like people need if they're leaving a country in peacetime. People had to prove they were English.'

Dad kept talking between mouthfuls of his dinner. Like he was desperate to get his story out. Like there had been no one to talk to about these memories for so long. I recalled what Mum had said about how whenever Dad and Uncle Bill got together, 'They had a lot to talk about'. I had wondered what they might have discussed. Even more so when Mum had added, 'I'll tell you another time.' But she never did.

'We tried to sell our furniture and other belongings.' Dad picked up his story. 'But we left our run too late. No one was buying any more. We withdrew our money from the bank. Good thing we did. Because the Brits ended up burning all the cash so the enemy wouldn't get it.' The smile across Dad's face conveyed his delight that he and his family had played a part in making a fool of the enemy, however minor.

'What happened to your car?' LeRoy asked.

'Uncle Bill and I sold ours. We kept Papa's Austin to get us around. We couldn't rely on the Chinese taxi drivers any more. Most of them had disappeared. We packed a few things in a couple of bags. My brother ferried us to Clifford Pier in the Austin, three at a time. We didn't know if there were any ships left in the harbour, but we went anyway.'

'Lucky you could get petrol,' LeRoy said.

'My brother was a building contractor. They had depots. Plus, we didn't have far to go. Singapore is a small city.'

'What happened to that car?' LeRoy asked.

'We left it for my other brother.'

'Why?'

'Because he was staying behind.'

'What? Which brother? We all screamed.

'Do we know him?' Glynis asked.

'My eldest brother. No, you don't know him. His name was Irwin. His wife and children had left a month earlier for Australia.'

'Why didn't he go with them?'

'Because his exit papers weren't ready. The authorities called it a hiccup. Said they would be done in time for him to leave with us.' I sensed a change in Dad. The colour that had returned to his face from the telling of his extraordinary story, had drained. He let out a little cough. Then paused to take a sip from his glass of water. Was he getting an asthma attack? Had we overdone the questions?

'So how come he didn't leave with you?' Glynis asked. 'What happened to him? Where does he live now?'

'He didn't get his papers in time. We left at the beginning of February.' Dad paused for a breath, then said, 'He died.'

Sweeping the back of his hand against the air was Dad's way of indicating he would not be saying anything more about that brother. Instead, he returned to his story. 'As the Japanese army drew nearer to Singapore, the bombing got heavier and heavier. Thousands of people were injured and killed. We joined a convoy of other cars just crawling along the road. Enemy planes were flying so low we could hear the noise of the engines from their aircraft, seconds before they dropped a bomb.

'Most of the people on the roads were on foot, running in all directions. Some were carrying suitcases. Others, just a few things wrapped in a bundle. Some looked dazed. Like they were in shock. Some tried to jump onto our car. In the end, the bomb craters were so big we couldn't drive any further. We had to get out and walk the last few streets, through the mess we'd seen from the car. The streets were littered with bodies. People hovered over them weeping. Rotting garbage. Broken glass. Everything seemed to be on fire. Cars, buildings, even people. The noise was deafening.'

Dad bit his lip. I sensed he might have done it to prevent another swearword escaping when he told us about the propaganda leaflets. 'They'd been dropping them from time to time since the very first air raid,' he said. 'But now, as if they could taste blood, they rained from the heavens. Landing all over the bodies and the debris.'

'What did they say?' Glynis asked.

'Oh, rubbish about how they'd save Singapore from the British. Create an Asia for the Asians. It was all hogwash, but they won over some of the treacherous Indians and Malays who wanted independence. The Brits had to fight them off as well as the Japs.'

Mum interjected. 'We had those leaflets in Malaya too. Mostly about the atrocities they were going to commit on women if they didn't surrender. Some of our neighbours ended up helping the enemy.'

A slow, measured nod indicated Dad's agreement with Mum. He recommenced, 'The smell was the worst part. The sky was filled with clouds of thick oily smoke from the naval base the British had blown up. They didn't want the Japs to get it.'

'Did you get asthma?' I asked.

'Yes. I was choking from the smoke. It smelt like burning rubber and chemicals. There was a sort of metal taste in the air. It was still day time, but it was almost as dark as night. I couldn't breathe.

'There was even more chaos when we got to the pier. Japanese planes had been dive-bombing the wharves. The waterfront was on fire. The ticket office had been bombed so the agents had to operate out of a tin shed. Someone from the shipping company made an announcement to the crowds that the authorities were no longer guaranteeing passage out of Singapore and that it wasn't free any more. Some of the people started screaming when they heard that. Some men were pushing women and children out of the way, to get to the head of the queue. When the sellers yelled that they had new orders to reserve all the berths for British people — well, that was the breaking point for some. The whole area erupted. They went crazy. People started attacking the sellers. Lots of Singaporeans were holding valid tickets for berths on the evacuation ships but they were stopped at the gangplanks crying and begging. The British women and children and lots of administrators evacuated in droves. The colonial administrators bungled so many things.'

'Like what?'

Dad shook his head from side to side. 'Oh, they were hopeless. Unnecessary delays for paperwork. And they didn't even advertise that exit tickets were free. Then they refused to grant berths to non-Europeans and Asians when they heard that the Japanese had reached the outskirts of Singapore. Thanks to them, some evacuation ships sailed as late as the middle of January with plenty of empty berths. It was very sad. They could have saved so many more people.'

As Dad continued his story, I imagined him, Granny Jones, two of his brothers, William and Terrence, their youngest sister Moira, and their married sister Violet and her children, following their papa onto a barge headed for an evacuation ship, which had been moored in the sea lanes outside of the harbour, carrying paperwork attesting to their British heritage and the tickets which they had purchased the day before,

Except for Papa, these were the same people who had immigrated with us to Australia. Was it the experience of war and the escape that had separated them? I thought it would have kept them close. As if she knew what I was thinking, Mum said, 'War separates more than it unites.'

'The Jap planes dive-bombed the whole time,' Dad continued. 'The noise from the shelling and buzzing aircraft didn't stop. Can you imagine the commotion on the water? Everything around us was on fire. All sorts of boats were trying to escape. Some people were on tugs. Others on Chinese junks, rowing boats, even yachts. We had to steer between ships on fire and half sunk hulls.'

Dad's lips came together in a thin line. He took a deep breath, sighed, then continued as if it was his duty to finally impart the story of his escape. 'We were in a terrible state. Our clothes were muddy. My shirt was torn. My lungs were heaving. As soon as we got on the barge, my sisters stopped wailing. They were shaking but they didn't make a sound. Only the children kept crying.

'Sailors raced us below deck. The bombers were harassing our ship. We heard the screeching dive bombers. There was so much commotion. We didn't talk much. We couldn't believe we'd made it,' Dad's words trailed off. 'We just prayed for the people left behind and thanked God we weren't one of them.'

Glynis and I both fell quiet. It seemed the right thing to do. A bit like how we practised the minute's silence at school each year on Remembrance Day. I thought about all the times I had watched Dad kneel on the ground and pray. I imagined his family doing this once they were on the ship.

Dad smiled. His demeanour changed. He sat up straight. He had reached the part in his story where the chances of falling into the hands of the enemy had been averted and he felt free to experience the thrill of the situation. 'When we bought our tickets for England, we were told the destination couldn't be guaranteed. But it wasn't until we boarded that they told us it was no longer safe to go there. The Japs were bombing everything headed that way.'

Despite his description of the uncertainty of their destination, the look of excitement I saw radiating across his face, prompted me to ask, 'Were you scared, Dad?'

'Of course. But I was a young man. It was very exciting to be on that ship. Once we were on board, I was just so happy to be escaping. They didn't tell us where we were going until we got out to sea.'

Dad's solemn voice returned to say, 'No more ships left Singapore after 12 February. The Japs bombed and sank everything in the harbour and the surrounding waters.'

He refused to say any more about the brother who had died in Singapore or his wife and children who had sailed to Australia on one of the early rescue ships. *How come we don't know them? Do they still live here? One day I'll find out what happened to them.*

'So where did you end up going?' asked Glynis.

'To Ceylon.'

'My family didn't get a chance to leave,' Mum said twisting her mouth to one side. 'After the British surrendered, we were cut off from the whole world.'

Allied forces left Malaya on 31 January. They fought all the way across the causeway connecting the two countries, before blowing it up to delay the enemy crossing over to Singapore. The action severed pipelines carrying water to Singapore as well as closing off routes for civilian evacuations. The Japanese quickly advanced into the area and began blitzing the garrisons from across the causeway and with increased air attacks. On 8 February, Japanese landing craft delivered artillery and troops on Singapore's north-west coast, then in the south-west the next day. The fresh troops and heavy artillery attacked Singapore with renewed force.

From airfields deserted by the British, the enemy increased air attacks, adding their fighters to the bombers. Allied forces commenced the same 'scorched earth' policy in Singapore, as they had in Malaya, which included the destruction of secret and technical equipment, ciphers, codes, documents, heavy guns, liquor, and millions of dollars in bank notes. Fire raged throughout the city, giving people the impression that the whole island was ablaze. Hundreds died each day. The decomposing bodies, litter, and rubble piled up in the streets along with the rodents, flies, and cockroaches. No-one was prepared to risk their lives in a clean-up. Whilst everybody waited for the surrender, the streets of Singapore became eerily quiet.

The British surrendered to the Imperial Japanese Army in Singapore on 15 February 1942 in what the world remembers as the largest military capitulation in British history. The Japanese were so confident of their victory, they made no copies of the documents relating to the unconditional surrender, which resulted in the incarceration of 100,000 Allied defence personnel. Thus, commenced the brutal occupation by Japanese forces which caused Malaya and Singapore to descend into darkness.

10.1

After hearing Dad's story, I was angry at the Japanese and understood the feelings of hatred he felt towards them. However, Dad's experience left me feeling bewildered. Despite their miraculous escape, my stomach churned at the anguish his family had endured as they waited for exit papers. It seemed so unnecessary. So unfair. Surely, when it is a matter of life and death, everyone is entitled to jump on a rescue ship. Surely, when the enemy is advancing, it does not simply come down to paperwork, money, or the nationality of your father.

The thought that even when they held the necessary exit documents in their hands, Dad's family had to endure the uncertainty of whether they would be permitted to accompany their father onto a waiting ship because of their mixed heritage; the way they looked, left me reeling. Even worse, if they did not leave on that ship, what could the sons of an Englishman, bearing such an overtly English surname as Jones, expect to endure at the hands of the enemy. Gosh! To the British they were not English enough and to the Japs they were not Asian enough.

I reflected on my early childhood in Australia, remembering the teacher who had told me that my siblings, and I did not look either Asian or English. And how Dad's experiences had confirmed that it did not matter what your paperwork said if your face told a different story. The worst prejudices I had encountered, had occurred at school. And they had come primarily from the immigrant teachers. Some did not seem happy to be in Australia. Perhaps they had they been passing on the prejudices they had experienced growing up in a foreign country. My family had been lucky to have the loveliest neighbours who had never made us feel lesser because we looked different. As far as I knew, our adopted homeland had never denied us anything. I wondered how that might change if Australia went to war with an Asian country.

I tried picturing the tumult on the water in Singapore harbour described by Dad. I imagined the boats of various shapes and sizes, weaving through the debris of half-sunk hulls and those on fire, in a frantic attempt to leave.

I imagined the silence of the members of his family as the barge carried them towards their evacuation ship. And Dad's words, 'Only the children kept crying.'

An image of Granny Jones came to mind. I had only ever seen her immaculately dressed and coiffured. Now I imagined her looking dishevelled, clothes dirty, stockings ripped, straggly pieces of hair slipping from her neat hair bun, a few wispy pieces sticking to her sweaty face as her sons heaved her onto a makeshift gangplank. Or was it a ladder? Dad had not said. I imagined the crew members waiting to bustle her below deck. Had Granny paused for a final farewell to her family's adopted homeland, I wondered. Perhaps at the sight of Singapore ablaze, she might have reflected on the torching of her father's plantation in Ceylon, twenty years earlier. I wondered what it might feel like to abandon everything you own, but for a few meagre suitcases, for the second time in your life.

But I knew enough about Granny's obsession with race. What she had said about Dad marrying a woman of Portuguese descent. How she had only ever described herself as a Dutch Burgher. Nothing about Ceylon or having Singhalese blood had come from her lips. And I was certain that despite the mixed feelings of sadness and relief at leaving Singapore, she would have been utterly devastated to discover at sea, that due to heavy bombing, their ship was returning them to Ceylon.

I never met my paternal grandfather, Frederick Walter Jones, nor did I understand why Dad could not bring himself to talk about him more. I asked a lot of questions but received few answers. When I pressed to know how and when his papa had died, Dad just said, 'He was old.'

The lump that formed in my throat was a difficult one to swallow after hearing those words about the grandfather we had never known. I could not help but feel that Dad and the members of his family, who managed to escape the unexpected fall of Singapore, despite the many blunders by colonial administration, owed their lives to the old Englishman from Devon, whom they called Papa Jones.

The hair-raising story of how Dad and his family had narrowly escaped the clutches of the Japanese left me with conflicting emotions. I tried to understand Dad's allegiance to the British. I bounced between feelings of gratitude and sorrow. Gratitude that being British had saved them. Sorrow at the ones left behind because they were not British or simply could not produce the right paperwork in time, which had included his brother.

No wonder Dad felt like he had been treated unfairly in the past. No wonder he resented people questioning his heritage. They must have made him feel inferior. Like how I had felt when the teachers disbelieved me. Though Dad was right about prejudice and discrimination, I had conflicting thoughts to him. There were times throughout my childhood when I had felt inferior because I did not look like other children. However, we had not experienced any bad treatment in Australia. Just the scrunching of eyebrows or the tilting of a head in response to saying we were British.

I tried to hold my gaze at Dad. Instead, my eyes darted around the table trying to conceal my feelings of guilt and ungratefulness. Guilt because I had fought Dad about his desire to feel so strongly about his heritage, considering his personal experiences with discrimination and prejudice. Guilt because I had disliked Granny Jones so much, considering what she had been through. Ungrateful because despite what Dad had done to bring his family to a safe country, I could not let go of my desire to return to Singapore one day where I could feel and look like everyone else.

Dad had stopped talking so I would have to wait for another time to get an answer to the many questions remaining. Like what would have happened if we had already been born in 1942. And what would have become of Mum's family if they had already moved to Singapore. Mum did not have a pure British father and neither did we. Would the authorities have let her and her family or any of us onto a rescue ship? And what of the other horrors of discrimination and displacement which Dad's family had faced in Ceylon? He had only ever touched on the torching of his grandfather's plantation on the west coast of Ceylon during the discrimination against supporters of the British in the fight for independence.

There were many more different looking immigrants at high school than I had encountered in primary. I wondered what conflicts their families had escaped, how much they had suffered, and in what ways it had changed them. Had the suffering changed Dad and his family? Had Granny Jones sought refuge in such an austere religion as Adventism to increase the chances of her family finding eternal peace in heaven? Maybe that was why Dad was so intent on his family following his religion. Until I knew the answers, I must simply trust Dad and have faith in God.

Revolutions

I had changed so much during second form, I hardly recognised myself in the mirror. I had become more reclusive at home, caring less and less about what was going on there. Mum and I now disagreed on anything and everything. I was angry with her, blaming her for never being around when I needed her. We were talking less than we had last year. She was always at work. Too tired when she came home. Ages had passed since she had accompanied us to church. I had not stopped to consider that she was the only working woman in our street and the only one with five children, three of whom had serious health issues. LeRoy had almost died from a serious blood disorder a few years earlier which resulted in him having his spleen removed. Wayne had developed into a chronic asthmatic like Dad. At the age of fourteen I did not have the time to think about the difficulties at home.

Even Dad seemed to have cut himself off from me to deal with Dewey who was demanding more attention. Determined to prove the education authorities wrong about his eldest son, he had stepped up his efforts to teach him to read. Evenings became a nightmare in our home. After an hour or more of persistence, Dad would give up. Sometimes, out of frustration, he would throw the books onto the floor. Mum did not always comment but whenever she did, it sounded like a criticism of Dad. 'Leave the poor boy alone,' was one of her usual remarks. And another, 'Can't you tell he's not even seeing the words.' No one asked about my homework any more. Not that I cared about that because there was a social revolution happening. A music revolution was broadcasting it to the world. The fashion revolution had collided with both. I was desperate to join any revolution. Preferably, a peaceful one to 'change the world' like the Beatles had recently begun singing about. But I was too young. Too disconnected.

The only way I could demonstrate my support for any movement, was by changing the way I looked. And so, I ripped the hem on my royal blue tunic to six inches above the regulation, then wore it to school without the yellow blouse underneath. The tuft I cut at the crown of my head stood up like a Mohawk. Every morning, I painted Twiggy lines on my eyes. The vertical lines drawn in black eyeliner, one by one, from the edge of my bottom eyelid to the top of my cheeks, had been named after the British model who had created the signature look. Some of the girls with whom I had made friends, hitched their tunics up to mini skirt length. At one point all of us had tufts at the top of our heads. However, I seemed to be the only one intent on wearing eye makeup. I wondered if it was because I loved watching Mum apply hers each morning even though it was never as extreme as mine.

Other than at school, I had little interaction with my friends. Religion continued to prevent us from mixing on Saturdays which left me out of many of their social events. My heart raced the first time my friends asked me to join them at the shopping mall after school. They went every afternoon. I wanted to say yes but I feared missing the bus. I would have to walk home alone. It might be dark. I had never walked that route. Nor had I ever been to the shops on my own.

They began to pester me to join them. 'Aren't we good enough for you? What's wrong with us?' One afternoon, I said yes. They each bought a can of coca cola. One smoked a cigarette. I bought a lemonade. Adventists shunned caffeine.

'You have to nick something,' one said. 'From the variety store.'

I froze. Then took it. A translucent, blue, acrylic ring. My eyes ping-ponged around the street. My face burned with shame, wondering if any-one had seen me. Certain someone had, I threw the ring in the bin outside the store. We walked a few steps together then I stopped. 'I've got to go now,' I lied. 'Before my father gets home from work.'

My legs wobbled as I walked away. My mind raced. Had that really happened. Maybe I was dreaming. I tried to imagine that I had not gone with those girls. Had not listened to them. Had not stolen the ring. That it had all been a bad dream. One I prayed no-one in the whole world would ever find out about.

A week later, I went with them again. This time, one of the girls got into a car with some boys. 'Come on,' she said. 'They won't bite.' I jumped into the back seat of the rickety old bomb. A thrilling shiver covered my body from head to toe. I had not felt this way since braving the roller coaster ride at Luna Park with Glynis. That day we had both screeched with fear. Today's reaction was a soundless shiver. They might not bite, but no-one in my family knows I'm in this car.

There were three boys. Two in the front and one in the back with us. I could smell their armpits. My friend sat in the middle. The shiver had made my head spin. It remained for the ten minutes it took to drive to my friend's house. By the time we pulled up, I felt dizzy. We got out and they drove off. I did not share the experience with anyone. Glynis was always in eldest child mode with me, which contributed to us having almost a parent-child relationship rather than friends. If I had confided in her she would have told on me.

Most of the prefects would ignore me at the gates if I wore regulation head covering. Students could choose between the winter and summer headwear at any time of the year. I had long since swapped the awkward Panama hat, which only the first form girls ever wore, for the soft navy-blue French style beret. Despite my free pass from the prefects, one of the teachers started harassing me. She was not our regular for physical education but had taken the class a few times. She dressed very plainly and wore no makeup on her face or eyes. Labelling my acts, and me, as 'non-conformist' she began stopping me to inspect my face and uniform. Each time our paths crossed, she would send me to the toilets to wash off my Twiggy lines, sometimes multiple times in one day, after I had reapplied them. One time, she forced me to wear a blouse from the lost property bin. I was confused as to why she wanted so badly to harass a good student into submission. My response to the onslaught was to stop learning completely. By the commencement of third term, my books were empty. In less than a year, I had gone from being an A-grade student to feeling confused, cynical, rebellious, and innocent, all at the same time.

Fearing the confrontation, I could not walk through the front gates of the school without breaking into a sweat. I hung my head whenever I passed the harassing teacher. Soon she cottoned on to my antics and would stop me in a corridor, in the quadrangle during lunch break, in between classes, everywhere.

The discovery of a few loose palings on the fence behind the Physical Education block, hatched the idea of escaping during the hour-long lunch break. The next day, just after the lunch bell, I swung the palings apart, then squeezed through the gap. I walked to the nearby shopping centre, bought a cup of hot chips for lunch, then returned before the bell rang to resume classes. It was the first time I had ever done such a thing, but when no one seemed to miss me, I did it again, and again. Until I was caught.

I had followed the same process on the fourth day before returning just before the bell. However, as I straightened up after bending over to slip through the palings, the tall, solidly built frame of the school's new Deputy Headmistress peered down on me. 'Hello Beverley,' she said. 'Please follow me to my office."

'You just can't leave without permission,' she said in a calm voice, assuaging my fears of severe punishment. 'It's extremely dangerous. Once you leave the school grounds, we can't protect you. Do you realise that?'

Her powerful build and tight brown permed hair had resulted in my friends and me christening her, Prison Ma'am. However, contrary to our impressions, she appeared to be the most even tempered of anyone whom I had encountered at the school. She was smart. I liked how she went out of her way to build rapport with me.

'Why do you want to go out at lunchtime anyway?'

Rather than broach the subject of the teacher who had been badgering me, I said, 'Because I want to buy hot chips.'

'You know that if you want something badly enough, you only have to ask.'

'Will you give me permission then?' I snapped back in a smart-alecky tone.

'We'll see about that,' she replied. 'I'll be talking to your home room teachers. However, you leave me no choice but to inform your parents.'

My body rocked slightly from side to side. I hoped she had not seen my chest rising and falling at her last remark.

11.1

My eyes bulged at the words reverberating from the pulpit. Our pastor's voice deepened like that of my principal when she was warning the girls about the 'consequences of their actions'. I was certain he was staring directly at Glynis and me.

'Beware temptation,' he screamed. Then in a steady, self-assured tone, 'Women and girls must dress modestly in knee length dresses with sleeves. Not wear garish makeup. Listening to modern music, dancing, going to the cinema is trivial, foolish.' After a long pause his voice softened. 'In fact,' he said with confident superiority. 'It's sinful for Adventists.'

My shoulders began rolling from side to side to relieve the feeling like two bare hands had locked around my neck and were squeezing the spirit out of me. I turned towards Glynis, seated on my right, for a reaction. She scrunched her lips together, batting her long black false eyelashes at me. I thought about how I had been using her lipstick, rouge, and eye makeup without her knowing, for months. The black liquid eyeliner was my favourite. She now wore a miniskirt to church. My thoughts flashed to Mum's shortened hemlines.

The image of Dad playing his beloved Bing Crosby record came to mind. According to this sermon, he was committing a sin each time he listened to *By the Light of the Silvery Moon*. None of these things had mattered when I was a child. Now they consumed my every waking thought, causing me to feel different from everyone I knew, other than this tiny congregation.

In retaliation, I rang my friend Rhonda that night and said yes to the invitation to go to Manly Beach with her the next Sunday. Rhonda had not been amongst the girls who stole stuff after school so I was confident I could convince Dad to allow me to go. I had the feeling he had started to realise that I was growing up and needed more freedom. I had been vocal about my boredom with school. And he was aware from Glynis, that I was six months away from being legally able to leave school for good. He seemed to be doing all he could to prevent that happening. So, despite seeming reluctant about my going on such a long journey by train and ferry, he consented.

'Of course,' I said with glee in response to Dad's conditions, which in addition to driving me to the station included keeping money for the telephone, ringing him before I bought the return ticket in case I forgot later, and waiting for him at Bankstown station if he was running late rather than attempting to walk home.

When Sunday arrived, I did not wake Dad. Instead, I snuck out of the house at six o'clock before anyone heard me, walked to the station, and met Rhonda. We caught a train to Circular Quay then a ferry to Manly. My first experience of being on a ferry on Sydney Harbour will remain with me forever. The new Opera House was still under construction. Sunlight flickered on the white sails of yachts. Our ferry rocked and rolled on the harbour swells. Topside, the two of us struggled to hear each other over the thunder of engines. I closed my eyes, pressed my face into the ocean breeze. The salt air matted my hair, made my face sticky, but dried my lips. Almost there, we clutched our beach bags and raced inside to brush our hair, clean our faces, repaint our lips.

At Manly Wharf, I saw young boys and old men quickly pull up their fishing lines as our ferry approached. Seagulls squawked overhead. Sea water, mixed with a bit of diesel, filled the air. Long before we came to a halt, passengers made their move, gathering up their clutter of beach bags and eskies, corralling Rhonda and me into the throng, then moving us along like a human wave, towards the ramps. If I had lifted my legs off the ground, I reckon the momentum could have carried me all the way off the ferry.

Rather than stopping at the wharf, the wave continued, past a merry-go-round, dodgem cars, and other carnival-like attractions, onto what seemed like a pre-ordained path. It spat us out onto the Corso – a part-pedestrian pathway, a few hundred metres long, leading passengers from the harbour pier to the ocean beach. A waft of salty, seaweedy air, much more delicate than what I had smelt on the ferry, reached me halfway along the Corso. A thin, horizontal, turquoise line appeared in the distance. Despite the humdrum of the crowds, I heard the echo of waves. Enticed by the wondrous smells and sounds, we quickened our pace.

On the Promenade, a cool zephyr re-tangled my hair. Girls in bikinis walked past. Blond-haired surfers assessed the waves, their black wetsuits hanging by their hips. I stared out to the endless jewel-sea. Breathed in the salt and seaweed; watched the gushing, white-tipped surf break on the sand.

Rhonda broke the silence. 'Let's walk up to North Steyne. It's where most of the *surfies* hang.'

Majestic Norfolk pines lined our walk to what was the middle of three main beaches on the foreshore. We spread our towels onto the soft white sand. Rhonda surprised me when she shed her clothes, stretching out her bikini clad body, before lathering herself in coconut oil. 'Got to get a tan,' she said. A group of surfers inched closer, like a flock of sneaky seagulls. Gaining confidence from her lead, I stripped down to my new swimsuit, a terry towelling bikini in white.

Mum had given me the money to buy the bikini when I told her I had outgrown my swimsuit. I had begun developing breasts at a rapid rate. Marvelling at how I had been as flat as a board one day, a D cup the next, she had said, 'You're taking after your Dutch Burgher grandmother. She has huge breasts. I better take you to buy your first bra.' With a lightning-fast quip of my lips, I had responded, 'I've already bought my own with my Christmas money.'

Two of the surfers came closer. They sat down on the sand alongside us. When they started chatting to us, Rhonda seemed to revel in the attention, even asking one of them to rub oil onto her back.

'White shows off your tan,' the other one said to me, eyeing my breasts. 'Are you Tahitian?'

'No. I'm Eurasian,' I said, picturing Dad's face as I smiled. It was the first time I had ever described myself that way. Neither of the surfers understood what that meant, nor had they ever heard the term. 'It's a mix of Asian and English. I was born in Singapore,' I added, remembering what I had heard Mum say over the years.

'I thought everyone in Singapore was Chinese?' one of them said.

Dad was right. Australians did not know anything about one of their nearest neighbours.

I did not respond to the question. They both seemed more surprised at the distance we girls were prepared to travel to get to the beach. Though neither of them had ever heard of the suburb where we 'Westies' lived, they both agreed that forty minutes on a train was a long way from Manly.

Rhonda's confidence in talking to the two surfers made me realise that I was naïve. Other than my brothers, I had no experience of talking to boys. Let alone a couple of beach-loving Aussie surfers a few years older than me. One of the boys said he was going in for a surf. When he jumped up, his friend followed. I watched them each grab one of the surfboards that had been resting against a pine tree near the footpath. I stole a look at the one who had asked me if I was Tahitian, through the corner of my eye. He looked very Australian with his blond hair. His skin was golden from being in the sun. He was nice, but not movie star handsome, had a bit of a pudgy nose. I watched them both sprint out to the surf. One carried the board under his arm. The other on top of his head.

'Which one do you like?' Rhonda blurted out as soon as they were out of earshot.

I shrugged.

'He likes you,' she said with a slight nod towards the left in the direction of the two boys. 'Let's get wet.'

We walked to the water's edge. The gritty sand crunched between my toes. She went in for a swim. I did not feel comfortable swimming in the ocean. I was not a good enough swimmer. I just let the frothy ripples wash over my feet.

When the boys finished their surf, they parked their boards back in the same spot, then returned to sit and talk with us. They hung around us for the whole day. We talked about school, where they lived, stuff like that. The four of us walked to a shop and bought cans of Coca-Cola. We left our towels and bags on the beach; came back to them untouched.

Rhonda jumped up and began shaking the sand from her towel in a panic. 'We'd better make tracks. It's three o'clock. We've got to get home before dark. She pulled her kaftan over her head. 'Ouch!' she winced. Despite over five hours of baking in the sun, her lily-white skin had not tanned. It looked like the inside of one of those papayas Dad had bought for Granny Jones.

'We'll drive you to the wharf,' said one of the boys. 'My van is just a street away.'

Rhonda's look, which said, no thanks we don't trust you, embarrassed me. I butted in and explained that we preferred to walk.

'Okay. We'll walk with you. We've gotta take our boards back to the van first.'

They surprised us by returning. Then accompanied us the same way we had come, along the Corso.

'Look, there's an ice-cream shop,' I said excitedly. In my haste to get to the beach that morning, I had not noticed the many shops and hotels that lined the Corso.

'There's a cinema too,' said the boy who had chatted to me for most of the day and who now walked by my side. 'Maybe we could go one day?'

I smiled in return.

'See you next Sunday?' he said when we reached the wharf. Then leaned forward and kissed me on the lips. My first kiss from a boy. It tasted salty. I thought about it for the duration of the ferry trip, almost walking past the public phone at Circular Quay without telephoning Dad.

Railway stations were scary to me. So many different types of people. Young men staring at Rhonda and me. Old men begging for money. Was it so obvious that we were from the sticks? The thought of the hour-long journey home to the western suburbs was horrible. Rhonda said I was being ridiculous about my fears. But I could not let go of Dad's words on the phone call after he had finished berating me for leaving without him this morning. 'Be careful of the louts that hang around the railway stations.'

Once inside the carriage, we kept to ourselves. The brown paper bags of greasy hot chips and cans of Coca-Cola we had bought from one of the milk bars along the quay, distracted us for a while. As we munched away, we dissected the day. Rhonda had found out a lot more about her guy than I had about mine. They had made plans to meet next week at the same spot. 'Are you coming with me?' she asked.

I wanted to say yes but I was not sure Dad would let me go again. I imagined he had been worried sick about me being out there on my own. I did not answer Rhonda. Instead, I stared out the dusty window at the hotchpotch of rusting corrugated iron rooftops, topping the procession of dilapidated houses that backed onto the tracks. Spotting an old woman pegging laundry on a makeshift clothesline, made me feel like a snoop. A pang of guilt shot through me when I thought of my family's immaculate home.

As our train headed further west, the 'safety in numbers' diminished with each stop. By the time it reached Bankstown, the sun had almost gone, and we were the only two passengers alighting onto the deserted platform. I raced up the station steps, with Rhonda in tow, letting out a sigh of relief when I spotted Dad's car parked in the bus zone.

'Can we drive Rhonda home?

'Of course.'

I loved that my dad was always happy to do stuff for me. It was not until after I had hopped in the front seat alongside him that I sensed his relief. Though his voice still wavered when he asked about our day. I inhaled and exhaled slowly, then licked my bottom lip. I do not remember how I described the day at Manly Beach. I was too busy thinking about the salt lingering on my lips.

With Dad's approval, Rhonda and I made the trek to the beach a few weeks later. And once again, until I discovered the two of us had little else in common. She did not like the music which was making my blood churn. She had no knowledge of world events which were becoming all-consuming to me. And strangely, she had absolutely no intention of escaping the suburbs where she had lived all her life. We both forgot the names of the friendly surfers. We never saw them again.

My stomach roiled, when I spotted an envelope sitting on the television addressed to Mr and Mrs Jones. I had half hoped the deputy principal had forgotten about me; that she had far more important things to do. Obviously not, because there it was, propped up with other envelopes that looked like the usual bills, waiting for Mum because she dealt with the mail. Except, this one had the dreaded school logo in the left-hand corner.

By the time Mum arrived home, I had chewed on the inside of my mouth till I could taste blood whilst replaying the events of the day on which I had escaped through the fence palings, a million times. On the one millionth and first time, I had fantasised that the incident had never happened; on the one millionth and second, that I had not been caught. Dinner was a quiet affair that night. Dad did not try to force Dewey to read. Neither Mum nor Dad said anything about the letter during dinner. When I left the table though, Mum jumped up and followed me to my bedroom with Glynis in tow.

'We received a terrible letter from the Deputy Principal at your school. What have you been up to?'

'What do you mean?'

'She says your books are empty. That you're not wearing the right uniform. And they want to know why you've cut your hair funny. Worst of all they're worried about you leaving the school grounds without permission at lunch time. They called it truanting. Is this all true?'

Mum did not wait for me to respond. 'We let you go to Manly with your friend. Your father and I are working hard to give you children a good life. Why are you doing this?'

'I just went to buy some hot chips.'

'You can't leave school without a note,' Glynis interjected. 'It's wagging.'

I cocked my head to one side and glared at her. Then crossed my arms and looked up at the ceiling rather than face Mum. 'I'm nervous at school.'

'Well, you're too young to leave so you must make the best of it. At least until you turn fifteen.'

'Oh gosh, Mum. I don't want to leave. I just hate some of those stupid teachers. They're hounding me.'

'I've made an appointment for you with Dr Novak.'

'What for?' I screamed, now staring directly at Mum. She did not respond.

I fell asleep listening to my transistor radio.

12

The Lion's Den

Dr Novak had visited our home many times over the years, at all hours of the day and night, to treat Dad and my brothers' asthma. Yet he had only come for me once. It was on the Sunday night after Mum had driven me to the hospital emergency earlier with an excruciating stomach ache. A female doctor, who did not speak good English, had diagnosed me as having constipation and told me to go home and eat lots of fruit. When the pain escalated during the night, and I started shivering, Mum rang the emergency number for Dr Novak, and he came straight over.

'Acute appendicitis, you have,' he said. Then, after removing the thermometer he had stuck in my mouth, listening to my chest and abdomen with his stethoscope, and pressing down hard all over my belly with his cold hands, which caused me to jump when he touched the side that was hurting, he said, 'You ate no fruit. Good.'

There were no rising inflections at the end of his sentences, so I did not know whether the doctor was asking me questions or making statements. Which was why I let Mum do the talking. Other than managing to squeeze in her opinion, of 'that useless doctor at the hospital', Mum had not had the opportunity to say much. Because, in a matter of minutes Dr Novak had diagnosed my problem, packed away the stethoscope, and was following Mum to the lounge room in response to his final question, or statement, 'You have telephone.'

From my bed, I heard him ring the local hospital for my immediate admission. No doubt he was responding to a question from a medical person on the other end of the phone when he said, 'Appendix. Organ soon burst.' After ensuring Mum was able to drive me to the hospital without delay, he left. The visit had been so fast that Mum and I were in the car behind him as he drove away.

Over a year had passed since the removal of my appendix when I found myself sitting opposite Dr Novak in his surgery with Mum by my side. The memory of his visit to our home flooded back as soon as I heard him speak. Mum had told us he was an immigrant from somewhere in central Europe who had escaped to Australia during WWII. Despite his accent resembling the 'useless doctor at the hospital' he spoke good English. Though Mum had faith in him, Dr Novak's sentences still sounded jumbled to me. After a gruff welcome, he invited us to sit down by nodding towards the two chairs in front of his desk, before tilting his head towards Mum, indicating he was expecting her to begin the consultation.

'Beverley has become anxious about going to school.'

Shifting his gaze to me he said, 'You are feeling like this, when.'

'I hate school.'

'She has begun menstruating, yes.' he said shifting his attention back to Mum.

'Yes.'

Ever since I began my excruciating menstrual period late last year, Mum had been blaming my hormones for anything and everything she considered abnormal behaviour. Now she had finally found an opportunity to take me to the doctor for a 'check-up'. Hearing her discuss my personal situation with this strange man made me feel like a freak. He came over to me and listened to my chest with his stethoscope, mumbled something about the removed appendix, said a few ah hums, then assured Mum, he could give me something that would help my situation.

It was the Sixties, so he prescribed Valium. Or *Mother's Little Helper* as I had heard the Rolling Stones call it in their song about the increasing popularity of doctors prescribing tranquillisers like the little yellow pill to women. I was living in an age where the adults disapproved of recreational drug use, yet even the professionals were endorsing and prescribing mind-altering drugs to housewives who complained about the difficulties of raising teenage children. And then, as in my case, to the female children of those women. All the while believing the problems must be related to hormones.

I saw Mum's lips moving in the car on the way home. But all I could hear in my head, was the new singer whom I had started following called Janis Joplin belting out 'Piece of my heart' from her song with the same name.

Throughout my ordeals at school, our pastor continued to search for opportunities to visit our home to encourage Dad to return to church, even without Mum, which Dad had refused to do. Mum referred to the pastor's actions as 'inexorable proselytising' which she explained meant his never-ending preaching. During those visits, he would allude to my baptism. A few weeks after my consultation with the doctor he made another visit.

I had prepared to tell him that I was unable to study for baptism due to a host of reasons. Like, my not knowing a single person who still went to Sunday School, my being too busy meeting surfers at the beach, listening to rock and blues music by singers who preached about alternative spiritualities, and taking drugs prescribed by the local doctor to calm me down. Until his new suggestion to Dad made my ears prick up. 'Have you considered sending the children to the Sydney Adventist College in Strathfield?'

Ever since the dreaded letter from school, I had been straining, extra hard, to hear what Mum and Dad had to say about me. Sometimes Dad involved Glynis in their discussions, which sent me into a silent rage, pushing me further away from her. I never heard him say anything about my wearing eye-makeup, cutting the tuft in my hair, or going to Manly Beach with Rhonda. However, I did hear him ask Glynis, 'What do you think of that music your sister listens to?' To which she had responded, 'She's just stubborn. Doesn't want to listen to the teachers.'

'Anyway,' Dad continued, 'I'm more concerned about protecting her from corruption than hearing about her empty workbooks.'

To what corruption was Dad referring. He could not have known about the incidents with my friends. I had been keeping my conflicts to myself by avoiding conversations with the whole family for weeks, maybe months. Had it really been a whole year. What had made him think the music was influencing me. I had not thought of it as corruption but maybe Dad was more aware of the potential dangers than me. Reflecting on some of the lyrics and their messages about anti-establishment, taking charge of my education by rejecting traditional methods and lessons, and experimenting with illegal psychoactive drugs, may have caused some of the music to be viewed by outsiders, like adults, as controversial. But corruptive? I did not believe so.

I had continued wearing eye makeup, despite being made to wash it off whenever the harassing teacher caught me, which had become a regular occurrence, sometimes several times in a single day. Valium was not a psychoactive drug, but I had taken it a few times after caustic interactions with her. I liked the feeling of calmness which had given me a break from caring about what she did or said to me.

My English teacher was okay, but she was young and new. It was her first job out of university. The class took advantage of her lack of experience in controlling thirty teenage girls. I was bored. I had been passing monthly tests without the need for study. And so, I became the ringleader at creating chaos in the class. Which, of course, led to my being in trouble with the English Master. The subjects of science, history, and geography all got a thumbs down from me primarily because I did not like the teachers. I just carried on as if in a dream-state, within the confines of the school property, wondering when I would be old enough to escape the sticks and join the counter culture.

Dad had resumed coming to church a couple of times a month. He had not expressed his reasons for doing so, except every now and then he mentioned the good qualities of the missionary girl whom he had named me after. I wondered whether it had been Dad or the pastor who had first raised the idea of the Adventist school.

Dad had taken to muttering the word 'fools' under his breath at the anti-war demonstrators on the newsreels. 'Those poor soldiers are fighting communism,' he said. And he laughed aloud at the images of hippies chanting in the streets. I had to take a deep breath to prevent myself from saying how much I longed to turn up at church wearing a flowing paisley dress and a daisy chain across my forehead. Anything to make me feel alive. A change from feeling dead in the suburbs. Was I making Dad's asthma worse?

My heart had skipped a beat when straight after saying grace one Sabbath evening, Dad looked over to me and said, 'I think it would be good for you to go to the Adventist school at Strathfield. If you go, LeRoy will join you.'

LeRoy looked up from his plate, staring at Dad, then me, at the mention of his name but did not say anything. I did not know how to respond. Instead, I started mentally tallying up the negative reasons. I did not like my current school, but what consequences might arise if I moved? I would certainly lose my friends. But since I had been hanging out with them, I had made some stupid decisions. I knew I did not want to become like them, doing all those bad things they did.

Changing schools might help me be a better Adventist. I would make new friends. Ones who did not steal, smoke, or get in cars with boys. Ones who would not press me to do stuff on the Sabbath. Maybe it would be a good idea. I mean, I was never going to stop listening to the music. It was the only thing that connected me to the outside world. My mouth was so dry, I had to swallow a few times before I could reply to Dad's suggestion. 'What about my friends?'

'You have that friend at church. Maybe she goes there.'

Meriden and I were the same age, but we only ever saw each other a couple of hours each week at church. Most of our time together was spent listening to the Sabbath school teacher or the divine service preacher. I vaguely remember going to her house one time for lunch. Other than that, we knew very little about each other. I was not aware that she had started at the Adventist High School until I asked. As far as private schools were concerned, my friends at school only talked about the Catholic ones. I wondered if we would even like each other outside of church. And if all private schools were the same.

Maybe if I was a pupil at that school, I could become more involved in the Adventist community. Maybe it could bring my family close again like we used to be. I was still angry with Mum for bringing the Catholic question into our lives. Maybe changing schools was fate. Maybe it will be like a fresh start. Maybe it will make Dad happy. If I decide not to go, I might be lost to God forever. I would not be with my family on the judgment day. The change might help me prepare for baptism – if that was still part of the plan.

'I've heard enough about religion from the old lady to last a life time,' Mum said after hearing Dad's question to me about changing schools.

Mum's negative comments about Granny Jones and our religion were becoming increasingly common in our household. So were the arguments about it between her and Dad. Tonight's comment came following Granny and Uncle's earlier visit to check on whether we had been to church. Mum had become braver since the visit from her mother. She no longer hid her feelings about her mother-in-law. Quite the opposite. Now she voiced her opinions for all to hear — even if only after Granny and Uncle had left.

The cause of the eruption that night, was a question Mum had overheard Granny ask Dad. I had heard it too. It was how I learnt that she had something to do with Dad's decision about schools. 'Have you spoken to the school?' was all Granny needed to say, revealing that the two of them had been discussing the subject. *Poor Mum, she must feel outnumbered. I hope I'm not wrong about this new start bringing our family closer.*

From my bedroom, I overheard Mum say, 'You know we can't afford this. We're struggling on two pays.'

In one of his *Onward Christian Soldier* ways, Dad replied, 'It's the Lord's decision. He will find a way. Beverley is in danger. If she goes to the Adventist school so must LeRoy. And Wayne when he gets older.'

I whispered to myself, 'Okay. Time to make your decision. You can do this.'

'Do what?' Glynis asked.

'None of your business.'

My mind raced with the possible consequences of my decision. I felt a sinking feeling in my tummy that Mum and Dad were arguing because of me. I fell asleep biting down hard on my bottom lip, praying it would all work out by morning.

12.1

There was no need for an interview to begin at the new school. The enrolment had been done on the phone because our pastor had referred us. All LeRoy and I had to do was turn up on the first day of the 1969 school year, which was still a few months away. Dad had trusted his faith in God and forged on with the investment in his children, despite Mum expressing her serious concerns about the family's finances. A few weeks before the end of the school year, Dad took the morning off work to take us to buy our new uniforms from The Greater Sydney Conference office for the Seventh-day Adventist Church, which was located a few streets from our new school.

Dad had remained silent during the drive. Inside the store, he stood, arms folded across his chest, as the assistant darted around the room handing LeRoy and me things to try on. There were tunics, blouses, shirts, ties, sports clothes, hats, a beret, socks, and blazers. I watched him unfold his arms, every now and then, to smooth down his hair before fiddling with his moustache. His thoughts seemed to be elsewhere. Like he was not with us. His expression lacked the vitality he had exhibited in reaction to my forced show of enthusiasm at changing schools. I had done it to keep him happy, make him proud. But now it only served to make me feel remorseful.

I looked down at the floorboards, but nothing could distract me from the mountain of crackling, crunching cellophane packets which the assistant had begun building atop the counter in front of us, sporadically punctuated by the ka-ching of a cash register or a sigh from Dad. School fees and textbooks were yet to come.

'Dad,' I said, hoping a smile would cheer him. He didn't respond.

'Dad. Are you okay?'

'Yes. I'm very tired Evvy.' He pressed his lips tightly together.

Dad worked so hard. Even after buying our uniforms then driving us home, he was heading off to the factory to work a couple of hours overtime to make up for the lost pay. Most afternoons, we could expect him to arrive home around half past four. On pay days, he would appear a little later, often with a loaf of freshly baked poppyseed bread from the local baker. After he had greeted us with a kiss and a hug, we would gather around the table as he cut thick slices then spread each one with generous layers of butter. I added lashings of Vegemite to mine.

I sensed this much-loved routine was about to change when Mum came to talk to me one evening before Dad arrived home from working late. 'Starting from next week, your father is going to need to shower and have a rest when he gets home from work. You and your brother's need to be quiet so he can sleep.'

Like clockwork on Monday, as Mum had predicted, Dad drove into our driveway at half past four as usual. After greeting us, he showered, dressed, then rested on his bed. At the incessant buzzing from the alarm clock, which he had set for precisely two hours from when he lay down, he came into the kitchen, dressed in a pair of dark grey overalls, ate the sandwiches

Mum had prepared that morning, kissed us goodbye, hopped in the car and drove off. Mum was running late, so missed seeing him. In addition to his day job, Dad had begun working the night shift at a chemical factory to save for the school fees, due before the beginning of first term.

LeRoy and I commenced at the Sydney Adventist College as planned. We caught the number 27 bus, which stopped a street away from the bottom of ours. Like the former bus to Bankstown, this was the only service that deviated from the Hume Highway. If we missed either the morning or afternoon service, we would have to walk an extra forty-five minutes.

At the sight of Meriden, I took a deep breath in and let it out slowly. She spotted me and raced over with her two best friends Esther and Rebecca. They were warm and inviting. Both had that sort of wholesome, *I'm safe in the arms of the Lord* look I had seen on other children at church. I fiddled with my hair, pushing it out of my eyes. 'Not used to wearing my hair out,' I said. Girls were not required to wear their hair tied back within the school grounds. It was one of the unexpected differences between this school and my last. Another was the size, which was significantly smaller. Instead of between five and eight levels per grade, there were only two. The most distinctive difference was that LeRoy, and I were attending the same school. Something about the mix of boys and girls made it seem more like a family than an institution.

The atmosphere, however, felt a lot more conservative. My old friends would have called it square. I felt like I had stepped back in time. Some girls wore thick ribbons in their hair. Female teachers wore simple, knee length frocks, no makeup, old fashioned hair styles. It was short-back-and-side haircuts for the male teachers. I was dressed like all the other girls, in the regulation summer uniform, belted at the waist, made of cotton, the colour of the sky. I sucked in as much air as I could, preparing for my dive into the blue.

Within a week, I became aware of the magnitude of differences between a public and private school. I had no idea if the nuances were linked to the Adventist religion or if they were in line with other private schools. 'They're crazy about the uniform,' I said over dinner one evening. 'Yesterday, the prefects walked along the lines at the morning assembly in the playground with a long ruler. They made some girls kneel on the asphalt while they measured how high the edge of their hem was from the ground. They never did that at my last school.'

LeRoy piped in, 'They're worse about the length of the boys' hair. It can't be touching the collar of our shirts. A prefect came and took away one of the boys from lines. When he came to the class room, he looked like a freak. They'd shaved his whole head. Worse than a crew cut.'

'Yeah. Apart from the seniors, we're not allowed to talk to the boys outside of the classroom. Not even my own brother,' I said, eyes widening. As far as the various practices of Adventism went, I realised that my exposure had been limited to my weekly church attendances, Dad's prayers, and any proselytizing delivered by Granny Jones.

'Oh Gosh, Mum. LeRoy, and I can't talk to each other for the whole day.'

'Why not?'

'Well, we just can't. It's the rule. They have separate buses to take the boys and girls to the station. Meriden said the buses go on strike every now and then and we've got to walk to the station on separate sides of the road.'

I stopped talking to consider how stupid this rule seemed. I dreaded the day LeRoy, and I would have no choice but to walk down opposite sides of the road. It was stupid because as soon as we got on the number 27 bus, we would be talking all the way home.

Dad had not raised his eyes from his meal. I wondered what was going through his mind. The only reason he could eat dinner with us that night was because he had been forced to abandon his second job. The noxious chemicals had aggravated his asthma, to the point we nearly lost him to some of the more severe attacks. However, he was already seeking another.

My regular seat at the dining table was two away from Dad. I wished I sat closer. I could touch his hand. Give him a hug. Tell him how sorry I was about his getting sick from the chemical factory. Anything to help cheer him up.

'Dad,' I said, raising my eyebrows as high as I could, 'Remember how you told us about all the fun activities you and your cousins used to do with the Adventists in Singapore?'

He looked up. 'Yes. I do.'

'Did you come across some of the rules LeRoy and I have been talking about?'

Dad did not seem interested in my question. He muttered something about not being lucky enough to go to the Adventist school. Perhaps the religion had changed a lot in the fifty years since his family had joined. Or perhaps the world has changed.

'Well maybe this is the Australian version,' I said, hoping to add some fun into the conversation. Then, quickly changed the subject to alleviate any concerns Dad and Mum might have about my ability to abide by the new rules and regulations.

The celebration of Prayer Week was the first religious ritual that LeRoy and I encountered a month or so after our start. Students observed the practice by forming groups of up to ten, into circles called Prayer Bands. The idea was for each of us to say a prayer out aloud, in succession, until the circle was complete.

'Let Beverley go last,' the mild-mannered but inappropriately named Mr Wild said. 'So that she can learn how it's done.'

Heads bowed, each of my circle said a prayer to Jesus which typically asked for something nebulous, like, 'Help us to remember the starving children of the world.' 'Bless all the hard-working teachers.' 'Take us home safely today.' 'Help the school raise the funds it needs for the new building.' 'Please help us find our lost dog.' Darn, I had planned to ask Jesus to help find our dog Chip, who had recently run away. Now there was nothing left for me to say. And I was next in line. I was in a pickle.

'Dear Jesus,' I began, then paused.

'Yes, Beverley?' Mr Wild said.

'Ditto,' I mumbled.

'Please leave the Prayer Band Beverley,' Mr Wild said without raising his voice or lifting his head. Mr Wild never raised his voice. He was one of the nicest teachers we had. After prayer bands he said, 'As this is your first experience Beverley, you're forgiven.'

However, some of the zealots amongst my classmates had not appreciated my humour nor the leniency of our teacher, denouncing me as 'a heathen'. One was adamant, 'You shouldn't be at this school if you're not a believer.' Another accused me of not being a 'real Adventist'. Perhaps they had a point because my attempts to debate and discuss the doctrines were out of the question. In such a highly religious environment, the teachers, as well as some of the students, treated every one of my requests for clarification as an attempt to refute, deny or mock the teachings of the Bible. Anyway, I reminded myself, there were more important things happening around the world than to waste my time worrying about petty rules and regulations. According to my transistor radio, the world was in a mess. And surely every thinking person had questioned how Noah had managed to carry all those animals on his boat.

13

Donovan

Though she still treated me like her annoying little sister, Glynis was responsible for lifting the weighty feeling that I was living each day inside a storm cloud, when she asked one Sabbath, 'Do you want to come with me on a double date?' I wanted to drop to my knees in front of her in thanks. But then she might think I had forgiven her for dobbing me into Mum and Dad.

Glynis had started attending some of the evangelical events held by the Adventist church for teenagers. Whilst the meetings were arranged to share the gospel, for most young Adventists it was one of the few opportunities outside of church to meet members of the opposite sex. My date was the younger friend of Glynis's date. He was seventeen years old. I was fifteen. He reminded me of the surfers I had met at the beach. He was cute, had blond hair, the early signs of a moustache, a solid build, baby blue eyes, and a jovial laugh. When he reached for my hand, my whole body broke out in goosebumps. I hoped he had not seen them.

At first, I thought he looked a bit like the singer Glen Campbell. Until later that evening, when he strummed folksy type music on an acoustic guitar. Then he looked more like the singer Donovan, which is what I have christened him. My Donovan lived with his family near Manly Beach, where he said he loved to catch a wave with other keen surfers. His family had converted to Adventism some years earlier, so he had completed his final school year at the Adventist school a few months before I joined.

Donovan and I quickly became an item and began seeing each other every weekend. Sometimes he would drive all the way from Manly to Greenacre then back again so we could attend his church. Other times we would go to our family church. Getting to know Donovan and his family was teaching me that, despite being born into the Adventist faith, I knew little about the machinations of the religion. The new converts like Donovan's family seemed to know much more. This could be an opportunity to help my family, I mused. Maybe I could lure Mum back to church. Before meeting Donovan, I thought my family had been adhering to all the rules except the one about sunset on Friday. Now I saw many differences between Donovan's family and mine. Like how his mother played a very different role to mine. She had not worked outside the family home since marriage. With five children, my mum did not have that luxury.

In addition to her weekly chores, Mrs Donovan set aside extra time towards the end of each week for cooking and cleaning, so the family could abide by the rules of not working on the Sabbath day. They were strict vegetarians. Sabbath lunch was always cold because it had been prepared the day before.

As new believers, Donovan's family were zealous about aspects of the Adventist religion that had never crossed my path until attending the school. For example, a hot dinner on Saturday night, of course cooked after sunset, invariably contained a home-made meat alternative called Gluten Steak.

When Donovan's mother discovered that I had never eaten this 'Adventist staple', she insisted I learn to make it. She did not need to follow a recipe. Instead, she stood by my side and instructed me on each step, pointing out the ingredients: gluten flour, Marmite which was a kind of Vegemite, dried Mediterranean herbs like sweet basil and oregano. I had never encountered those herbs. They smelt funny to me, like something mouldy. Mum would have added fresh coriander leaves, spring onions and garlic.

The instructions continued, 'Sift the dry ingredients together in that large ceramic bowl, add a little water, then mix it with this wooden spoon.' When it became a sticky dough, she helped me empty it onto a plastic baking sheet, showed me how to knead it lightly, then how to cut the now springy mound in half. We each took one of the pieces and rolled it into a log shape. Then I followed her lead and cut mine into half inch slices. We placed them together into a huge saucepan called a pressure cooker, added hot water flavoured with more Marmite and dried herbs. The pressure cooker had done its job in about twenty minutes. When Mrs Donovan lifted the lid, the slices had trebled in size. We dipped them in egg and breadcrumbs before frying them in vegetable oil. Then she served the steaks with saltless boiled vegetables and gravy.

Before Donovan and I left for the long trip back to my house, his mother wrapped a few pieces of the gluten steak in foil. 'For your Mum and Dad,' she said. 'If they like it, I'll write out the recipe.' Remembering Portuguese Granny's revelation about Mum 'never coming home from the market with the meat order' made me eager to introduce it to her. Perhaps it could encourage her to come back to church with us.

That night, Dad had barely finished saying grace, when I leaned forward and the words tumbled out of my mouth, 'Hey, did you know that we're not meant to be eating meat? The canteen at school is strictly vegetarian.'

Dad stopped slicing his lamb chops. We all turned towards him. With the cutlery still in his hands he said, 'That's not true Evvy. Many Adventists eat meat. We just don't eat animals that the Bible says are unclean, like pork, rabbit, or shellfish. Some families I knew in Singapore were vegetarians. At that time people throughout the world were eating wild animals which, in those days, were full of disease. The Bible does not say we can't eat meat.'

'Well anyway, I helped Mrs Donovan make a special dish. It's called Gluten Steak. They eat it all the time. She gave us this to try,' I said, removing the lid to reveal what now looked like springy strips of rubber.

'Don't eat it,' Mum said. 'I don't like the smell. It might give you asthma.'

Dad ignored Mum and tried a small piece. When he finally swallowed it, he smiled in my direction. 'It's very nice. Please thank Mrs Donovan. However, he did not eat any more. Neither did anyone else. Including me because I had already eaten it twice over the weekend. It remained in the centre until Mum cleared the table and threw it in the bin.

Mrs Donovan continued trying to convert Mum and Dad to vegetarianism. And here I was thinking that they were the new believers. Though the gluten steak had failed to impress, I often returned home after a visit to the Donovan's home with a variety of tinned vegetarian products. One day it was a product made from nuts which had been designed to replace minced meat, and which I liked a lot. Another time, it was a sort of log that came out of the tin and was meant to replace deli meats. I detested that one. Mum and Dad did not like either, saying they upset their stomachs and provoked Dad's asthma.

Eating meat did not concern Donovan as much as his parents. After all, they were the ones who had chosen to become vegetarians. On the weekends we spent at his home, we either ate dinner with his parents or ventured out to one of the many small cafés near the beach. At one, we both ordered the speciality of the house, Vienna Schnitzel, made with veal. The cook pounded the meat so thinly it covered the large dinner plates. The crispy, salty coating crackled as we sliced through to tender, juicy, pink meat, which melted in my mouth. We adopted the café as our special place, keeping it a secret from his family, but returning often.

On Sundays, if the weather was good, Donovan liked to search for waves at the various beaches on Sydney's northern peninsula. I was not a good swimmer so rarely ventured into the surf. Other than at the height of summer, I found the water too cold. I preferred to laze on the sand, watching him surf, dreaming that we were on the west coast of America in California if we were on a busy beach, a tropical island if it was a secluded one. Being at the beach never failed to kindle my desire to be near the ocean. I knew that my Asian ancestors had raised their families on the coastal towns of Ceylon and Malaya. Also, that my family had roots on the island of Singapore. Though I knew little of the lives of my European ancestors from England and Holland, I was aware that the ones who had immigrated to Asia had also chosen to live close to the coast. Perhaps it was possible to inherit ancestral desires.

Like many other young Adventists, Donovan and I adopted the popular pastime of visiting a different church each week to meet people in our age group. Donovan would collect me on Saturday morning in his little grey Morris Mini-Minor and we would either drive back to his church at Manly, a different one, or up to the Adventist College near Newcastle. If we were not having lunch at his house, a family at one of the other churches would invite us home to 'break bread' with them, referring to the Bible story of eating a meal with Jesus.

It was a first for me to visit so many different homes. I do not know why our family did not mix with other Adventist families. Perhaps it was Mum's adage of not taking five children to someone else's house. Donovan's parents and mine had got together for lunch on a few occasions at each other's homes. The drive was a four hour round trip before the freeways were built which was one contributing factor to the limited visits between them.

Meals at the various homes each Sabbath were similar if not identical to what Donovan's mother served. They consisted of some kind of meat substitute, salad greens, nuts, and dried fruits. The women dressed in a manner our pastor would have called 'modest'. They did not wear makeup. Not even lipstick. I wondered what they thought of me with my Twiggy eyes, miniskirts, and platform heels.

But my family were Adventists too. Dad said we children had been dedicated to the church which is like infant baptism in other religions. Yet these families seemed far stricter than ours. Comparing their lives to mine, weighing the pros and cons, became something I could not help doing. They seemed content to live a simple life, as the church doctrines encouraged. I saw it in the way they dressed, the way they were content to leave their lives in the hands of God. But I had decided to do the same, now that I was going to the same school as their children.

After the long Sabbath day, Donovan would drive me home before driving all the way back to the north shore alone. To supplement the meagre trainee wage he was earning at a large insurance company in the city, he had taken a second job, cleaning offices two nights a week. The amount of driving soon became dangerous and expensive. Seeing him so exhausted caused me to worry about his health. The drive each of our parents had undertaken to each other's homes had helped them realise the distance he was travelling to see me each weekend. To abate their concerns, we began spending Friday and Saturday nights at each other's homes.

Mum and Dad had taken to Donovan.

'He's such a lovely boy,' Mum raved. 'So polite. Such good manners. He's never any trouble. Eats whatever I cook. Never complains about sleeping on the settee.'

Dad nodded his head. 'Yes, he's a good Adventist boy.'

13.1

The assassination of John F. Kennedy happened when I was nine years old. The execution of Che Guevara when I was 13. The next year it was the assassination of Martin Luther King, then Robert Kennedy. The deaths of each of those prominent people stopped my world for a time. But when Cousin Andy died, something inside me broke.

The news came to me, on a bitter winter's day in the early part of July 1969, halfway into second term and two weeks before my fifteenth birthday. Wayne ran out to meet me in the street when he spotted me arriving home from school. His face spelt out the news that something terrible had happened before he had even opened his mouth.

'Andy died,' he screamed. 'He had an asthma attack. He burst out of Violet's house screaming for air. Then he collapsed on the footpath.'

My school bag dropped to the road upon hearing Wayne's words. My legs started shaking, gave way, joined my bag. My first thoughts were about Dad, remembering all the times he had been rushed to hospital in an ambulance from similar attacks. The memory seeped through my eyes.

In my opinion, Andy had died at a most inconvenient time. He had left his home with Granny Jones, to move in with Violet and her family. Violet was our only blood related Aunty in Australia. However, the siblings, including Dad, had become estranged. They must have been, once again, at a point of estrangement in their intermittent, unpredictable relationship because Andy's funeral, which was held at a small Adventist church in a north-western suburb of Sydney, turned out to be a frosty affair.

Glynis, and I had a fondness for Violet, no doubt because she was our Aunty. She had been nice to us on the few occasions we had seen her. Must have been during a cease fire. I remember the time she made me laugh. 'I almost won a lot of money today,' she said, drawing out the almost so long I thought she would run out of breath. 'I was on my way to bet on a certain horse, and I changed my mind when I got to the TAB.' I did not know what that meant but I recalled once hearing Uncle Terence say, 'Violet drinks beer and gambles on horses.' Sounded to me like she was just trying to be like everyone else. Was it an Adventist thing that had caused them to be enemies, I wondered.

Violet had seven children. Andy was similar in age to her sons. No doubt he preferred the company of her young family to that of his old grandmother. I would have too. Now that Andy had died, they were our only cousins in Sydney. Mum had been right about losing track of whom in Dad's family we were talking to at a given time. I could not help but wonder why we had immigrated to Australia with a family who hated each other so much. We should have stayed in Singapore with Mum's relatives.

Andy's death was my first encounter with the loss of someone so close. No one in the family could comprehend the uncanny coincidence that both Andy and his mother had suffered a fatal Asthma attack in their early twenties. I wondered about the life he had lived with our grandmother who had taken him away from his father to bring him to Australia.

'God has forsaken me,' Granny Jones had cried, when we called in to see her after the service, her eyes still moist and red. We were in the dark as to why she had not attended the service for her grandson, because Dad had refused to answer any of the questions Glynis, LeRoy and I had asked in the car. And though Mum's response did not explain enough, the mumble we heard from her about 'blaming God' would have to suffice. At least for the moment.

Andy's passing deepened the suffering of that winter. Our house became deadly cold. I imagined seeing shadows on every wall. We spoke in whispers, and only when necessary. Dad cast his eyes to one side whenever we children passed him in the house. He still bent his back to stiffen against the cold. Except now he was so hunched I could see his shoulder blades through his clothes. At first, I thought he might be trying to protect his heart. But other times, he walked out to the car, straight and tall, in the freezing cold, without wearing a jacket or cap.

I felt sorry for Dad, but I was also angry at him and his family. At a time when they could have given each other comfort, been close, the tragedy of Andy's death had driven them further apart. And what about us cousins? How I would have loved to have confided in at least one of them that this was the saddest time I had known in my life. Instead, I had heard the chatter at the funeral.

'No one is to blame for this.'

'He drank too much. There were empty beer bottles strewn around the room.'

'He smoked too much. His bedside table was covered in empty cigarette boxes.'

'And what of the carton of empty Ventolin inhalers the police found under his bed?'

'No. No one is to blame.'

Had Granny Jones failed Andy, I wondered. His uncles too. Dad included. Andy had no siblings. But there were plenty of cousins. And yet, the family had allowed their dead sister's only child to die. I could not fathom why God had allowed this to happen.

A flutter of nerves in my belly made me feel guilty at what I was about to ask Dad. I knew how much he had loved Andy, so I took a deep breath, carefully weighing my words before speaking. 'I don't understand why God couldn't have saved Andy.'

'His death was an accident. He's with the Lord now. He's safe.'

I did not like Dad's answer. It was not going to bring Andy back. I cried for weeks. More so, when I thought about how Andy had moved in with Violet to be close to his young male cousins, though they never acknowledged him as such. And, like us, he never called Violet, Aunty. I guessed it was in preference to living with Granny Jones who no doubt would have badgered him about going to church.

Going to school after the funeral was terrible. I felt, and looked, like a zombie in mourning, now that I had to wear the drab winter uniform. A new style had been introduced that year. Mine had been on order. The tunic was an A-line shift with two inverted pleats at the back and front in the same stiff dark grey wool as the boy's trousers. A new beret style had been introduced as well. The flat, rigid top looked like a flying saucer which I reckoned could have propelled a girl upward in a strong wind.

The whole outfit was ugly. I could not bear wearing it. The tunic had been designed without a belt to prevent the girls from hitching it up. However, I managed to thwart the wicked intention by adding my own belt, which I concealed under a regulation pullover. My actions pacified me for a time. However, knowing I had no choice but to go out into the world in such a ghastly outfit made me cry. I started to notice the prefects staring at me. Which added to my feelings of sadness. I wanted to pray for help, but I was angry at God for taking Andy. I would have prayed to the devil if it had eased my suffering.

My fifteenth birthday came and went without much ado. I do not remember if anyone gave me a present, lit the candles on a cake, or cooked any special meals. Except for Donovan who took me for a schnitzel at Manly, surprising me with a boxed set of perfume and matching powder. Then later, played his guitar and sang the words to Simon and Garfunkel's, *I Am a Rock*, as well as providing a shoulder on which to lay my head.

The girls at school had been excited when I started dating an older boy who worked and had a car. I had begun mixing with a couple of different, more sophisticated girls at school. Come Mondays they waited with beaming smiles, to hear news of our romance. I did not see my friends outside of school. One reason was because they lived far from our house. The Adventist College at Strathfield was the only one of its kind in metropolitan Sydney at the time. Students travelled from all over Sydney and as far as the Central and South Coasts. The other reason was because Donovan and I now spent every spare moment together. Oh, how the two of us could talk for hours on the phone during the week yet still have so much to say when we saw each other. Together with the increased load in homework, my time on the telephone, and weekends with Donovan, there was no free time to see friends.

After three months of dating, Donovan and I began joking about getting engaged, proclaiming our love to the world, and all that stuff. Admitting that it was a first for both of us, we committed to going steady, a signal to others that we were in an exclusive relationship. We were both too young to commit to anything beyond that.

The memory of Donovan reaching for my hand so tenderly on our first date, could still make my arms look like chicken skin. Something about the way he could quirk an eyebrow and smile at the same time, made my stomach flutter. Our commitment to not seeing others, meant we both felt the same about each other. Since then, there had been a lot of kissing and heavy petting.

In my first year at the all-girl high school, my friends and I had whispered about boys in hushed, excitable tones. The next year most of our conversations had involved sex, the forbidden fruit. Despite no one daring to admit it, every girl wanted to experience it. The routine sex education that year had consisted of little more than explaining the male and female reproductive systems and how we girls started menstruation. However, not a single soul had told me how to have sex or how I might feel afterwards.

Being at a co-educational school seemed to make it less weird about having a boyfriend. Half the girls in my class were going with someone in the same year. I had done the same with a boy in a form above me. We had never been on a date. We just talked at school and on the phone, until I met Donovan. Despite the communication rule, both sexes managed to communicate within the school grounds. The favoured method was to walk around the sports field whilst the boys were playing soccer in the centre. As we passed by, whomever we liked, we would shout out messages. 'Hi…See you this arvo on the train…See you on Saturday at church…Talk tonight on the phone.'

Too young to know about the sexual repressiveness of earlier decades, I had nothing with which to compare my attitude to sex. Though I knew it would never be one of shame or regret. I had never heard any fire and brimstone stuff about sex. Not even at church where the sermons about girls not wearing makeup, miniskirts, or listening to music, had only served to anger me. If the music had influenced my views, I did not care. I had not analysed it. I was following my heart.

Mum had been forthright in ensuring her daughters had some form of sex education from a young age. I remember the Sunday afternoon she decided she would deliver her first lesson. 'Come inside Evvy,' she cooed at the back steps. 'I have something important to tell you.' Her look had succeeded in tempting me away from the war game I was enjoying with my brothers.

Glynis was already seated on the settee in the lounge room. It irked her that despite being two years older than me, Mum often lumped us together when it came to important matters. Glynis had a point because when Mum proceeded to tell us both about how babies grew in a woman's stomach and from where they emerged, my first sex education lesson left me a little surprised, mostly disinterested. I was ten years old. If Mum had said anything about intercourse, it had gone in one ear and out the other. Or, she had continued to divulge more to Glynis after I had resumed playing with my brothers.

Two years later, the sex education for Grade six, had consisted of little more than what Mum had told me, with the addition of scientific drawings depicting menstruation and the production of ovum. Our lesson did not include the boys. I never uncovered what they had learnt. Later that same year, when one of the girls in the class showed a few of us the pictures in a book about the facts of life, which her parents had bought in America, most of us pretended we had seen it all before, rather than admitting it was completely new to us. I had seen my naked brothers often, but it was the first time I had seen explicit drawings of men and women having sex.

By the time I was fifteen years old, no one, including my parents, teachers, friends at school, or even our pastor had told me that it was a sin to have sex. I had expected to hear something about intercourse in the sex education class that year. However, the prescribed lesson consisted of a female teacher showing a few hackneyed slides, depicting animated drawings of a wiggly spermatozoon penetrating an ovum, resulting in the creation of an embryo in a woman's stomach. Though she informed us that the spermatozoa came from a male, she did not tell us how it was sexual intercourse between a male and a female, which caused it to reach the ovum. That detail was left to us to learn on our own through whispers, magazines, or experimenting, which I was about to learn other young Adventists were doing.

Donovan and I had made a few visits to the church at the Adventist college near Newcastle to catch up with friends he had known from high school. On one visit, we were staying overnight, he in the men's dormitory with a friend and me in the women's dormitory with the girlfriend of that friend. At one point a few of the boys in the group were joking about the drama caused a few weeks earlier at the college. A blockage in the pipes at one of the dormitories revealed the cause to be a build-up of condoms. Clearly someone was having sex.

Social norms were changing about sex outside of marriage now that the pill had been invented. I had learnt that in general, the attitude of protestant religions was the complete opposite to the Catholics about the use of birth control measures. Although some considered it a sin, as far as I knew, the Adventist church was not against birth control.

Sex continued to be a taboo subject throughout my school years. No one ever talked about falling in love or the lustful feelings that could drive us teenagers to distraction. Not how or why they began, nor how they manifested. And no one talked to us about birth control. We learnt everything from our friends and magazines.

At school, my friends and I had uncovered the important point of difference between the Protestant and Catholic religions in relation to the concept of "Original Sin", a term coined by Saint Augustine. Considered one of the great Catholic saints, Augustine linked Original Sin to the lust and sexual intercourse between Adam and Eve in the Garden of Eden. His proclamation resulted in the belief that babies were born out of sin and that a priest must baptise them at birth to absolve them of that sin. In contrast, the doctrine of Protestants considers Adam and Eve's act to be one of disobedience resulting in the belief that sex is a human weakness rather than a sin.

'How come they tell us we can't listen to modern music, wear miniskirts or makeup, but no one says we can't have sex?' joked my older friends at school. Armed with the new discovery, that Adam and Eve had merely committed one of numerous human acts of disobedience, and with no clearly stated rules for sex, we assumed our own.

Donovan and I were both virgins. We understood what was happening between us. I had no fears about sex, other than how I might feel afterwards or falling pregnant. I did not want to regret it. Though it was Donovan who pushed for sex, I made up my own mind. I was not reticent about him being my first sexual partner. He was perfect. We loved each other. We were going to use protection. Nobody had told me it was wrong. It seemed the most natural thing. And so, when the opportunity came, it just happened. In the same way, I imagined it had for many teenagers – on the settee in my parents living room. It was not an overly erotic experience. But it was tender. We were both breathless.

13.2

Sometime during third term, photographers arrived to take the annual class photos. It was Spring which meant we girls were once again wearing our sky-blue summer tunics rather than the awful grey ones. A couple of weeks after the photos, my science teacher summoned me to the staff room. 'I'm really sorry,' she said. 'But your uniform is not going to look nice in the school photos.'

I did not understand what she was saying until she handed me a piece of film. My hand rose to temper the gasp that escaped from my mouth. Most of us in the class had thought of this teacher as young, hip, someone with whom we could relate. But really, she was just like the others. I scrunched up my brow. Shook my head from side to side, fighting hard to stop the tears that had begun to fill my eyes.

Sensing my confusion, she added, 'I had no choice.' Then elaborated that she had been given an order by one of the department heads to alter the length of my tunic in the photo. In response she had used a white liquid correction fluid, the type used by typists, to paint a false hem onto the negative. I stared at the image. My summer tunic looked like my parents had bought it from the second-hand shop, then tacked on a piece of off-coloured rag to the edge of the hem, which now dangled at the top of my shins. My mouth opened to say, 'You're a rat'. But no sound came out. Instead, I dropped the negative at her feet, turned away and ran to the lockers to avoid her seeing my welled-up tears.

By approving the doctored photo for the annual school album, the science teacher had delivered a punishment in perpetuity. For evermore, classmates, parents, officials, former teachers, in fact anyone connected to the Adventist community, could see the photo. What would they think might have happened? Other than the perpetrators and me, I imagined they would feel sorry for this girl whose parents had been too poor to afford a new uniform as she grew taller.

Donovan played an important role in helping me block out my feelings of betrayal. It was true that he had broken a little of the magic for my first sexual experience by asking, 'Do you feel any different?' A better thing to say would have been I love you. Nevertheless, the experience of being held so closely by him had delivered a welcome distraction from the pain and confusion following Andy's death, the uniform disaster, and the new alliance, which I had sensed developing, between the department head and the science teacher.

The two culprits had commenced a united tirade against me. Each one stopping me whenever our paths crossed, ordering me to 'kneel on the asphalt' so they, or a prefect whom they had enlisted, could measure the length of my tunic — even interrupting a lesson one day to do so. The science teacher, who admittedly had simply been carrying out orders, seemed to be so guilt-ridden, she had begun seeking opportunities to justify her actions. 'Don't sit there Beverley. Stop talking in class. Read that passage again.' I felt certain her actions were payback for causing her to perform the dastardly deed.

The actions of both teachers were pushing me away from school. I no longer wanted to be there. So many stupid rules. I could not follow them. So much trivia. No answers. Nothing made sense any more. Though I had not told any of my friends about the photo, I knew they would find out soon enough. The looming revelation made Monday mornings intolerable. I walked to the bus stop full of apprehension of what the week might bring. Some days, my legs struggled to carry me off the bus. My school bag felt like it had been filled with rocks.

Dad continued to work two jobs to pay the school fees. Thank goodness he had left the chemical factory. I could not have lived with the guilt of him dying from an asthma attack caused from the inhalation of chemicals. Instead, after doing as much overtime at his work as he could, he went to another factory a few nights a week. I must keep going, make him proud, fulfil his dreams for me, be a good Adventist. I simply must.

14

Arising to a New Life

The busy weekend schedule of Donovan driving all over Sydney, took its toll on both of us. His parents never stopped pestering him about the hours he spent in his car. I had less time to listen to my music. When we were together, he played the guitar to some of the folksier styles which I liked but not the sort of psychedelic rock, soul, and blues that had captivated me. Though I had never completely stopped listening, I felt myself being drawn back to it, seeking comfort, and answers, with a new intensity.

The Top 40 charts kept me informed. They were compiled by various radio stations who logged the forty best-selling records of the week then published the results in the local newspapers. Dad knew how much I hung out for those charts. 'Here you go Evvy,' he would say after reading the newspaper containing one.

The attitude of the church towards modern music had been emphasised, once again, during one of the services that Donovan and I attended at my family's church. Our pastor delivered a service aimed directly at young people. He deepened his voice and leaned forward on the pulpit. Waving his finger at the congregation he warned us to 'shun any melody partaking of the nature of jazz, rock, or related hybrid forms, or any language expressing foolish or trivial sentiments'.

I sat up straight. Had he spoken directly to me. If he had, his words were having the opposite effect. It was as if they had rekindled a fire that had been smothered. I had been trying hard to ignore the music that fuelled the counterculture movement. But it had been bubbling along in the background, growing in strength and following. It had given me answers before. Now I wanted it back in my life.

The lyrics from the music of a rock festival called Woodstock, which had been held on a dairy farm in Bethel, New York, were too profound to ignore. One night I listened to some of the songs on my transistor in bed, hiding under the covers so no one would disturb me. I was still awake when Dad came home from his second job. I heard his key turn in the lock of the back door, his shuffling through the laundry in his socks so he would not wake anyone. As he crept past my bedroom, he leaned in and whispered, 'Go to sleep now Evvy. School tomorrow.'

Another time, I watched the newsreel images of the festival beaming from our television. I ran up close to the screen so I could see the faces of the singers. I liked how the music thundered in my head, numbing my senses, blocking my thoughts about the next day at school.

Mum laughed at me. 'What are you doing?'

Without turning my head to look at her, I said, 'Did you know that almost half a million people went to Woodstock? They starved. It poured. They slept in the sludge. Had no toilets.'

'Why?'

'Because they didn't expect so many people to turn up.'

'I mean why did they do all that?'

'For the music, Mum. Just for the music.'

'Oh my gosh, it's Janis Joplin,' I screamed. She had become my favourite female singer. Her raspy voice made my insides quiver. Janis Joplin singing "Try (Just A Little Bit Harder)" and "Piece of My Heart." won a piece of my heart forever.

Listening to the music helped me cultivate solitude. I became quieter at home. It was hard to talk to Dad. He was often tired and overworked. Mum too. And I did not want to bother either of them. On the nights Dad was not working, he would continue his efforts with Dewey. As usual, many of those sessions ended in frustration with the books and pencils on the ground and Dad retreating to the bedroom.

One night, I overhead Dad's response to Mum's usual comments about 'when he was going to stop with the poor boy'.

'He'll be at such a disadvantage if he can't read,' Dad said. 'I need to prepare him for when we're not around.'

Dad's words about not being around upset me, causing me to feel guilty that I had also been avoiding conversations with him since the trouble at school. I had thrown the letter requesting payment for class photos and the school album in the bin. That photo was never going to be seen by my family. I knew if I spoke to Dad, it would come out when he asked how school was going. Better to avoid him.

Mum and Dad were not aware that I was becoming obsessed with the music again. I was certain that Dad was happy that Donovan was keeping me entertained. He hoped we would marry one day. But they did not know how hard it was getting at school. I had been hiding it from them. It was easier to do with Donovan helping me escape each weekend. Mum and Dad thought everything was going well. They were working so hard they had not noticed that their fifteen-year-old daughter was spending every waking hour listening to music about escape, freedom, and psychedelic drugs. And, despite the churches attitude to modern music, the weekly Top 40 chart had become my Bible.

14.1

The feeling of something jerking my shoulder, woke me to Dad's face almost touching mine. 'Evvy. Quickly. Wake up. I think Donovan's having a fit or something.'

I jumped out of bed and the two of us rushed to the lounge room where Donovan had spent the night on the settee. Dad was now whispering, 'I heard a noise and thought he was dreaming. Then it sounded more like he was choking.'

The sight of my boyfriend's body jerking from side to side on our settee scared me. I knelt by his side, feeling so numb I failed to hear Dad leave the room until he was handing me a soup spoon and suggesting we use it to prevent Donovan from swallowing his tongue. We tried to get it into his mouth, but his teeth had clamped together so tightly we could not pry them apart. He did not know we were in the room. When he stopped moving, his eyes became vacant, staring at the ceiling. Like he was in another world.

Though it seemed like an eternity, the episode had only lasted about five minutes. It was all over by the time Mum came into the room. 'Should we call an ambulance? she asked. 'The doctor won't be at his surgery because it's Sunday.'

Donovan overheard her and began shaking his head from side to side. He managed to squeeze out a faint 'No.' He sounded like the times the wind had been knocked out of him after a long and taxing surf. But this was different. He fell asleep, did not stir for hours.

Whilst he slept, I explained to Mum and Dad how a doctor had recently diagnosed Donovan as suffering from a rare form of brain seizures. This was his third or fourth, but a first for me.

'What do you plan to do?' Dad asked.

The memory of his uncontrolled shaking, not even being aware that we were in the room, became overwhelming. 'I love him,' I sobbed. 'This doesn't change how I feel.'

When he awoke, Donovan told me about the medication the medical specialist had prescribed. Also, the recommendation that he maintain a diet high in proteins, including red meat. Despite the diagnosis and counsel, he said his parents had refused to serve meat. I was angry at them for this decision. He was my boyfriend. I loved him. I had a say.

Before the next weekend, I bought an eye-fillet steak, placed it in Mrs Donovan's fridge on Friday night when I arrived and pleaded with her to cook it during the week. When I returned the next weekend, I found it hidden at the back of the fridge, green and smelly. I wondered about these new believers and their strict adherence to religious rules. I preferred how Mum and Dad bent the rules in line with the changing times, necessity, and survival.

On Sunday we drove to the northern end of Avalon Beach, off Barrenjoey Road for Donovan to surf. I lay on the sand, watching him. I thought about our blissful times together, how much my life had changed since meeting him, and the extent to which he had helped lighten the pain of the terrible winter my family had endured since Andy's death. In my opinion, Donovan was the perfect boyfriend. I always felt like I belonged to the world we frequented, whether that was at the beach or meeting other young Adventists. When he smiled at me, held my hand, opened the car door for me, or kissed me, I was in heaven. Donovan and I belonged together. I felt certain my dating Donovan was a time in Dad's life when he too was his happiest.

The waves that day were gigantic. I thought about Donovan's last medical check-up. The specialist had warned him against getting overtired as it could trigger more seizures. Though he looked exhausted, he jogged out of the water, placed his surfboard on the sand, and dropped to his knees in front of me. The freshness from the last wave clung to the air around him. His face almost touched mine. Cold droplets of water trickled from his hair, onto his face, then onto mine. I felt his saltiness as he kissed me, then whispered, 'I'm in love with you.' Better late than never.

14.2

The veil of darkness engulfing our family after Andy's death lifted for a time, when Mum shared the news that her youngest sister Juliet had applied to immigrate to Australia. Though I had heard little about this aunty from Mum, Portuguese Granny had explained during her visit that Juliet had been by her side since the age of twelve, which was when Granny became a widow.

Mum had been acting differently since her mother's visit the year before; more confident, more in charge. She had started learning new accounting techniques at work and taken charge of the family finances by paying the bills. But in tandem with the new changes, I felt as if she was becoming distant from us. Perhaps it was my imagination. I did not know. Mum and I had not been close for a few years. She was a good mother. She tried hard. But sometimes I had the feeling that my parents were sort of bumbling through raising us children in an adopted country. They had both worked so hard to give us the material things for a good life in Australia. The sacrifice had been our time together. Going to church had kept us close but now, even that had taken a blow.

The newsreels were reporting society's concerns about the growing political and anti-establishment movements throughout the western world which they had labelled a counterculture. However, my generation did not know anything different. We were watching the hippies, Hare Krishnas, anti-war protesters, and music festivals on television. And if Dad had been concerned about my becoming further influenced by the music of the era, he never commented. Nor did he say anything to LeRoy who had begun listening to similar music but more heavy rock like Jimmy Hendrix, Black Sabbath, and The Doors. I sensed it was because, like many parents of the era, Dad did not know what to say or do.

The anticipated arrival of a new aunty forced me to contemplate how Mum must have felt leaving her family in Singapore. Thirteen years had passed since then. Had she felt alone, powerless? She must have. Because having her mother near, for just a few weeks, had changed her so much that even after Portuguese Granny had left, Mum continued to do and say stuff she had never done or said before.

Despite being at least two years away, Aunty Juliet's arrival became the primary topic of conversation in our house. Mum began recalling memories of Singapore and Malaya, some we had never heard. One time we heard more about her beloved paternal grandmother who had married the Englishman who had given the family their name. Another, she talked about the harsh French nuns at the Convent of The Holy Infant Jesus where she had completed her schooling.

I had not forgotten about the Catholic thing in our family. It was just something I had pushed deep into the back of my mind, still hoping and praying God would not hold it against us. Especially now that LeRoy and I were going to the Adventist school where it had been reinforced about Catholics being the enemy. It was a feeling that varied amongst the staff and students. Some never mentioned it. Others raised it often. Like the teacher who admonished a group of students, which included me, one afternoon as we walked out the front gate, 'Don't look right because Saint Patrick's Catholic College is up that way.'

Mum's mention of the convent she had attended in Singapore rehashed the shameful reminder that my parents had married in a Catholic church. I became curious as to what had caused her to change after being raised in such a strong religion as Catholicism. One time, when Glynis and I were sitting on the end of Mum's bed listening to her stories, I was thinking the same as Glynis when she asked, 'Why did you become an Adventist Mum? If you don't want to go to church?'

Mum curled her lips right up to one corner of her mouth and looked away as she spoke. 'After the wedding, your grandmother visited with a minister in tow, every single day. She's a terror. They might as well have made me a prisoner. I was so young. And silly. I gave in to her and got baptised.'

Mum's words stunned me. I did not know why learning that Mum had been baptised had come as such a shock. Perhaps because it was because she had never raised it before. Not even before Glynis's baptism two years earlier. The revelation forced me to think about how little I knew about my parents. I had never thought about these things before. I had been too caught up in my own trials. Despite the new disclosure, I singled out the word 'they', wondering if it had included Dad.

'My parents were heartbroken,' Mum continued. 'My brothers and sisters felt I had betrayed the family and our faith. They thought I should have married a man from my own religion. My father was a devout Catholic. He was a good man. Always ready to help those in need. He gave money to his sister and even his cousins.'

'Then why did you … ?'

Mum's eyes glared the blackest I had ever seen them. Cutting off Glynis mid-sentence, she yelled, 'To keep the peace. That bloody old lady threatened to expel your father from the family forever if I didn't.'

Despite Mum's concerns about upsetting Dad, it must have been playing on her mind. Because later, in the silence of the night, Glynis and I heard her say, 'You lied to the bishop. He only gave us permission to marry because you pledged to raise our children as Catholics.'

'Well, I could never be married to a Catholic,' Dad whispered.

'You signed the papers.'

My body went limp upon hearing the new revelation from Mum. Her words somersaulted in my head like the songs on my records whenever the stylus got stuck in a groove. If I had been standing, I would have collapsed. Learning that my parents had married in a Catholic church had been enough of a shock. Despite feeling some pity for Mum that she had been forced to give up her faith, I had rationalised that it had been for the greater good of our souls that our mum was no longer a Catholic. Unfortunately for me, the new leak had arrived on the eve of my last Bible study lesson in preparation for baptism where I would be accepting the Lord Jesus Christ as my saviour, Adventism as the one true faith.

I racked my brain about what this might mean for me. What trade-offs God might expect. I feared He might consider my siblings and me to be sullied because we had been promised to the torturers. After tossing and turning throughout the night, I awoke to realise that my concerns had been in vain. Because Mum had converted before we were born, we had been born Adventists. Whilst I was able to breathe a sigh of relief at my newfound insight, I felt ashamed about Dad's betrayal of Mum. Also, that the annals of the Catholic church in Singapore would contain his written promise to the bishop for eternity.

'I'm ready for baptism,' I lied to our pastor that weekend after making the decision to move forward in the same manner as I had often lifted the stuck stylus on the record player to continue playing a song.

'After being buried in the water, you will arise to a new life in Jesus.' Those were the last words I heard before the pastor put one hand on the small of my back, covered my face with the cloth in his other, then dunked me backwards. Cool water flowed over my head, trickled down the nape of my neck, then engulfed my body in the baptismal font which was a marbled wading pool the size of six bathtubs. Within seconds he was raising me upright. Water rushed over my face as it broke the surface, and I gulped my first blessed breath.

I spotted my family in the front pew. Dad's face looked contorted from his desire to hold back tears. Mum sat by his side dressed in a pantsuit. The satin swing dress had long since gone out of style. Donovan smiled and winked at me. Glynis and my brothers were sitting next to them. My baptism had brought my family together.

Minutes earlier I had been a dilettante, in a line-up of sinners, clad in sombre, ash-coloured robes, distinguishable only by my hot-pink speedo cap and black waterproof eyeliner. Grid-locked teeth helped prevent the escape of a nervous giggle that inched its way from my belly to tickle the insides of my throat.

The deed done, all I felt was guilt. With one hand firmly gripping my arm, and a deathly stare that penetrated all the way to where that guilt lay, Pastor reminded me of my affirmations, of the chronicles I had been studying to prepare for today. 'Full immersion in water is a symbol your sins have been forgiven. That you will now be received by His church.'

Dragging my water-logged robe, I exited the font, disappearing into the arms of women waiting to dress me, amidst a gaggle of 'congratulations' and 'praise the Lords'. In the distance, the congregation had erupted into a hymn about 'being buried beneath the yielding wave in the arms of the Lord.'

Vanity was my first new sin. It occurred when I looked into a mirror and saw that my hair was a tangled wet mess, despite the speedo cap. And the joy I felt when I realised the waterproof eyeliner had not failed me.

15

Principles and Principals

The slow-motion swoop of a hand grabbed at the piece of newspaper floating from my textbook. She had been faster than me; I was still looking at her foot tapping on the wooden floor. When I raised my head our eyes locked. She smiled like she was about to win at hide-and-seek, 'Afternoon detention Beverley.'

During the lunch break, a friend and I had been reading the latest Top 40 music chart. 'Hey, I've got a cool idea,' she squealed, throwing her hands up in the air. 'Let's match a song to everyone in the class.'

'Yeah. That's a cool idea. And we'll add the teachers too.'

In between hurried bites from sandwiches and slurps from plastic drink bottles, we spent our lunch break giggling about some of the couplings. I chose the psychedelic pop hit *Hair* from the musical with the same name for my song. I do not remember the song chosen by my friend. When the bell rang, I shoved the dog-eared chart between the pages of my textbook.

I never learnt whether it was my being in possession of the music chart that caused the science teacher to indict me for the crime of pursuing pop music, or if it was her anger at seeing her name written against the hit song *Bad Moon Rising* by Creedence Clearwater Revival, which was number four on the chart that week. She never shared her reasoning.

Legs shaking with each step, head pounding with each thought, I made my way to the maintenance room, the designated meeting place for detainees. Despite my run-ins over the length of my uniform, including the liquid paper fiasco, this was my first detention, and I was scared. More about how I would get home than writing lines or being humiliated for listening to sinful music. Bus number 27, from Strathfield via Stacy Street, was the only afternoon bus that went near our house. I caught it each day with LeRoy. That day he rode it alone, with no clue as to the reason for my absence.

A metallic jingling awoke my straying mind. It came from the gigantic bunch of keys held by the Deputy Headmaster as he turned the lock in the door of the maintenance room. I felt his burly hand against my back as he pushed me towards a line-up of mops, buckets, and grubby cloths, waving his hand along them. When I did not react, he pointed a fearsome finger at me. 'Grab what you need,' he bellowed. 'You're cleaning all the windows on the ground floor. Inside and out.'

That was how I learnt my school did not have cleaners. Each afternoon, students swept and mopped floors, cleaned windows, emptied bins. My mind shot in a million directions. Surely, this could not be the way other private schools cleaned their buildings. If so, the teachers must have some sort of scheme to meet detention quotas. There was no need for further contemplation. No need to chew over my thoughts. I simply said, 'No.'

'What?' the Deputy Head's screwed-up face snarled.

'I'm not washing the windows.'

His face turned scarlet. His spectacles fogged. One of the other detainees whispered something indecipherable. My legs were shaking uncontrollably. Nerves made it impossible to say what I was thinking. *Perhaps I could write lines, stand on one leg for a whole day if need be. Anything other than clean the school.* But I had barely finished those thoughts when he roared, 'How dare you. Get to the headmaster's office.'

It must have been steely resolve alone that carried me all the way to the principal's loft, for I have no recollection of the climb which landed me in front of his desk. Minutes earlier, I had stood at the bottom of the concrete stairwell for what seemed like an eternity, trying to stop my ski-pole-legs from shaking long enough to tackle the first step. So close, yet worlds apart, I sensed his rebuff when he ignored my entry, imagining for a second that it might have been his principal persona. Although, I got the distinct feeling that my unexpected appearance had caused him to miss the window for avoiding the peak hour traffic. Just like me, he was eager to get home.

The first movement in the room came from his bushy black eyebrows. They sloped slowly towards each other before springing up, at lightning speed, to hover over thick, black-rimmed spectacles, revealing a set of beady, blue eyes. 'Why are you here?' he said.

I started to explain about the deputy head asking me to wash the windows and how I had refused. I watched his eyes veer towards the right. With as little movement as possible, I glanced left to see what had drawn his attention. A white-faced clock, rimmed in steel, with numerals large enough to see from the back of a classroom, stared down at me. It's tick, tick, tick, seemed to be in slow motion, amidst the now deathly silence.

Together, we watched the bright red second's hand jerk towards the 11, before reflex drew my eyes, and his, back to the meeting spot, over the desk. I swallowed, involuntarily, from the glare he shot me.

'You have sixty seconds,' he said through an expression that made it clear he did not care to hear anything in my defence. 'To accept the Deputy Head's punishment.' After delivering this missive, he cast his eyes downwards, shifted some papers on his desk, looked up again, straight through me, as his final words tumbled from his mouth, 'Or leave my school forever.'

My heart began pounding in tandem with the ticking of the wall clock. I tried to keep it still by holding my breath, on and off, to no avail. I stole another look at the clock. I did not know how many times the red hand had gone around but it was back at the 11 when the unexpected words sliced through me. 'Your time starts now.'

My muddled mind could not think. My legs wobbled like jelly. My cotton mouth had no spit to lubricate the lump that had grown in my throat. Not prepared to surrender any more precious seconds, I drew my fingers up into fists, felt them quaking from the tension as I blurted out, 'My father is working sixteen hours a day for me to go to this school and I'm not washing the…'

My body flinched when he cut me off, midstream, to reinstate his proposition through a grimacing growl. 'Clean the windows or immediate expulsion.'

His ultimatum was as clear as mine. He was not giving in. I was not washing the windows. I pursed my lips, turned, and left his office, ahead of the allotted time. Insouciance on the outside, masking what was the loneliest moment of my teenage life.

I returned the same way I had come. Except that now I took two steps at a time. My fists remained clenched the whole way down, my mind replaying the principal's references to Christianity, forgiveness, and compassion. Hackneyed words no doubt rehashed on a regular basis for similar encounters.

At the bottom of the stairs, I felt the pain from my fingernails digging into my skin. My body felt hot as I tried to fend off tears. I wanted to hit something as my feelings vacillated between disbelief, hurt, and rage at the principal who represented the religion that had baptised me into their fold just weeks earlier, assuring me of a place in their congregation, telling me I was one of their children. And which now was willing to abandon me.

The audience with the headmaster was not the end of the saga. I still had to break the news to my parents. Mere words would never be able to convey to them how it had felt to have someone force me to choose a path in sixty seconds. No time or experience for measured thought. No opportunity to consult a supportive adult. No capacity to comprehend the potential far-reaching consequences.

The rule which separated boys and girls meant LeRoy knew nothing of my situation. Missing the bus, which stopped at the end of our street, had forced me to walk forty-five minutes in the fast-fading light from the stop on the highway. By the time I turned the corner into our street the sun had set. I had arrived home over two hours later than usual.

Mum and I came face to face at the front door. She had come home from work only minutes before me. With no response to her telephone calls to the school, she was preparing to drive to the local police station to report the unexpected absence of her teenage daughter. The build-up of anger and fear caused her to rage, not at me, but at the Adventists, whom she regularly blamed for all the hapless events that occurred in our lives. Dad had already left for his second job.

'They can't do this to you,' Mum said. 'They don't mean it, or they would have contacted us. You're too young to leave school anyway.'

'But Mum,' I squealed feeling the furrows on my brow multiplying. 'They told me not to come back. The principal said I don't belong there. Maybe he's right. I'm an idiot for ever going to that stupid school.'

'Don't worry. I'll drive you tomorrow.'

Donovan telephoned around seven o'clock that evening. Thank goodness it was one of the nights on which he did not work. We had spent the weekend at his house, but I missed him already. Even more so, now that I needed someone in whom I could confide my fears about the future. So, it annoyed me when he laughed out aloud at my situation which he found 'hysterical'.

'Well, it's not funny. I've been sick with worry. Mum's insisting on driving me back there tomorrow morning.'

'Oh really? Do you think they'll let you in the front gate?'

Donovan sounded like he was back-pedalling on his initial reaction but hearing the doubt in his voice made my insides quiver. 'Well, I told Mum, word for word, what the principal said. But she reckons he can't expel me because I'm too young.'

'Are your parents thinking of talking to the school?

'What for? I think this school is a law unto itself. No one would even listen to my parents. Either way, can you please come on Friday night. I'm worried Dad might not let me go to your place. And there's no way I'm going to our church on my own. One of the bossy teachers goes there. And a girl from my class too.'

'Of course I will come to support my girlfriend.'

I liked it when Donovan called me that.

I do not think anyone in my family had expected the extreme rules, regulations, and religious rituals of the Adventist school. Perhaps all private schools were the same. Nor how far the principal was prepared to go to enforce them. I certainly had not. I cried silent sobs under the sheets so Glynis would not hear me. She had already chided me about what had happened. 'How could you do this to Mum and Dad? Mum's right. You are stubborn.'

It was bad enough we had to share a room. No doubt she felt the same. I was always going to be the annoying little sister who borrowed her makeup and clothes. But right now, I did not need to hear any more of her badgering. Nor did I have the energy to argue. My thoughts were about Dad. He had been gone all night, working to pay the school fees.

Must have been midnight when I heard the usual sounds of him arriving home, beginning with the squeak of the back door, the shuffling of his overalls and work boots as he removed them, then the trickling sound of water from the laundry tap as he washed his hands, arms, and face as quietly as possible before tiptoeing to his bedroom.

I sat up in bed. My head was exploding from all the things I wanted to say to him. I'm sorry Daddy. Sorry I've let you down. Sorry about all the money you've spent. Sorry about the chemical factory. Please don't die. But my body had turned to jelly. I could not get out of bed. My head fell back onto the pillow.

Sleep eluded me that night, to the point I contemplated jumping out of the bedroom window and running away from home forever. Instead, morning came, and the telltale sounds of the members of my family starting another day echoed all around. Like Dad's car revving out of the driveway, Glynis being the first dressed and out the door because she always bagsed the bathroom first, Dewey, LeRoy, and Wayne bantering at the breakfast table over their cornflakes.

Mum's voice reigned over the top of everything ensuring adherence to the daily routines. I snapped shut my eyes when I heard her approaching.

From the door, she yelled, 'I've told your father, and he said you must go back. He said it couldn't be as bad as you think. And they're Christians, they'll forgive you. Get dressed and I'll drive you and LeRoy.'

Before I knew it, we were on our way to Strathfield and all I could do was continue to protest in the car. At several stoplights, I touched the door handle, imagining I was brave enough to open it to escape. Mum drove on, her eyes on the road ahead.

I looked across at her several times but even the intimacy of the car could not reveal her true thoughts. Though I guessed from her furrowed brow that she was concerned about arriving late at the office. I had seen that look over the years, whenever she had no choice but to take leave without pay if we children had a serious illness. It was well known that companies discriminated against women with children for fear of them bringing their domestic problems to the workplace.

To get this job, Mum had been forced to lie that she had no children. I smiled at the memory of hearing the tremor in her voice the day she had telephoned her boss at her last workplace to inform him of her absence for at least a week because her children had contracted German Measles. By the time she returned to work, her friends had revealed that there were five of us. Mum must have been good at her job because they did not fire her. Instead, following the incident, her boss said with a smile, every morning forever after, 'Good Morning Margaret. Hope the children are well.'

My mouth dropped open when Mum delivered the blow that she was now almost an hour late so could not come in with me.

'No way,' I screamed as LeRoy jumped out.

'Seeya,' he said.

'Everything will be alright,' Mum insisted. 'Schools are not allowed to do this sort of thing without contacting the parents.'

I took a deep breath hoping it would calm me. Arguing with Mum seemed futile.

Time seemed irrelevant in the other-worldly place I had entered on the footpath outside the front gate. I felt numb. Except for the trillion ants crawling on my skin, attacking my helplessness. As I watched Mum's little white Cortina vanish, I felt their twelve trillion hairy talons crawling over my skin, then under it. Armies of them began clawing inside my socks, on my calves, then scaling my stomach, some making for the tender flesh of underarms and all the way to my neck, before swarming onto my scalp and through my hair. The tingling, numbness, and itching became so unbearable, I started to scratch. It might have continued had the bell not sounded to jolt me out of my illusory hell. Now, with legs like wet concrete, and a heart just as heavy, I made my way to morning assembly, obeying my mum — against the tsunami of instinct screaming at me to get the hell out of there.

Morning assemblies took place outside, in the quadrangle. Hemmed in by the towering classroom buildings, I stood in my form line, side by side with classmates. Some were in a febrile state having learned about my situation, others whimpering. The daughter of the Deputy Head was in my class, so I imagined that the news had carried like wildfire. Something like this had never happened to anyone they knew.

Hearing my name over the loudhailer, bouncing between the buildings, brought me back to reality. Not one of the banal daily briefs had made any sense. I had not been listening anyway. I was being summoned to the principal's office. At that moment, I knew Mum and Dad's judgement had been naïve. I vowed, right then, to only trust my own, for the rest of my life.

My footsteps tapped a melancholy drumbeat as I passed empty classrooms. I raised my head high, pleased for the rescue from certain drowning in the clammy pool of consolation from classmates.

The principal was not in his office when I arrived. 'You can stand there,' said his secretary, pointing to an area on the open balcony. I stood *there* for over an hour. 'Stay where you are,' he barked when he arrived. By the time he called me in, I felt calm. The familiarity of his office comforted me. This time around, I noticed his proclivity for fiddling with his spectacles.

When he began, 'I'm a good Christian…' my thoughts left the room, preferring to wait in the corridor for my body to follow. He was simply repeating his edict from the previous day. Replaying the drama and forcing me to experience the terror all over again. His lecture seemed to have no end. Unlike the first time, he moved around the office, gathered and signed papers, even took a phone call. I paid no attention. I had stopped listening.

My hearing returned, when I heard the order, 'Make your way to the lockers, remove your possessions and prepare to leave the grounds of the school.' Poking a tongue into my left cheek, I inhaled a long breath, then strode out of his office. I was an old hand at this expulsion thing.

Alone, in the bowels of the administration building, where the girls' locker room resided, I heard the recess bell ring. I felt exhausted. Hours had passed since Mum had left me at the front gate. I sighed at the thought of having to appear stoic in front of my classmates when all I wanted to do was run to the station and jump on a bus, feeling relieved that I would not be going home in the dark like yesterday.

I gazed at the contents of my locker. A dozen or so text books, stationery, navy sports tunic, freshly whitened sandshoes, and my beloved blazer stared back at me. On a hook on the door, hung my one-summer-old white Panama-style hat, adorned with a band in the school colours of royal blue, bordered with a thin, azure-blue strip on each side and a crimson strip down the centre. Symbols representing membership of a cadre, now with no place to belong, but for which Dad had paid dearly. I gathered them up, intending to make as grand an exit as possible.

Eager to camouflage my trepidation, I climbed the stairs in double time all the way to the top floor balcony outside the staffroom, where the infamous liquid paper artist hid. My friends, who were now on lunch break, called out from the quadrangle below, where they had gathered to hear my fate.

I stood at the bow of the top floor balcony and with one fell swoop, threw everything over the rails. My hat, a lone Frisbee, glided over their heads to land on its own, in tribute. However, when the remaining items flopped to the ground, the intended drama fell flat. Nonetheless, my former friends rushed for them like vultures, a little too quickly for my liking. In my haste to escape, it had not occurred to me to sell the items for some small compensation.

There was no next act in this tragedy. I was on the outside now. I had stood my ground and paid heavily for what might seem a small victory. Within weeks of being baptised, one of the bastions of the Adventist religion had cast me out. By Sabbath everyone at our church would know.

Walking towards the station, felt unnatural at that time of day. It was too early to see the girls I had befriended from other private colleges who caught the same bus. I could not have revealed what had happened to me anyway. They would have been shocked. Even the drizzle that began as I rounded the corner to our street was a pathetic attempt at washing away the slime of shame that clung to my body. I felt certain the neighbours were staring at me. And that they knew I had been kicked out of school. My head was spinning from the memory of the many instructions from Mum and Dad over the years to dress well, speak clearly, and behave. 'Must not bring shame on the family,' they said. 'Must hold our heads up high.' My eyes dropped to the ground.

From a pocket deep in my memory, a verse from the Bible that I had learnt in my recent preparation for baptism, leapt to mind. The one when Jesus answered a question from his disciple Peter about forgiveness. "Then Peter came to Jesus and asked, Lord, how many times shall I forgive my brother when he sins against me? Up to seven times? Jesus answered, I tell you, not seven times, but seventy times seven." Matthew 18:21-22.

15.1

Unspoken words percolated throughout our house, penetrating the flimsy, fibro walls. I heard them, louder than the hubbub of everyday life amidst a family of seven. The Bad Moon Rising incident had plunged me into a nebulous no-man's land — within the sanctity of my own home. Though nobody wanted to talk to me, I was sure everybody was talking about me.

Yesterday, I had arrived home before Dad, which was not unusual on a typical weekday. We had not spoken since the incident, so he did not come to my bedroom to ask about my day. He simply yelled out his customary hello to my brothers and me, then followed the usual routine for the nights he went to his second job. I must have dozed off because the next sound I heard was Mum's car driving into the carport. She came straight to my room. When I told her the news, she took in a huge breath, sighed, then walked away to change her clothes before cooking dinner. In the early hours, I heard murmurs from Mum and Dad's bedroom. I could not decipher the full conversation other than the word Adventist, repeated several times by Mum.

When daylight came, I remained hidden under the blanket, marinating in the comforting smell of toast wafting from the kitchen. Not game enough to join in, I lay there listening to the rumbles of others setting off for places where they had something to do, people to see. I had no reason to don a tunic that day, catch up on homework, nor run for the red bus. I was not going to show my head until everyone had left the house.

Finally, Wayne slammed shut the front door. He was the last to leave for his walk to primary school. Thank goodness he had gone. Alone in the house, I scratched at the twinge of fear that itched my scalp. I leapt out of bed, hoping to prevent a similar ant experience to yesterday. I swaggered to the kitchen, made Vegemite toast and a hot Bonox, which I brazenly munched and slurped back in bed.

All was quiet, save for the anthems from my radio. 'The controversial Ballad of John and Yoko has leapt a whopping 20 points in the charts to take the number one spot,' screamed the announcer. I sat up at the sound of the nasal, Merseyside accent of John Lennon about his latest song, lamenting how hard it had been for him and Yoko to get married. When he reached the part about being crucified by the authorities, I yelled out, 'Gosh. I should have chosen it as my song instead of Hair.' No one heard me. The house was empty, silent. I slid back under the bed covers with my radio booming out the usual songs about good times, psychedelic drugs, sex, war, and politics. And Lennon singing about a revolution to change the world.

The lyrics were speaking to me in the same way they had before I had changed schools, forcing me to regret how I had put aside my thoughts about joining a revolution for almost a year, whilst allowing myself to be closeted in our conservative religion, far away from the hype. Now, escaping the shackles of school and family, rebelling against religious dogma, casting off conservative ways of dress, embracing sexual freedom, and listening to modern music, sounded like words that had been penned especially for me. They were also amplifying the pace of change throughout the world, which I felt certain was leaving me behind.

Through the fog of thoughts, one pushed its way through the doubt, the fear, the shame. My desire for a little freedom to dress the way I wanted and listen to modern music was all I had been seeking. I just wanted to be me. Though, I was no longer sure who that was. Up until now, the ideals of my generation had come to me solely through the mediums of music and television. Now I wanted to live them.

The media had attributed the new wave of violence erupting at some of the demonstrations against conscription for the war in Vietnam to communism. A memory came to mind of Dad's outburst whilst watching the evening news one weekend. He had not been able to hide his anger upon hearing the reports from America about the radical Marxist political movements that were taking place, primarily amongst college students which had been tagged as the 'New Left'. 'The West will end up like Malaya,' he had said. 'Another Emergency.'

Dad seemed to be on the same wavelength as John Lennon who was using his song *Revolution* to warn people with "minds that hate" they could count him out of their violent movements, whilst advising his followers not to donate to those same people. I did not want to be involved with those groups either. My family followed conservative, traditional beliefs. Would it be a conflict of interest for a baptised Adventist to participate in a revolution?

The thought of participating in a peaceful, worldwide revolution did excite me. It made me feel invincible which was a far cry from how I had felt at school. I recalled the bloody-minded attitude of the principal, forcing me to decide in one minute on a course that could change my life. He did not care about me. Made me feel insignificant. Like a tiny nobody. Come to think of it a lot of teachers had made me feel that way. Always standing over me, looking down, never letting me finish a sentence, or explain myself. My mind cast back to Miss *Strongarm* and how I had felt, at the age of six, when she said, 'You're no different to the other kids.' She was wrong. I was different. And it was not only because of the way I looked.

Dad's silence since the expulsion had begun to annoy me. If he was thinking he could decide my future without discussing it with me first, he was wrong. For the first time I wished he had screamed. Instead, all I had seen was the same twist of his mouth he would adopt to suppress a swear word or prevent himself from becoming embroiled in an argument. It was true that Dad tried hard to be a good Adventist. I wondered if he had given up on me. Or whether his disheartened look was because of how his religion had treated me. I had no idea what he was thinking. More so, what he was planning for me, for my life. His words about being a good Christian, not drinking alcohol or smoking cigarettes, working hard, saving money, buying a car, and marrying a good Adventist man of European heritage echoed in my head.

My chin dropped to my chest. I had studied the Bible teachings, got baptised, been a good student, was dating an Adventist boy, doing everything right. Despite my efforts, school had rejected me, telling me I did not belong. If not within the bosom of the religion into which I had been born, and was now baptised, then where did I belong?

Maybe I should not be an Adventist. Maybe I did not need the faith that gave Dad strength. After all, I had not suffered like he and his family had. I had not been persecuted nor had my home burnt to the ground like his parents had. I had not been forced by invaders to flee from my country. None of my siblings had died a terrible death.

In contrast to Dad, Mum had never been as vocal about what I should or should not do with my life, which I had interpreted, during my early teenage years, as her not caring or showing interest. I had found it difficult to get close to Mum during those years. We were not friends who discussed feelings or opinions. Apart from giving Glynis and me a lesson on how babies were born, Mum and I did not discuss boys, hair, makeup.

Mum had opposed Dad about religion primarily because of his overbearing mother. She scolded him for his strictness with us children. Refused to allow him to take a belt to my brothers when they did something naughty. Was it possible that Mum felt as caged as me. With five children, I guess she did not have the opportunity to change her life. But I did.

So why did my heart race at the impending discussions about what came next. Why did my eyes well in the knowledge that my personal desires had become all-consuming. How could I ignore the back-breaking efforts of both parents to provide a good home for my siblings and me in Australia, pay for a private school education for LeRoy, me, and eventually Wayne, and try so hard to give us so many comforts. Why were the feelings of restlessness so overpowering that I was prepared to break their hearts. Would they ever forgive me.

Yesterday, Mum had been so outraged at the actions of the school, she had resigned herself to giving our religion the flick forever. Though I knew I would most likely never forget being abandoned at the school gate, I got the feeling Mum was on my side. Dad's silence had made it difficult to know what he was thinking. Perhaps he was planning to send me to one of those reform homes for girls he had once threatened me with when I had been rude to Mum. At the onset of the most fearful outcome, that he might insist I attend yet another school, I decided to get out of bed and dress. If there was going to be a confrontation when he returned from work, I did not want to be lounging around in my pyjamas.

I jumped out of bed, feeling angry. I stepped into the shower and turned on the water, rolling each shoulder under the stream before letting the beads massage my back. With my face turned to the jets, I closed my eyes, letting the water cascade over my body, thunder in my ears. I felt safe in the confines of our bathroom. Like I had escaped to some sort of refuge. Had yesterday really happened. Could it have been a dream. When I turn off the water, will I be transported back in time, be given a second chance.

The clingy, nylon shower curtain stuck to my leg, annoying me back to reality. A sob burst from my lungs. I hung my head. It had not been a dream. There would be no fleeing from this situation. The weight of my anguish brought me to my hands and knees. The torrent pummelled the top of my head, reverberating at the bottom of the bathtub, gurgling towards the waste. I opened my eyes to see the water disappear down the drain, recalling the ten months I had spent as a student at the Adventist High School.

Safe in the steamy bathroom, I lost all sense of time. Had I emptied the water tank. Poor Dad's going to want his afternoon shower before leaving for his second job. Would he even need that job now. I reached for the tap. Turned off the water. The mist dissipated. Along with it my sorrowful self-pity. I dried myself and dressed. I had made up my mind. If Dad insisted on my going to another institution, I would run away from home. The thought caused my tears to return. To what magical place would I run. I had let go of my old friends from my former high school. I would never again see the ones from bus number 27. My new classmates had abandoned me. Not even the most Christian of them had telephoned to ask how I was coping. I was a student without a school. A teenager without friends. I had nothing to do. Nowhere to go.

I spent the rest of the day listening to music and stressing about whether the uprising could even find me out here in the sticks. When LeRoy arrived home, he rushed to tell me how his teachers had warned him not to con-template 'copying your sister's behaviour'. Last night, all three brothers had whispered their support for me despite their heartfelt fears for what might happen next. LeRoy was now repeating his support.

'Shush,' I said at the sound of Dad's car entering the driveway. 'Don't say that out aloud. The last thing I need is Dad hearing you glorifying my behaviour. At least not until I tell him my decision that my school days are over.'

My mental preparation for a showdown would have to wait. Because when Dad came in, he showered, had something to eat, lay on the bed for a while, then got up, dressed, and left for his second job. We did not speak.

Donovan called. 'Hi. I'm in between jobs. Thought I'd call to see how it's all going?'

He had barely finished speaking when I blurted out, 'Well, since we spoke, I've contemplated jumping out of Mum's moving car, been attacked by killer ants on the footpath outside school, been forced to endure a repeat performance of the principal kicking me out, thrown my uniform and books over the balcony in front of the whole student body, and made up my mind I'm not returning to school. Any school. Ever.'

'I'm so sorry. It must've been terrible.'

'Scary would be more like it.'

'What are your Mum and Dad saying now?'

'I don't know. I've adopted a self-imposed persona non grata status. I don't leave the bedroom until everyone's out. Dad hasn't spoken to me. I haven't seen him since I made the decision not to go back to school. So, he doesn't know. I've told Mum. She's going to tell him when he gets home tonight. I don't know how he's going to react. I'm worried he might not let me leave the house. At least if you're here, he won't over react. Anyway,

I can't talk now. You know our phone is in the lounge room. The whole family is listening. I'll see you on Friday.'

'Yeah sure. Can't wait to see you and hold you. I love you.'

'I love you too. Bye.'

Hanging up the phone felt like disconnecting from the world. I hovered over it, trying to maintain the link with Donovan for as long as I could. Waiting for Friday was going to be like anticipating the second coming of Christ. I trudged to the bedroom. Slumped down on my bed. My head pounded so much, both hands shot up to hold it. The weight of a million thoughts was bouncing between one ear and the other. How would I be received at church. Would everyone know. Of course they would. That teacher at our church would have told them by Saturday. After this Sabbath, I will ask Donovan to take us to some of the far away churches. Hopefully no one will recognise me as that heathen who got expelled.

The members of the congregation were not the only people I did not want to face. I dreaded what Dad would tell Granny Jones. Had he already told her. We had not seen a lot of Granny and Uncle since Andy's death. Mum said it was because the old lady felt like the family blamed her for his death. It was true that she had indulged Andy. She had bought him a car, given him money, allowed him to move out. Was I going down the same path. Is that why Dad was so quiet. I imagined Granny preferred to avoid being judged by others. Like me, she was holed up in her new apartment, a different one to where the mosquitoes had eaten my ankles.

I felt lost. It had been an emotion-charged few days. Now the turmoil had begun to subside, I felt empty, lost, devoid of energy. I no longer jumped up at the sound of Mum or Dad's car arriving home. So, I failed to hear Mum come to my bedroom until I saw her standing over my bed with a smile from ear to ear.

'There's a vacancy for an Office Junior at my work.'

The buoyancy in Mum's voice made me feel like something wonderful had transpired in the world. Had someone announced the end of the Vietnam War. I sat up to listen, wondering what on earth I could possibly do in an office. Having been prevented from working on the sabbath meant I had zero work experience. I opened my mouth to start asking questions, then decided to wait until Mum had finished speaking.

'My supervisor is willing to give you a start. You must come for an interview first but that's just a formality.'

'What does an Office Junior do?'

'They will train you.'

My eyes circled around Mum's face. I wanted to appear enthusiastic, but I was wary. Having met Portuguese Granny I could say with confidence that our mum still harboured some of her mother's beliefs about the important things a girl should know, which did not include a tertiary education. However, Mum seemed to be a contradiction. In some ways she had become a modern woman which was evident in the way she dressed, wore make-up, entertained her friends from work, and listened to Johnny O'Keefe on the popular music show called Bandstand. In contrast, she had never shown much interest in further education for either my sister or me. She had convinced Glynis to leave school two years earlier. And there was the saving of hundreds of dollars a year in school fees if I did not return. Not to mention her contempt towards the Adventists because of her pushy mother-in-law.

'What about Dad?'

'I'll tell him when he gets home.'

Dad and I had not yet spoken. He had hardly been home because of his two jobs. I felt sad for the hurt I knew I was causing him. But I could not help it. My skin still burned with fury at the teachers for hounding me about the length of my uniform, plotting the photo fiasco, painting the negative with whitener, serving me a late afternoon detention, and then expecting me to perform a ridiculous punishment. Like a volcano, things had been bubbling since Andy's death. I had reached boiling point. The eruption had been inevitable. But I felt sad that the events had led to the disappointment I knew I was causing Dad. I wished I could have dealt with my feelings before reaching this point.

I had difficulty falling asleep that night. Thank goodness Mum had taken on the mantle of breaking the news to Dad. The look of sadness on his face, that his Evvy had failed him, would have been too much for me to bear. I wondered what Mum planned to say to him. What words she would choose. How Dad would react. Exhausted, I fell asleep in the early hours, failing to hear any whispering between them.

The next morning, I heard Dad in the kitchen snapping at Dewey. Was he taking his anger out on my brothers. Another time, when I passed him in the passageway, his shoulders seemed hunched. Was he sad, feeling defeated. Had I betrayed his faith in me. Or did he fear for my safety, my future. The night that he did not have to work, I decided not to join the family for dinner. Not a sound from the table reached my room. The silence was unnerving.

Donovan held my hand extra tight as we walked into our church on Sabbath morning. I saw neither Meriden nor the teacher from school. We glided into a pew side by side, then left as soon as the service ended. It felt good to breathe freely again which had transpired last night after hearing the cheery tone in Dad's voice when he called out, 'Evvy. Donovan's here.'

Dad had always been so welcoming to Donovan. The two of them were having a good old chinwag when I entered the room. I reflected on why so many people warmed to my parents. They had always been inviting and friendly towards visitors. Today, Mum had invited Donovan to stay for Sabbath lunch, but we were heading over to Manly for the rest of the weekend. Whatever Mum had said to Dad seemed to have worked.

The two of us spent the weekend talking about the expulsion. It was the first opportunity to speak freely. When I told him the details about the music chart and the song I had assigned to my teacher, he roared with laughter. On Sunday morning, we drove to the beach for his early morning surf before setting off for the long drive home to my house. I was relieved when he accepted Mum's offer to stay for dinner. I had been eating alone in my bedroom and needed an ally by my side for the first meal with the family in a week.

When I looked at Dad at the head of the table, I thought about the week of silence. A huge fissure had almost torn me apart from him. Now it seemed to have mended itself without the anticipated drama. Perhaps Dad had considered my recent antics at school as the lesser upheaval compared to the tragic death of his beloved nephew. It came to mind that no one had mentioned his name since the funeral. Until that night, when in response to Dewey saying, 'Poor Andy,' Dad sucked in his lips so tightly they disappeared into a dead straight line, before he took a deep breath and said, 'He brought it on himself.' After dropping that clanger, he stood up and left the room without finishing his dinner. There had been many deaths in Dad's family. This must have been the only way he could deal with the hurt.

After Donovan had left, my curiosity at Dad's true feelings about my being expelled, forced me to raise the subject. As soon as I knew he was alone in his bedroom, I approached. He looked up at me a little surprised when I entered. So, before he could say anything, I said,

'Dad. I'm really sorry about what's happened but I…"

'It's finished,' he said cutting me off mid-sentence. 'Let's not talk about it.'

At first, I wondered if Dad could simply not find the words to discuss his disappointment with me. Though now when I looked into his eyes, they seemed deeper and darker than they had ever been. Like he was sad. But his beautiful smile told me he loved me as much as ever. That he was on my side. Mum confirmed that his anger had been with the school. Firstly, for not contacting them. Secondly, for not being more forgiving. Now that I had made my decision there was no point in pursuing the issue. Neither Mum nor Dad, ever raised the subject again. And as Dad had said many times, 'Forget about the past.'

16

I'm Out

A jittery feeling overtook me in the reception area of the office where my mum worked. Unlike at school interviews over the years, I would be on my own today. I had followed Mum's suggestion and worn my Nehru-style dress. The Beatles had made the style popular when they adopted the look from India's first Prime Minister. Mine had been a Christmas present from Mum and Dad. Shaped like a coat, it was made of cream coloured cotton with a stand-up Mandarin collar, and a long row of shiny metallic buttons at the front opening. I wore it the same way I had to church, with nylon stockings and my black patent mini heels, also part of a Christmas present.

Last night, my heart had raced at the prospect of earning my own money. Until Glynis admonished me. Was she trying to be a killjoy, or had it been a genuine warning when she said, 'Remember, I worked there too. It was a good start, but you won't like it. The industrial suburbs are terrible. And you'll have to walk through the factory. All the men whistle and yell out. It's awful. They made me cry.'

It was already going to be a challenge joining the company where latitude for women with children was non-existent. The one that had warned Mum that taking time-off to attend her children's school events could put her job in jeopardy. The one that had caused her to leave me stranded on the footpath outside school where a colony of ants had attacked me. I lifted my chin, pulled back my shoulders, hoping to replace Glynis's words with positive thoughts. Working here would rescue me forever from wearing a school tunic that hung around my calves, balancing a flying saucer on my head, fighting inane rules and regulations that had marred my love of learning, or having to face teachers, whom I now despised as a whole. I commenced my first job a week later.

Everyone was friendly towards me because Mum had worked there for five years and was well liked. Despite that, there was a formality in the air that made me nervous. The men dressed like they were going to church, in suits, collars, and ties. For the women it was either a dress or skirt. Wearing trousers for us was against the rules. We were required to refer to the men as mister, despite them calling us by our first names. They held all the management positions. They sat in wooden cubicles with frosted glass around them. The women worked in large groups in open spaces on typewriters or calculating machines.

There was little interaction between the sexes. Except when a 'boss' called out. Then one of the women would jump up and run into the office with papers, a file, or a cup of coffee. The only time I got to see the men was when I dropped off their mail. That was one aspect of my job which allowed me to roam through the hallowed, teak-panelled corridors.

The positives outweighed the negatives. There was the weekly pay packet, somewhere in the vicinity of $16 and some cents. Enough to buy clothes, makeup, and begin paying board to my parents. And meeting Lee, a delightful older woman, who operated the automatic switchboard. Lee took me under her wing, teaching me everything she knew about the company's state-of-the-art PABX switchboard. It was one of the most advanced in the world.

Lee and I shared a passion for clothing, although we had quite different ideas about style. Like a former siren of the silver screen, Lee wore calf-length dresses and skirts made from breathless chiffon, in soothing pastel colours like baby-pink, duck-egg blue, mint, and lavender. 'The reception-ist is the first person whom visitors see. One must dress accordingly,' Lee said, through the plum in her mouth, gained from attending drama classes as a teenager. I never told her for fear of hurting her feelings, because Lee had a gentleness towards others, but sometimes her bouffant, platinum blonde hair and over-powdered face made her look like Bette Davis's desperate character in the scary movie, which we had recently watched on television, called Whatever Happened to Baby Jane.

I alternated between the two dresses I owned. The Nehru one and a buttercup-yellow safari-style suit which Mum had bought second-hand from a friend who had bought it in London. After my first pay packet, my wardrobe grew by two dresses and another pair of shoes.

In addition to learning how to operate the switchboard, my duties as an Office Junior included the tasks of maintaining a Xerox printer the size of a small bedroom, ordering stationery supplies I had never heard of such as file hangers, Kalamazoo ledgers, punch cards, and powdered toner cartridges before distributing them when they arrived, sorting gunny sacks of mail then delivering it down the rabbit warren of corridors and using a franking machine to print a stamp on outgoing mail. Operating the switchboard with Lee was the highlight of the job.

There were a host of smaller tasks like delivering files to different people, typing envelopes, and being a general dog's body. The variety and importance of the duties helped me gain confidence working with people and procedures in an office environment. Though it was better than being at school, I missed the companionship of young friends. I now had none, other than Donovan. The opportunity to escape to the beach suburbs with him at the weekends helped me endure the new loneliness. We continued to visit different churches. I no longer felt embarrassed about the possibility of crossing paths with former students, though I never saw any, ever again. I recognised a few teachers but never acknowledged them.

Being Adventist was one of the things Donovan and I had in common. Despite the expulsion, he had encouraged me to continue going to church. Another was not having friends. Neither of us had any of our own. The few people he knew were friends of his older brother. Like me, he had changed camps from the public system to the Adventist school halfway through his high school years. And like me, he had not remained long enough to be considered part of their clique. We just had each other which pushed us closer. Though we had talked about getting engaged, perhaps marriage one day, for now we had both agreed we were still too young for that kind of talk. However, we did talk about also being too young to have a baby together.

Perhaps it was because of the era but I did not feel guilty about sex. I never thought of it as bad, forbidden, or something to be enjoyed only in marriage. I had read about the birth control pill, which people were calling the pill, in Mum's Women's Weekly magazine so I telephoned Dr Novak's surgery to enquire about it. When the same doctor who had prescribed Valium to me at the age of fourteen said, 'The pill is only for married women' I was outraged. I had heard on my radio that some husbands had refused to allow their wives to take it. Also, that some religions had banned it for their believers, whether married or not. Many socially and morally conservative men amongst the political and religious leaders were blaming the pill for the sexual revolution. Some even dared to say in public, "It's a woman's duty to have children to increase Australia's population."

Despite the public outcry, the Australian government followed the line of the conservatives, by imposing a whopping 27.5% luxury tax on the pill, which remained in force until 1972. Their actions seemed ridiculous to me as they only served to make, what was fast becoming the century's most revolutionary medical breakthrough after penicillin, unaffordable to those whom I suspected needed it most. Dr Novak relented and agreed to give me a script if I had permission from my mother. When I told Mum I wanted to go to the surgery, and why, she did not question me about my decision, agreeing with me that she did not want her daughter to endure the hardship of an unwanted pregnancy. After all the bother, the pill did not agree with me as it caused crippling migraines which prevented me from ever using it. Despite my personal situation, in my opinion, birth control pills removed many of the obstacles that stymied a woman's life and prevented many unwanted pregnancies.

Working with Mum helped to improve our relationship. I was grateful to her for my first job. It had given me the opportunity to buy new clothes and shoes. It also provided an opportunity for us to be alone to talk in the car each morning and evening. It was how I had found the courage to discuss my decision to take the pill. I never said the words I'm sleeping with Donovan or I'm having sex. Mum was not like a girlfriend with whom I wanted to discuss my personal life. She was my mum. I do not remember the exact words I used but it was more of a statement than a request. Something like, *I need you to take me to the doctor to get the pill.* Which she did.

I wished Mum and I could have been closer, like friends. I wondered why we had never talked about girlie things together or gone shopping for pretty clothes. I still had the feeling my mother did not like me, but I did not know why. Was it because I had supported Dad in his religion, complained about the instant foods she had cooked, spurned her offers to curl my hair, or reminded her of her mother-in-law because she said we had similar features. Or was it because she was just plain exhausted from working and raising five children whom she had given birth to in quick succession, long before the availability of the pill. Mum always seemed to lack energy, be fatigued, sleepy. When she was not working at the office, she was working in the home. Some nights, after cooking dinner for us, she would be so tired, she would go to bed without eating.

Now that I was getting older, I liked that Mum did not interfere in my life. I had assumed the lack of interest was due to her not caring but now I could see evidence of the concern that raising five teenagers in a foreign country, and without family support, had caused both parents. I wondered how they had coped with some of the challenging decisions the five of us had forced on them. Like allowing me to stay overnight at Donovan's, not questioning Glynis's decision to go on a date with a guy she had met at work, permitting LeRoy to hang out with his mates on the weekend, and letting Wayne catch the train to the beach to go surfing.

When my siblings, and I were younger, Mum had made it clear she would have liked us to play sport as she had at school. She had often defended our pleas against Dad's refusal to let us join any of the sports teams for the Saturday matches, to no avail. How different might our lives have been if we had been permitted to participate in more social activities or if we had spent our teenage years in an Asian dictatorship like Singapore. I wondered if it was more difficult for parents to raise children in a western democracy. I started to wonder if the social, cultural, and political changes that were challenging traditional norms and values across the western world had even reached the East. Or had it been simply that Mum did not want to be the decider of our fates. I had not forgotten her stories about how Portuguese Granny had been so strict, it had caused Mum and her siblings to leave home as quickly as they could.

Despite my gratefulness to Mum for the job, Glynis's premonition, about the factory, the whistling, and the drab, grey industrial suburb, came to pass sooner than anticipated. In less than six months, it had become difficult to get out of bed in the mornings. Alas, even my fondness for Lee could not prevent my feelings of being trapped. Nor dispel my fears that the revolution would never find me because of where we lived.

Neither winding the window up and down nor fiddling with the sun visor had elicited a reaction from Mum on our drive to the office one morning. In desperation, I drew in a deep breath and let it out with a sigh. 'God, I feel like one of those sardines.'

'What do you mean?'

Was Mum so oblivious to what I was going through. I had allowed my simmering feelings of restlessness at school to reach boiling point for fear of upsetting Dad. I was not doing that again.

'You know,' I said. 'Like how those little fish all look the same when they're pressed into a tin. I'm going to become like all those women at work. A few are not much older than me.'

'That's not nice. Everybody at the office likes you.'

'Well, if I stay there much longer, I reckon when they pull back the ring, I'll be lying there looking as dead as them.'

Mum did not respond. And I was not going to reveal that I had been romanticising about moving to the northern parts of Australia to join the hippies. I had seen them on television talking about dropping out of society. I swung my head to stare out the window. I longed to ask her if she remembered the time I wanted to jump out of her car on the way to school. But Mum would not know about that, because I had never confided those feelings to anyone other than Donovan. I had also never confided how I felt about working in the industrial suburbs. Nor how I had begun dreaming about coming to a sudden stop in the middle of delivering the mail one morning, running out of the building, then continuing until I reached – I don't know where. I felt caged. I wanted to roar. I just did not know how.

That night, before I had a chance to continue my melodrama, Glynis came to my rescue. 'There's an opening for a Junior at my office,' she said as soon as she arrived home from work. 'That's if you want to work in the city. They'll give you the job if I recommend you. You don't even have to come for an interview.'

I resigned the next morning. A week later, I joined the Australian arm of Levi Strauss & Co., the world's largest maker of pants, noted especially for its Levi blue denim jeans. The change in jobs coincided with my turning sixteen, and Mum returning *back home* to Singapore for her first visit in fourteen years.

16.1

Hard to believe that an article of clothing could fuel a global revolution, but blue denim jeans did just that. In western society, where men still wore a shirt and tie to the shops and women only wore dresses, wearing jeans had become a symbol of rebellion and non-conformity. Behind the Iron Curtain, where they were hard to obtain, owning a pair of Levi jeans represented status and liberation – everything communist governments worked hard to stamp out.

I had joined within the first year of the American based company establishing a corporate office in Australia, based in Pitt Street in the heart of the city of Sydney. It was a marathon to get to work from our home. Glynis and I caught a bus to Bankstown Station, which took about twenty minutes, then we spent forty minutes inside the steel carriage of one of Sydney's famous red rattlers.

The city offered an oasis of trendy boutiques, beckoning me to expand my love affair with clothes, cementing the belief that what I chose to wear defined who I was, or wished to be. The fire still burned inside me from my run-ins with teachers over wearing a uniform or the constrictions that had applied at the company in the suburbs. Now I could match my clothes to how I felt, my personality, my identity and how I wanted the world to see me. I could change my look in line with the changing trends if I chose to. I had olive skin, I had long dark hair almost to my waist. I was a petite dress size 8. I wore a mini skirt one day, a maxi dress or jeans and a t-shirt, the next.

My lunch hours were spent traipsing through boutiques like House of Merivale and Hides. Merivale had been attributed by many as the first store in Australia to sell the mini, which was a dress or skirt with a hem of four inches or more above the knee. Housed in a six level Victorian-style building, the boutique was a beacon to teenagers like me. Sauntering up and down the twirling wrought iron staircase, amidst the bohemian architecture, mesmerised by the music, I searched for what I could afford to buy with my new salary of $21 per week.

Gliding through the doors of Hides made me feel like I was floating onto the stage of the controversial new musical called Hair. Sales assistants, wearing sandy coloured buckskin, transported me to an imaginary San Francisco. Suede fringes and tassels brushed the wooden floorboards from their skirts, pants, and boots. Nut brown tans and big hair were the order of the day, as the words from the title song of the musical about flaxen, waxen, curly, fuzzy, snaggy, shaggy hair, filled the store.

The news reports were broadcasting about how young people in the western world had become as enchanted with clothes and makeup as we were about the social, economic, and political revolution. And that billions were being spent on both during the affluent post war decades in which we were living. The mini craze had made skirts and dresses so small women began buying children's clothing. At a height of 169 centimetres, I had become too tall to wear them, but I remember Glynis buying tops and skirts from the children's section at department stores. The new trend caused a problem in England where clothing with a length under 24 inches did not attract tax. In response, new Customs and Excise rules changed the assessment of women's clothing forever, from length to bust size.

No one knew what outrageous trend might hit the scene next. *Hotpants* arrived just when society thought the mini skirt had crashed all social boundaries. When they became acceptable office wear, my wardrobe consisted of a pair in pink suede, one in black velvet, and another in denim. At the same time, companies in the suburbs like where Mum worked continued to insist women wear dresses or skirts and tops to the office.

Everything about working for the iconic jean manufacturer was electrifying and controversial, from its connotations of rebellion to its provocative use of sex, religion, and music to advertise its products. I remember relishing the news that my new employer's controversial advertising had crossed paths with schools and churches. I had cheered in silence for the brave students who had refused to wear anything other than Levi's, forcing their headmasters to telephone about the possibility of manufacturing our jeans in grey. And when the calls flooded in from religious representatives beseeching the company to retract disrespectful advertising campaigns – well.

Within a year into my new life of working in the city, I began to question my commitment to any form of religion, whilst Donovan was strengthening his. It followed that I became unsure about my feelings for him. We had been dating for almost two years. Rather than excite me as it had once done, his talk of solidifying our relationship with a ring, now pushed me away. I started to search for opportunities where I could distance myself from him. The change in me had coincided with Levi's moving its office out of the city, where I was certain a piece of me would remain forever. Plush offices meant nothing when they were situated in an inner-city industrial suburb near the airport, surrounded by manufacturing companies. Though the move had left me gasping for the vibe of the city, Donovan had welcomed it because it meant he could drive to collect me after work which he had begun doing most Friday nights. We would stay at his parent's house, in preparation for the Sabbath.

I had become bored with our weekends. I no longer enjoyed the visits to various churches where kind Adventist families invited us into their homes. They were always nice but now their lives seemed like carbon copies of each other. They served the same food, asked the same questions or rather, did not ask questions. They never questioned anything about the bible, the rules, the beliefs. I had started seeing that the world I had been imagining through my music, really did exist. Though whilst I was with Donovan, I was never going to be a part of it.

The last time Donovan collected me after work, an early sunset had begun to veil the nearby factories which had long since shut-up shop for the day. I raised a hand to shield my eyes against the final rays as I searched for the old grey mini minor I had once loved, then remembered he had sold it. I had felt safe and secure in my perfect first love. But things were different now. A car rounded the corner. A shiny new white Holden with Donovan behind the wheel.

Dad could not talk about my breakup with Donovan without those crystals filling his eyes. Mum said it had broken his heart. She, on the other hand, took it in her stride, 'It's normal. You're young.' Portuguese Granny sent me a lovely card saying similar, 'Don't be sad. You're young. I will be in Australia soon. Granny loves you.'

Shortly after the breakup, I met and became good friends with Louise, a girl about seven years older than me who lived in Paddington. Louise introduced me to the pick of Sydney's wine bars and restaurants in the city and eastern suburbs. I ordered my first alcoholic drink when Louise invited me to meet a group of people at the Piano Bar at the luxurious Wentworth, Sydney's first 5-star hotel. Despite my being under the legal drinking age of eighteen, no one asked for identification.

After hearing others in the group ordering tequila shots, I asked for the same from a waiter who said, 'It's come all the way from Mexico.' His comment meant little to a teenager who did not even know the name of an alcoholic drink. Until that time, I had adhered to the Adventist belief that drugs, tobacco, and alcohol were unclean chemicals, never to be ingested.

The drinks arrived, served on a plate accompanied by a tiny mound of salt, and a wedge of lemon. I glanced around to see most of the people in our group performing some sort of ritual with the ingredients. When I looked across the table at Louise, she was licking the soft fleshy area at the base of her thumb. I watched her sprinkle some of the salt onto the same spot before licking it again and throwing back her head to swallow the full shot of tequila before quickly sucking on the lemon wedge. It was all over in a matter of seconds. I mimicked her. How else could I mix with social groups who were beyond my age and experience. Rather than radiating a similar grin to hers, I gasped from the shot I had thrown down my neck. A flame raged inside my mouth, spreading to my throat. The fireball screeched all the way down to my stomach. I feared the toxic brown substance might have damaged some of my internal organs in its path, but I suffered in silence. Rather than reveal my innocence, I ordered a second.

Partying wildly in the city at the age of seventeen, with my new, much older friends, meant it was not long before I encountered some of the fashionably "beautiful people" whose worlds flowed with the mind-altering substances of alcohol and marijuana. Both substances were a popular pastime for a generation living at the edge of a revolution. One that was eager to experiment and explore the counterculture ideals of peace, love, harmony, music, and mysticism. And me, just wanting to experience — well, anything. My new friends lived each day as if the rules did not apply to them. As if they were above the law. Until then, everything I knew about this world had come through song lyrics, magazine images, television and radio.

Those people drew me into their world. I wanted to be a part of their exciting lives. It was an opportunity to wear the trendy clothes I had bought and mingle with personality-types I had never encountered. Everyone I met was older than me, though I never felt intimidated or in danger. Some had eccentric or pretentious personalities. I found them all interesting, some quite fascinating. I wanted to spend more time with these people. I just wanted more. And so, I plunged into their hedonistic decadence, without an anchor.

'Free love' the morally conservative called it whenever the media displayed images of young people dressed in miniskirts or hotpants. I did not see anything wrong with wanting to dress this way and resented the tags and negative portrayal of my generation. At times I wondered what the media meant when they reported about a 'sexual revolution for women'.

Most of the television and newspaper articles were about the pill allowing women to have sex without the consequences of conception. I did not feel as restricted as I was certain my mother's generation had. However, I did start to question the notion of women's liberation. I got the distinct feeling that from a man's point of view, the movement was giving more freedom to them to have sex without feeling any guilt or making a girl pregnant then being forced to marry her. On the other hand, I liked hearing about the aspects of the feminist movement which emphasised the many other benefits of liberating women other than sex. Like women having more control over how they dressed, helping them achieve higher education, equal employment opportunities, and improvement in a range of health issues.

Despite the proliferation of recreational drugs and alcohol, I never encountered any 'drunken orgies' as were implied by the never-ending headlines splashed across the front page of Dad's afternoon newspaper. Most of the girls I met admitted they were having sex to appease their boyfriends. Was this the real reason behind those men supporting the so-called liberation movement? It seemed like a difficult struggle during a time I simply wanted to have fun.

Although I had the perceived freedom to have sex with whomever I chose, hearing men assigning the tag 'sleeping around' to women who had chosen to grab the new so-called freedoms, infuriated me. It was a term I never heard applied to a man. This contributed to my preferring to have a steady boyfriend or none. Louise was engaged to man who had been conscripted and sent to the Vietnam War. It made her the perfect friend because we were able to have some riotous nights out without needing to include men.

My new acquaintances lived in a world that seemed alien to me. One I now ached to be a part of. They came from many walks of life. Some were immigrants from England and European countries of which I had never heard. Their attitudes and respect for different cultures were broad minded. Through the glamorous events that Louise and I attended, I met lawyers and their model girlfriends, the children of wealthy entrepreneurs, celebrities, famous photographers, and publicists. I went to rock concerts where I met like-minded music lovers. At one I met Billy Thorpe. At another Marc Hunter. During the years that Levi Strauss sponsored the Holden Racing Team I went to car rallies where I did photo shoots for the company wearing jeans and a logo t-shirt; one time at the Bathurst 500 with the famous driver Peter Brock.

They were halcyon days. Like others who were prepared to work hard, I was benefiting from the immense success of my employer in Australia and throughout the world. I had a well-paying job, money to burn. The company had been good to me. Recognising my mathematical prowess, they had trained me in financial analysis. Skills that would remain with me forever.

Now that Glynis and I were working in the city, and mixing with a wide range of people, we had begun debating with Dad about our race.

'We must be Eurasian.'

'We don't look English.'

'We have brown skin.'

'There are Eurasians coming to Australia now.'

'I like being Eurasian.'

Those discussions angered Dad. He rehashed the responses he had always given.

'You are English. Like me.'

'My father was from Devon in Cornwall.'

'How you look does not make you Eurasian.'

'Race is based on your blood.'

It seemed like we were never going to reach any consensus about the subject. So, both Glynis and I just stopped discussing it. We were too busy getting on with our lives.

Mixing with older people at exciting events made it tough to dutifully go home to Greenacre after a night or day out. Almost everyone I knew lived miles away from me which made it challenging to get home. There were no trains from Bankstown to the eastern suburbs. The ones to and from the city stopped running at midnight. I was frightened to catch a train at night anyway. Louise owned a car and often drove me home. Sometimes I caught a cab, which on occasion cost me a week's pay. The drive from Paddington to Greenacre took around forty to sixty minutes. Each time I arrived home after midnight Dad would interrogate me about where I had been and with whom.

I do not remember whether Dad was doing the same to Glynis. I was not paying a lot of attention to her life. Except that both of us had stopped attending church. It was not because we did not believe in God, or the Adventist teachings, but rather that we had other things to do on the sabbath. Mum had long stopped attending, Dad also. Now, he simply drove our three brothers to and from the services. I wondered what would happen as soon as one of them started driving. Though I had seen the tears in his eyes about my breakup with Donovan, I did not know if they were because Dad was hurt by it, or disappointed with me. Either, because of those feelings, or the fear that he was losing control, he had begun reacting badly to my attempts for autonomy.

One evening I said yes to a drink after work with a man whom I had met amongst the new group of older people with Louise. He took me to a party where we smoked a lot of marijuana. It was well after midnight when I realised that I was stranded in the eastern suburbs without transport home. My friend drove me home, complaining about the distance all the way.

'My father's going to kill me,' I said to change the subject. I had not meant it literally which was how my friend had taken it when he responded, 'If he lays a hand on you, I'll beat him up.' Of course, Dad was not going to kill me, but he had bolted the door. My key was useless which forced me to ring the bell to get into my own home. The instant scrape of the metal bolt drawing back meant Dad had been standing behind the door all along. We came face to face, Dad in his pyjamas, his lips clamped tight, jaw clenched. He tried hard to look me in the eye, but I turned away.

'Who was that?' he said, looking behind me to see if the car was still there. Remembering my friend's offer to beat-up my father, I was glad he had gone.

'A friend who drove me all the way from Paddington. Why?'

'Your sister said you left work to meet a man you've been seeing. Is that true?'

I looked at Dad, remembering Glynis telling me I 'must go home with her' when I told her outside the office that I was not getting in her car. My eyes narrowed, wary of what other stories she might have told Dad about me.

'I met a friend,' I said with defiance. 'That's all.'

'Your sister is worried about you. Can't you understand that?'

I did not respond. I was seething. I started mentally justifying my actions. *I'm working...I'm old enough...We live so far away...I'm not going out with Donovan any more.* Better not tell him tonight that I will be spending the weekend in Paddington.

Dad fiddled with his moustache. When he said, 'You must come home straight from work from now on. Is that clear?' I decided I would not be forewarning him. 'Please switch off the light,' he said, turning away from me and heading towards his bedroom muttering something about having to get up early in the morning.

I stood still on the spot. My chest hurt, like I could not breathe. I might be having a heart attack. Was that even possible for a seventeen-year-old? Arguing with Dad always unsettled me. I knew he had been upset since my breakup with Donovan. I felt both indifferent and annoyed at his reasoning. Donovan was a boy not a man. It was inevitable the relationship would not last. He would always hold a special place in my heart but Donovan being an Adventist was not enough reason to marry. Dad should not have attached so much to his dreams of my being safe in the arms of the Lord, being rescued from heartache like his sister Moira, and marrying a man from, what he beleived was, the right race and religion.

I was ambivalent towards Glynis's concerns about what Dad had called my 'antics'. I did not want anyone to watch over me. Least of all a sibling. But the last thing I wanted to do was argue with her. Especially as we had to sit together in her car tomorrow all the way to Mascot. Since the company's move out of the city, Glynis now drove to work, collecting two other employees on the way. I loathed the boring drive, loathed being driven, and loathed living in the suburbs.

I undressed and got into bed. I had a lot to think about. Especially the offer from a girl called Olivia whom I had met that night. Olivia was looking for someone to share accommodation with her on the south coast near Wollongong where she lived. It would be almost two hours by train from Central Station. It was not the city, nor near my new friends, but it was the first tangible opportunity to escape. I had already said yes to the offer.

17

Leaving Home

The music was lauding the changing times, telling the world there was a new order coming, telling the children they were no longer under the command of their parents. For me, living at home became more and more constrictive and isolating. Other than the threats of sending me to a reform home for girls, which no longer scared me, Dad had failed to tell me how he planned to punish me if I disobeyed his orders. So, I was stubbornly sticking to my decision to resign from Levi's and move to the south coast.

Olivia, who worked in a supermarket, had assured me she could get me a job with her. I could not tell Mum and Dad about working in a shop. They would be devastated. Upon hearing of my thoughts about resigning, a manager at Levi's offered to finance a commercial arts course after being impressed by some of my drawings. I had continued my love of art since leaving school and Glynis had encouraged me to take a few of my sketches into the office as a suggestion for new marketing ideas. Though I sent away for brochures, I knew I would not be taking up the offer. I was not ready to return to any kind of learning institution.

Dad was eating dinner when I broke the news about leaving my job, and home. I watched his lips come together in the thin line I knew so well. He placed his spoon and fork either side of his plate and started coughing, almost choking on the spoonful of rice he had just put in his mouth. 'You will not leave this house,' he spluttered. 'This is the last straw.'

I had not realised the anguish that had been building in Dad. I did not argue with him that night. The next morning, I calmly told him that I was going and that no one could stop me. We did not talk again that day but two weeks later he drove me to the station to catch the train south. He helped me take my suitcase out of the boot, carried it up the ramp to the ticket office, then hugged me tight. His voice crackled, 'Be safe my Evvy. Telephone us as soon as you get there.'

My head rattled in unison with the train. I did not know if it was from the adrenaline pulsing through my body, but I had the sensation of being both scared and excited at the same time. I remember feeling exhausted enough to sleep but afraid someone might steal my suitcase. The decision had been mine to leave home, my job, and Sydney. I had not asked for money or help. Best not to be beholden to anyone. Though as the train drew nearer to my stop, reflecting on what I had done and the fear of what I was getting myself into caused my head to spin out of control.

The ancestors on both sides of my family came to mind. They had ventured to the far-flung corners of earth and Empire not knowing what awaited them during an era when many never returned home. As if following their lead, my parents had left our birth country to start a new life in another colony of the British Empire with four children under the age of five. I pointed my chin towards the roof of the train as it clunked towards its final stop, hoping it would disguise the cascade that churned inside me.

Olivia had taken a three-month lease on an old garage which had been converted into a small flat situated a few kilometres inland from the coast. The freedom of living away from home was exhilarating; everything a new experience. We showered in a roofless, defunct, concrete water tank under blistering heat one day, a southerly bluster the next. We smoked marijuana every night. Those wild nights never stopped us from dutifully waking up on time to prepare for work, then walk the hundred metres or so to the main road where we would hitch a ride to our jobs in the nearby town. Hitchhiking, or hitching, as we called it, soon become our preferred method of transport. It was at our disposal because most cars headed towards the town, and it was free.

Almost everyone I met on the coast was around my age or a year or two older. Most of them did not appear to be doing much with their lives. 'I'm trying to find myself,' was the standard response to my questions about what they did for work or pleasure. Could I ever be like them I wondered. Content to live an effortless life in a laid-back town where the primary pastime was getting stoned on marijuana. For many of them it had become a popular alternative to alcohol. Those who favoured it considered it the lesser of the two evils. It was always easy to obtain. Everyone knew someone who either grew or sold it.

Marijuana delivered me an overwhelming feeling of happiness. Smoking it gave me the courage to get up to all sorts of mischief with new friends on the coast. Like sneaking into pubs because some of us were underage, driving cars without a licence, swimming in the ocean at night, hitching in the dark, and a host of other dangerous antics. I doubt I would have had the courage to push the limits without it. I think I laughed more during that period than I had in my whole life. Many people scorned us for smoking marijuana, despite so many more social issues arising from alcohol, or addiction to prescription drugs. The drug scene at that time was like playing in the sun in the garden when I was a child. I imagined I had not a care in the world. Like I had finally escaped the ropes that had bound me. When Olivia told me she had some friends on the coast who had paid for their cravings with their lives, I never considered that sort of thing happening to me.

The novelty of living in a beach town with people closer to my age group soon wore off. As did the joyful feeling from being under the influence of marijuana. Within a few months, I was in desperate need of intellectual stimulation, sophistication, and fashion. I resigned from the fruit shop after two months when the owner told me I could not sit on a stool, even when there were no customers in the shop, because I must stand whilst the doors were open. Despite looking through the newspapers and visiting the unemployment office, the only job on offer was serving in a butcher shop. My first thought was imagining someone I knew from Sydney walking in and how I would have died from embarrassment. It was time to leave the coast.

The week before my planned return to Sydney, I went to a party on a remote farm property situated about an hour out of the town. Marijuana joints appeared like *pass-the-parcel* treats at a children's party. We all participated in the free offer. Everyone was stoned. When the host announced he had received a tip-off that the police were on their way, the fifty or so revellers almost trampled each other in their frantic attempts to escape.

Eager to make a getaway, I jumped into the car of someone I had only met that night. In the pitch black of night, on the road back to town, his car crashed and somersaulted. Afraid he would be tested for drugs, he insisted we walk to the nearest telephone box to call his friend, who dropped me off at the flat. Olivia did not return. I spent the night alone hoping I was not going to die. The next morning, my arms and legs had turned into a motley pool of black, blue and green. I packed my belongings, hitchhiked to the station, and caught a train back to Sydney. I never saw anyone from the south coast again. Not even Olivia.

Dad welcomed me at the front door with the tender smile he always had for his children. He hugged me so tightly, I could smell his familiar hair oil. Mum and my brothers gathered around us. I could hardly get my bag in the front door. Despite my telephone call to inform the family about the accident and that I was returning to Sydney immediately, everyone gasped at the sight of my bruises.

'You could have died, Evvy,' Dad said. 'How did it happen?'

Explaining the crash was not something I wanted to do. The family did not need to know the details of what could spoil the revelry of my return. My brothers were hanging on to my every word, firing their breathless questions at me as if I had returned from a pilgrimage or been found after having been kidnapped. The familiar aroma of Mum's cooking exuded its welcoming warmth.

So much love radiating around me from our big family made it impossible not to compare it with the past few months. It took all my strength not to burst into tears at every familiar sound, smell, and loving gesture combining to remind me that I had not fitted in with the vibe amongst the people living on the coast. Compared to those young people, I felt different, more mature. If I had grown up in the sticks, then they were living in the wilderness. Working in a shop where I had to deal with the public had been the worst part. However, the chance of an international fashion company relocating to the coast was implausible. As for the horror crash which almost killed me, that should never have happened.

'I've got early Christmas presents,' I said to divert attention and questions about the accident. 'I had to put them in the mail because I couldn't carry them. There's an embroidered bedspread for you and Dad,' I said smiling over at Mum. 'An electric shaver for you Dewey. And a curling wand for you Glynis. I left before I had a chance to buy anything for LeRoy and Wayne.' They both looked disappointed when I said, 'Sorry but you'll have to wait.'

'Why did you buy anything for us, Evvy?' Dad said. 'You didn't need to. You should save your money.' His comments made me realise I had spent a significant portion of my weekly wage buying presents for my parents and siblings.

My eyes darted around the lounge room soaking in the familiarity. Dad had hung posh-looking wallpaper on the white walls and painted the French-style louvre doors glossy white. I smiled at the sleek stereogram on which I had played my favourite records. They were all reminders of my parent's hard work to provide a quality life in Australia. Only a few months had passed, yet I was now a visitor. I had avoided peering into the bedrooms on my way to the bathroom, wondering if my bed would still be there.

At some point, I would have to deliver the news that I was only staying until I found a job in the city. Then I would be looking for something to rent in the Eastern suburbs. The thought of how Dad might react caused the butterflies in my stomach to flutter, making me feel light headed. When Mum said she had to check on something on the stove, I jumped up to avoid any talk about my plans. I whispered to LeRoy who had followed me to the kitchen. 'Which is the best glass to use?' Was it okay to touch things that no longer belonged to me I wondered. I balked before opening the fridge, then restrained my hand from lifting the lid on the saucepan to see what was causing the glorious smell wafting throughout the house. Mum must have sensed my hesitation.

'Don't eat anything Evvy, I've cooked your favourite, tripe curry. I got the butcher to add lots of those knobby bits you like.'

I smiled, glad that her eyes were on the saucepan. But when she turned towards me, I was certain she had caught the exaggerated gulp as I swallowed a mouthful of cordial. Mum was smart. She knew I was not staying. She told Dad later that night.

The offer of a receptionist position for a law firm in Elizabeth Street, paying twice as much as I had been earning on the coast, was too good to refuse. Dad's parting hug lasted longer than usual, Mum's too. I moved into a share house in the eastern suburb of Double Bay, Sydney's answer to Los Angeles's Rodeo Drive. My new home was close to Bondi Beach, a short bus ride to the city, the Domain, and Kings Cross. Places where I soon began my obsession with the art of people watching. Though they would have preferred I lived at home, Mum and Dad were content I had remained in Sydney.

The areas I began to frequent beat with a general feeling of euphoria. The people whom I met talked about the Summer of Love, the Sexual Revolution, the Swinging Sixties, the Hippie Movement, and living an Alternative Lifestyle. Fashion and music continued to be major influences in my life. Behind them both lay Flower Power, the symbol of passive resistance and non-violent ideology. A façade for opposition to the Vietnam War, it really represented opposition to all traditionalist values. I embraced the symbolism, dressed to broadcast it to the outside world.

My choice of clothing for the law firm was fashionably zany. It included a flowing, forest green maxi dress that swept the floor, miniskirts, and my newest addition, an American style, red, white, and blue, stars-and-stripes hotpants outfit with matching top, plus several pairs of six-inch platform shoes. In contrast, my weekend wardrobe overflowed with hypnotic pastel coloured paisley, peasant blouses, flowered bandanas, embroidered bell-bottom denim jeans, tan suede moccasins, Indian kurtas, beads, flower patches, and all manner of representations of peace, love, freedom. I wore yellow sunflowers in my hair and painted the Twiggy style eye makeup that I had adopted several years earlier. My dark hair flowed down my back.

Shortly after my breakup with Donovan, I stopped attending church. For the first few Sabbaths I had caught a train to a couple of different churches, even attended our local church as an opportunity to outrage the parishioners with my outfits. One Sabbath I donned my faded jeans and Indian kurta and hitchhiked to the annual Adventist camp in Blacktown to catch up with Donovan to explain why I had sent him a letter saying, 'I'm not sure I believe in God any longer.'

Back in the city now, I spent my weekdays in the conservative world of the lawyers. Then on Saturdays I hitchhiked from Double Bay to Speakers Corner at the Domain in Sydney's Hyde Park to hear the philosophies of the fundamentalists. Anything could be on the menu from Darwinism, the Vietnam war, socialism, anarchism, religion. The speakers represented and argued all points of view. A tiny old woman called Ada from the Salvation Army was my favourite. Ada stood on the top rung of what looked like a ladder she had carried all the way from her kitchen. Banging on a tambourine, she sang Bible songs in the rain, hail, or shine. I recognised those songs. I had not forgotten them.

The domain buzzed with a powerful energy. It radiated throughout me. Just being there made me happy. I did not have a boyfriend, nor any close friends at the time. Louise had left Australia for America. Most of the people I socialised with were either my housemates or just acquaintances.

Sometimes I would hop on the back of one of their motorbikes for a thrilling ride through Kings Cross or down to Bondi Beach.

Years would pass before the glow of neon from the famous Coca-Cola sign illuminated the way to Kings Cross. Though by the beginning of the 1970s, the hippies, painters, poets, writers, film, and rock stars had begun drifting there, seeking to be a part of the change in Sydney. I too flocked to the *Cross*, as it was now mere minutes from where I lived. Kings Cross introduced me to a diversity of humanity the likes of which I had only read about in the news stories. Most of those stories were about the sleaze, the crime, the prostitutes, the strip clubs, the gambling, and the illegal drugs and alcohol for sale.

The negative reports kept both the fear and fascination with Kings Cross alive. Especially the stories about the crooked cops, the gangsters, and the mysterious disappearances of people who had flocked there to see if the hype was real. Though many of these things were happening in front of my eyes, I never crossed paths with either the world of the sordid, seedy, dangerous or deadly. Instead, I soaked up the bohemian buzz, sipping espressos with the lawyers and academics who frequented the European style coffee shops. I listened to the live rock music and buskers in the street; hung out with the hip artists and their other followers at the Yellow House artists' collective; sat cross-legged with the beatniks and rebels that popped into the Wayside Chapel.

I had become a bit of a loner, enjoying my own company. Though I loved hanging out with the hippies at the Domain, I had no interest in their philosophies. Sometimes they heckled me, called me a plastic hippie because whilst I joined them at concerts, rallies, and other events, I was not committed to their cause. I was free to join the counterculture ideals. Yet I felt restrained by my deeply conservative upbringing which urged me to be self-reliant, resilient, earn a living. 'You work for the man,' some of them taunted, referring to the taxman. They were correct. I was non-conformist in all aspects of my life, so I was not prepared to conform to the ideals of the anarchists any more than I was to the conservatives.

I had chosen to wear tie-dye, faded jeans, and bandanas because I liked the look. Smoke pot because I liked how it made me feel. Adorn myself with peace signs because they made great jewellery. I wanted to be free to do whatever I chose. Political opinions were not in my purview. When Monday morning came around, I was as keen to get back to my well-paid job as I had been to escape it on Friday. I never felt the need to join any club or group, including religious ones.

I was not serious about much in my life. I liked it that way. Which was why, when the senior partner offered to sponsor me to study law if I completed my university entrance exams, I declined, still wary of committing to any school-like studies. The offer triggered my restlessness. The idea that the people with whom I worked were suggesting I needed to get serious felt like something poking at my freedom. I was happy. I wanted to stay in the moment.

Midway through 1972, and totally out of the blue, the cute blond American named Jack, a friend with whom I had lost contact for over a year, walked into the law firm. We had struck up a friendship because, following the example of Dad, I had a love for everything American which had drawn me to the ideals of that country. It had fascinated me to learn that the United States had been the first major colony to successfully revolt against colonial rule, making it in a sense the first new nation.

Jack was leaving Sydney with his younger brother to live with a group of young people in a communal farmhouse in a town called Tully, 140 kilometres south of Cairns, in Far North Queensland. 'Come up,' he said, handing me a one-way bus ticket. I resigned my job at lunch time, left a week later.

18

Where is FNQ?

On a winter's day in July, mere weeks after seeing Jack again, I jumped onto a bus to commence the forty-eight-hour trip to Tully, hoping not to reveal to my fellow passengers the series of sinister scenarios spooling through my head about the small, plastic zip lock bag, one third full of marijuana hidden in my suitcase. I had purchased it for $30 from an acquaintance. It was the first time I had bought marijuana.

Flaunting the law may have been part of the thrill for some, but not for me. My fickle anxiety gauge became the antithesis of the rhythm of the bus, receding as it accelerated, rising as it slowed. Each time we stopped to allow passengers to disembark or to collect new ones, which happened either in a town or somewhere along the highway, I felt my heartbeat skyrocket. I imagined the driver's puzzled look, wrinkled brow, and screwed up nose sniffing at the strange smell coming from the luggage hold. Were he to insist his passengers alight to identify their suitcase, I was certain he would notice my heart palpitating double-time or at the very least my sweaty palms.

My neck hurt. It had become stiff within a few hours of leaving the depot in Sydney. With every twist, my back felt like it had broken. Having an aisle seat made it worse because I had nothing on which to lean. Unlike some of my fellow travellers, I had not taken a pillow. More than once, my head flopped onto the shoulder of the woman sitting next to me. All discomfort paled however, against the obsession with what nestled in a corner of my checked suitcase.

We were an affluent generation in the western world during the Sixties, with money to spend on pleasure. Marijuana had been accessible to me since leaving school. To many of my generation it was preferable to alcohol. People freely shared their joints. Like buying the drinks at a bar, most guys brought the marijuana with them. We girls smoked whatever was going around. I had heard it called by a variety of pseudonyms. On the coast they called it dope or weed. In the city we usually referred to it as grass or pot. I often smelt its sweet earthy smell wafting wherever young people had congregated, like boutiques, bars, parties, rallies, parks.

My friends, and I never thought of smoking pot as illegal. However, during my late teens, the production of the illicit drug had soared, largely to satisfy the demand from US servicemen arriving in Sydney on leave from the war in Vietnam. To stem the growth, law enforcement agencies had increased their efforts to hunt down organised drug traffickers as well as introducing stronger prohibition and criminal laws for users. As part of a growing defiance towards society's rules, young people had surprised many of the lawmakers by flocking to the areas where the police had discovered major crops of illicit marijuana, rather than avoiding them.

Consistent with the police crackdowns, I had heard stories about arrests for possession. Those who could afford it hired expensive lawyers to avoid a criminal conviction. Though most were released with a hefty fine, some of my friends had been mistreated by the police, whom they said had punched them in the stomach through a phone book, kicked them in the back, or spat on them.

Learning that people I knew were being charged, mistreated, or were having their young lives tainted by a criminal record fuelled my fear of getting caught. Over the past year, the fear had turned to paranoia after finding myself in a few scary situations of my own.

Like the time I had jumped out of a window at a friend's house in Paddington at the sound of the front door bursting open. Grabbing my handbag, I ran to the old sash-style windows facing the street, turned the brass latch at the top of one, heaved it up, then jumped onto the front lawn. Once on the street, I hailed a taxi home to Double Bay.

Jumping out of a window was not my normal behaviour and I hoped never to have to repeat the performance. However, I had just watched my friend empty a metre-high mound of marijuana onto his dining room table from two shopping bags. He had been carrying around the bags with a group of us as we traipsed through the city shops one Saturday morning, but I had no idea what was inside them. Heavens above, with that much pot, I ran the risk of getting busted for something in which I had no part.

The intruder turned out to be the landlord. Suspicious of his young tenant because of the blaring music and comings and goings, he had telephoned the police whose arrival occurred within minutes of my escape. I learnt that after interrogating everyone in the apartment, they had only carted off the owner of the bags. Though they charged him with possession and intent to traffic, a criminal lawyer managed to keep him out of prison.

Once I had felt safe in the taxi, I reflected about the car accident on the coast months earlier which had almost killed me.

A sickening feeling washed over me when our driver announced we were crossing the border from New South Wales into Queensland. The thought of how far away from home I had travelled made me feel like something was gnawing at the insides of my stomach. I recalled the discussion I had with Mum and Dad on the day I had told them the news about Tully. How I had avoided contact with them throughout the conversation.

'What are you thinking?' Both had cried out in unison. 'You're leaving a good job to go thousands of miles away. And with two American boys you hardly know?'

I had travelled alone to the south coast and been living away from home for over a year, but this was the furthest I had ever been from my family. Despite all the anguish I had caused them they were the only people in the world who had my back. They were prepared and willing to support and defend me no matter what I did. There was the time the two of them had driven to the south coast without question when I telephoned crying that someone had stolen my handbag containing not only my week's pay but my precious eye makeup. Dad had driven around the town searching for a pharmacy that opened on Sundays to replace what had been stolen. And Mum had given me some cash to tide me over until my next payday.

Turning to stare out the bus window, I took a deep breath, letting out a sigh. I dwelled on the thought of the two of them driving the long journey home yesterday, after ensuring me safely onto the bus for Tully. After selling my bed at the share house, I had gone home for two nights before the bus departed from the depot at Central Station. I imagined the car would be silent. There was nothing left to discuss. I had left home forever.

Mum and Dad had a point about Jack. I did not know much about him. We were just getting to know each other before my move to the south coast. After that we had lost contact. Now there was plenty of time to think about what I was heading into, what the house would be like, who else lived there, whether I would have my own room, and what Jack might be expecting of me. Despite the feelings of melancholy, the questions about what I was heading towards, and the anxiety caused by that darn plastic bag in my suitcase, I knew in my heart that nothing in the world could have kept me from jumping on that Greyhound bus.

When we arrived in Brisbane, my neighbour disembarked. No one replaced her, so I slid across to the window seat. Though gazing outside made the trip a little more bearable, the mental image of wailing police sirens from a motorcade pulling up alongside the bus to arrest me for possession of the illegal substance in my suitcase remained with me for the entire trip.

Heading further north, the temperature during the day hovered around 25 degrees Celsius, dropping to around 17 at night. The bus had air conditioning and a bathroom with a portable toilet. It stopped at certain roadhouses along the way for those who wanted to buy a meal. Feeling something catastrophic was imminent because of what I carried in my bag, I was happy not to leave the bus until my back felt so numb, I had no choice. When we stopped a few hours north of Brisbane, I jumped off for a much-needed stretch.

We ploughed further north. I had only ever seen images of sugarcane farms in books at school. Now, the willowy green and yellow grasses fringing the stretches of highway between the towns of Rockhampton, Mackay, Proserpine, Bowen, and Townsville, were close enough to touch. Though the sheer size of Australia had captivated me, it had been an arduous trip.

On the verge of feeling that neither my body nor mind could take much more discomfort or anxiety, I turned away from the window towards the crackling sound of the driver's microphone which we passengers had learnt would signal an important announcement.

'Not far t'go to FNQ now folks,' boomed the most Aussie accent I had ever heard. 'That's what we locals call the Far North. Eye-est ever annual rainfall for a populated area of Australia. Tully's got the record, ain't it.'

This had been the third or fourth driver since our departure. And his first address to us. We had picked him up on a lonesome stretch of the national highway. Some of the drivers had provided a commentary along the journey, others hardly spoke. I had found the changeovers curious. They seemed to take place at remote locations and odd times. This driver had joined us on one of the eerier late-night exchanges.

The sound of wheels crunching on loose gravel had intrigued me. I saw a man standing on the roadside. We were in the middle of nowhere. There was no car in sight, so I wondered how he had arrived there. The other driver had hopped down from the bus to join him. I watched as the two men shook hands, lit up cigarettes, then started chatting through a haze of smoke. They swapped some papers, then walked around the bus together. I assumed they must have been checking the tyres. As soon as our fresh driver boarded, we drove off. I stared into the night as hard as I could but there was no trace of the man we had left behind. *Must have been taken by aliens.*

On the outskirts of Tully, our new driver told us that during the erection of the sugar mill in 1924, officials had named the little agricultural town, which grew sugarcane and bananas, after a nearby river. In recent years it had lured the hippies, university bond absconders, and city dropouts with the promise of an alternative lifestyle. Tucked away in the far north, it still offered shops, pubs, and people. I guessed a town like this had just the right amount of remoteness a young city dweller was prepared to endure. I smiled to myself at the thought that Dad would have called it a 'backwater, worse than Malaya'.

As the bus came to a halt for the last time, the driver, whose accent had warmed me up for my adventure in FNQ, straightened out of his seat to face us. Head tilted to one side, he said, 'It's winta here now folks. So yous'll be roight. Unless yous'a planning to stay longer. Then fair dinkum yous'll know what's what.' A hearty belly laugh swallowed up his next words as he stepped off the bus to begin unloading the luggage.

My eyes followed him from the window. My stomach started turning somersaults as he got closer to the luggage compartment. The second the other passengers started shifting in their seats, I jumped up and moved into the aisle to escape. My thoughts melded with the swampy humidity which hit me before I reached the open door. *Jack better be on time. I don't want to be hanging around town with marijuana in my suitcase. What will I do if someone comes to search me?* Oh gosh, what was I thinking.

Jack had borrowed a little white sedan to collect me from town. It was a joyous meeting. We hugged and kissed each other. He fussed around me, offering to carry my hand luggage, seeking my suitcase. I had missed his infectious smile, his positive nature. In the brief time I had known him, he had always been in high spirits. And I adored his American accent.

'The farmhouse is about fifteen minutes out of town,' he said. 'Everyone is at work till about four o'clock. You'll meet them then.' He proceeded to give me a run down on the others in the house, 'Michael and Minnie, a couple of teachers from Perth' and 'Casey my younger brother. He's only sixteen.'

A waft of grassy air hit me as I stepped out of the car. My new home was a wooden farmhouse built on stilts, sitting smack in the middle of a wide-open cane field, like those I had passed on the journey north. Jack took my suitcase out of the boot and motioned towards the steep staircase leading upstairs. 'I'll show you the bathroom later. It's through there,' he said with a nod towards the wooden slats, which I noted made a poor attempt at concealing the area underneath the house.

Trinkets of silver and brass jingle jangled as we stepped through the front entrance. 'This is the common area,' he said. 'It's where we spend most of our time.' I saw that it included a long bench with a sink. There were no cupboards. Just shelves with curtains across them, I guessed to protect the crockery and food from dust.

'Oh my gosh, what's this,' I gasped at the site of the vibrant images that covered one side of the passageway wall from ceiling to floor. Blood red and majestic white robes, chestnut and black stallions, brass helmets, and swords had transformed crumbling stucco into a magnificent mural of mayhem, majesty, and marauding troops.

'That's Alexander the Great and his army. Michael's an artist. It's not finished yet. Cool, isn't it? He and his girlfriend sleep over there,' he said motioning to the opposite side of the house. 'The other rooms run off the verandah. Let's go outside and look.'

We exited through the jingles. 'This is yours if you want it.' I peeked inside a dingy enclosure that looked stark and empty, but for the hospital-like bed with its thin, striped mattress. The door swung shut as he stepped over to a larger area facing the cane fields.

'Or you can share mine,' he beamed as he pushed open the door to his bedroom. A silk parachute billowed from the ceiling over a large waterbed which lay on the slatted floor. Mosquito netting trailed from the parachute. The aroma of sandalwood seeped throughout.

'This is for you,' he said as he grabbed a coat hanger with a flowing calico dress hanging from it. Giant field mushrooms had been painted across the front. Gothic-style sleeves swept the floor as he dragged it across to me.

'I got it at a market in Cairns. One of the hippies painted it especially for you.'

'I love it. It's gorgeous.'

A glance at my suitcase, followed by a swift nod towards the mystical space, was enough of a hint to Jack that I had accepted the invitation to move in with him. He smiled, dropped my bag inside his door, and doubled back to kiss me on the lips.

The farmhouse being on stilts gave the impression it floated. The woody aroma from sandalwood joss sticks was a constant. It fused with the musky smell of elephant dung mosquito coils during the nights. Just like our bedroom, everything about the farmhouse made me feel as if I had been lifted above the clouds and transported to a far-off land.

There were days I felt as if I had been suspended in time. The music assisted in creating the illusion. It was 1972 but we only played music from the Sixties. Dylan, Simon & Garfunkel, Donovan, and Van Morrison, drifted from a record player which rested on a stack of bricks in a corner of the living room. Whenever the needle reached the end, someone either replaced or replayed the record. It just seemed to happen by magic. It was one of the phenomena of the farmhouse.

Fabrics and cushions originating from mystical lands like Nepal, India, and Tibet set the living area ablaze with purple, crimson, yellow and orange. I could not wait to see more when Minnie told me they came from the market in Cairns.

My new housemates seemed to have much more purpose to their lives than those whom I had met on the south coast. Everyone in the farmhouse earned a wage picking bananas on the plantations, rather than applying for welfare, which was what many people believed of the so-called dropouts. I was fortunate that my steady job in Sydney had enabled me to have a little cash in the bank. Because, although the others chided that I was a snob I was able to decline the offer to join them picking fruit. Learning that the cane fields and banana plantations harboured a plethora of dangerous animals had sealed my decision.

'Oh my gosh,' I had said to Jack earlier. 'Mum and Dad would be horrified if I picked bananas. If I wanted to do manual labour, I would have gone to a kibbutznik in Israel like one of the girls from the law firm has.'

When my fellow housemates left for work the next morning, I ventured under the house to investigate the machinations of the bathroom which doubled as a tool shed. Farming implements hung on the wooden slatted walls, with gaps wide enough to let in sunlight, as well as the whistling winter wind howling outside that day.

Jack had told me it was a drip heater and that after turning on the oil tap and allowing it to drip into a metal shaped saucer, I just had to light it. 'I'll work it out,' I had said to his offer to light it before he left for the day. Thinking it sounded simple I had undressed and was ready to shower. The archaic technology was far more difficult than expected. I felt annoyed at myself for being so self-assured and refusing help. This contraption bore no resemblance to the gaslit system at my parent's home, which magically produced hot water with the press of a button.

I found the tap and spotted the saucer. Naked and cold, I lit the first of many matches, but the wind kept blowing them out. Trying to comprehend how to make the odd-looking heater work, whilst trying to keep a match alight against the wind, took close to an hour and many tears of desperation. I had almost emptied the matchbox when at last the oil caught alight. I quickly turned up the oil tap then woosh, the flame burst into the metal tank above the saucer. I jumped back in fright. Without ever realising, or caring, how the heater worked, I turned on the water tap, closed my eyes as the glorious liquid gushed over me, smiling as I rolled my shoulders under my first hot shower in three days.

My arrival in Tully had coincided with the commencement of the sugar cane crushing season. Each day, during the working week, a cane train traversed the fields surrounding the house, pulling behind it several metal crates called bins. Men came with the trains, workers who either cut the cane or gathered and threw it into the bins for transporting to the central mill.

I watched the workers from a window, fearing that if they knew I was alone in the house when the others were at work, they would pay me a visit. They scared me so much that most days I spent hours hiding inside. Only venturing out when the others returned home in the afternoon. On the days I was certain no one could see me, I kept myself occupied around the house, cleaning the kitchen, sweeping the floors, making our bed, or washing clothes in the kitchen sink. Every now and then, someone would arrive from town. A few days after my arrival, I hid inside at the sound of a car horn beeping. Turned out to be the man who delivered fresh eggs every week. I felt silly when my housemates laughed.

On weekends, we hitchhiked into town. Sometimes the trip was to shop for staples like toilet paper, soap, milk, bread, and butter. Other times, just to have a milkshake or catch up with people with whom Jack, or one of the others from the farmhouse, had made friends. Food did not seem to concern anyone in the house. On those nights when no-one had offered to cook, we ate toast and Vegemite. If someone came home with lamb chops, or vegetables they cooked for everyone. I do not remember cooking anything. Most meals were simple, like boiled potatoes on their own, or fried eggs. Everyone seemed to want to eat something different. We all ate a lot of bananas because they were free.

Every now-and-then, I would telephone Mum and Dad from a phone box at the Post Office in town, or on the road if we were hitching around, letting them know I was safe. On the occasions when one of my brothers answered, I could hear the background noise of Mum and Dad rushing to talk to me before the coins ran out. The conversations consisted mostly of questions about my safety, where I was at that time, did I have enough money, warnings not to hitchhike, and if I had enough food. Once I rang to tell Mum we were going to the markets in Cairns. 'Make sure you buy a mango,' she said. 'They should be good up there in the tropics.'

It was winter and although the local growers displayed some magnificent fruit, mangoes were not in season. Instead, I bought strawberries. The stalls set up by the hippies interested me more. They sold all sorts of handmade and imported clothes and trinkets. Jack showed me the stall where he had bought my hand-painted mushroom dress. Looking around the many stalls and people at the market, I realised that despite being far from the frenzy of Sydney, I looked different from the others. My clothes looked different. Even my most casual jeans and T-shirts seemed out of place. I did not own a pair of thongs. I was still applying my eye makeup and styling my hair with the blow dryer I had brought with me. To fit in, I bought a pair of brown leather sandals, some clips for my hair, and a homemade remedy which promised to combat frizzy hair in high humidity. Despite the time of year, Tully's humidity was averaging around eighty percent.

Jack, his brother, and I ventured out of Tully every so often with an American girl named Kelly, who lived nearby and owned a Kombi van covered in hand-painted yellow and white sunflowers. One time, Kelly drove us to the major town of Cairns, 110 kilometres north. We climbed up the fire stairs of a pub to sneak into a dance. We had the money to pay the admission, but we preferred the thrill of the illegal entry. Alas, we were confronted by the proprietress at the top of the stairs who forced us to exit the same way we had entered. Another time Kelly drove us to Mission Beach for a swim.

Tully was where I experimented with the popular psychedelic drug of the time called lysergic acid diethylamide, also known as LSD. It came as a soft pink droplet suspended in a clear gel called a microdot, also known as acid. It arrived via one of the visitors in a car. Unlike the egg man, he came bounding up the steps of the farmhouse calling out our names. Recognising him as someone I had met in town with the other housemates, I came out of hiding. He said he was dropping off a packet of *acid*, which was something I had never seen. When the others returned from work, they had brought a couple of friends with them. As the sun began setting, we each took half a microdot. I followed the others, allowing the substance to melt on my tongue.

I do not remember the time that lapsed between the calm conversation on the verandah, to the sensation that the wooden chairs we had brought out from the kitchen were melting from under us. I jumped up to prevent myself from falling to the ground, screaming at the others to do the same. The sensation was unlike the lackadaisical effects of marijuana. Instead, I had an intense feeling of euphoria. The others said they felt the same. Exhilarated. Invincible. Unstoppable.

'Turn up the music,' someone yelled. No one moved, yet it mysteriously blasted louder. We had all left our melting chairs to dance, but no longer content to do so around the house, we bounded down the stairs in a frenzied state, into the inky night. We formed a conga line to follow an elected pied piper as he danced up and down the furrows separating the sugarcane. All the while, laughing hysterically at the realisation that as we ran, the rows of cane moved with us, so we could never reach the end.

I had a sensation that whatever had caused us to repeat our actions was out of our control. I felt like I was on a merry-go-round, passing the same things again and again. My head began spinning so fast I had to lie down on the ground. Others lay around me. We stared up at the stars, searching for Jupiter, Mars, and the celestial Gods. The crisp night air was intoxicating. The smells emanating from the fields were mind-blowing. My senses were on high alert. At one point I was certain I could hear the swooshing sound of stars moving across the night sky. Others said they had heard it as well. This must be the feeling I had heard people call hallucinating. I did not know how long I had been lying there. Seemed like an eternity.

'Let's fly,' someone shouted.

We rose in silent agreement. With a newfound energy and determination, we made our way to the house. Once there, we gathered blankets. Some preferred the coolness of their white cotton sheets. A pair of scissors appeared. We began folding the blankets and sheets in half, then cut a hole in the middle of each, just big enough to fit over our heads. We ran back to the field, sprinted up and down the furrows, our capes fluttering behind us. Despite trying as hard as we could, no one managed to fly that night.

Like one of the side effects of marijuana, we all became ravenous at the same time. We wandered back to the farmhouse in the clouds in search of a feast. But there was never much food in the house. On our last trip to town, I had bought flour. So, just like Dad had done on rainy days at home, I made pancakes, eating mine with Vegemite whilst the others ravaged theirs with bananas and sugar.

After cooking the pancakes, I had the feeling that my head was weighing me down. I was not sure I could hold it up without removing the thoughts and music inside it. The events of the past couple of years were overflowing and I had to get them out. I searched for pen and paper. In between carrying on conversations with the others and eating pancakes, I sat at the kitchen table and began writing poems about all the people I had met. At the appearance of the first rays of daylight, we had been talking for hours about our audacious efforts under the influence of the psychedelic drug. And I had written a dozen or so poems. We all agreed with the illusion that days, rather than a single night, had passed. Despite the exhaustion, my mind churned, relentlessly.

'Valium,' yelled out one of the housemates. 'It's the only way to come down from a trip.' We each took two, or three, or four. I lost count. Anything to stop the relentless ticking of my mind. Sometime during the next day, we sheepishly gathered up our bedlinen, which now had giant holes in the centres. I questioned the reckless behaviour that had caused me to enter the sugarcane fields, oblivious to the presence of the snakes, spiders, rats, foxes, and wild pigs living there. I did not enjoy the sensation of being out of control of my mind or actions. I never experimented with psychedelic drugs again.

Apart from the LSD, everything about the little river town of Tully was eerily appealing to my senses. I was certain that the smell of sweet molasses wafting from the mill that crushed the sugar cane would find its way into a compartment of my memory. And that the slightest whiff of it would resurrect my experiences of dancing in the cane fields, the vibrant colours throughout the farmhouse, and the smell of machine oil as I showered under the house. However, I also knew that the memory of entering the dangerous sugar cane fields at night under the powerful influence of mind-altering drugs would have the power to make my stomach churn with fear.

18.1

Motionless air. Nothing to stop my body from overheating. Sweat oozing from the top of my head, creeping through my hair, dripping down the sides of my face. Clothes so wet, they stick to my body. Nowhere to sit or hide. In the looming haziness of dusk, I have no way of clarifying who, or what, is approaching. That is what it was like standing on the side of a spooky, remote highway in Australia, praying for a ride.

Jack had been given some tips by another American for hitchhiking in Australia. According to him, there were two primary dangers. The first was the harsh weather, for which his friend recommended carrying water. The second was the issue of safety for personal belongings, especially your passport and wallet, for which he urged travellers to carry on their person in case they needed to bail out. I thought they were pretty good tips. I had not thought about the water, but I did once have to bail out of a stranger's car when it stopped at the traffic lights, leaving my backpack behind.

Many young people seemed to be hitching. It had become my primary mode of getting from one point to another since my breakup with Donovan. There was no other way to travel to some destinations, especially when I was living on the south coast with Olivia. Dad had taught Mum, Glynis, and Dewey to drive but I had left home before he had the chance to teach me.

The freedom to move around had been exhilarating, despite the potential danger of landing in a life-threatening situation. Admonitions from Mum and Dad about being wary of strangers since childhood never left my thoughts. On the occasions when I hitched alone, they weighed extra heavy. I wondered what strangers in fast cars saw as they approached the mere tendril looking girl, in faded denim jeans, on display for viewing, vulnerable.

I knew I was putting myself at risk but with adventure tapping one shoulder, safety the other, I knew which side I would follow. On some occasions, I had decided to step back from a car, when intuition said not to get in, even after taking hold of the door handle. When that happened, the driver usually drove off in a huff, whipping up dust in my eyes.

Olivia and I had hitched every day because there was no other means of transport to get to our jobs in the nearby town. We followed a few guidelines before accepting a ride like assessing the number of passengers, the condition of the car, and whether we thought the driver looked normal. For us, normal meant a guy aged in his mid-twenties or younger, sporting long rather than short hair. Nonetheless we had found ourselves in a few dangerous situations. Like the time we got so stoned we hitched at night to a local dance being held at another beach town. After the dance, sober and scared, we had no choice but to beg a patrolling police car to drive us home.

Another time, the same middle-aged woman who had offered us a lift several times in her small, white two-door sedan, pulled up to offer us another. I hopped in the back seat which was a position that always made me feel trapped. She took off the handbrake and pulled away from the kerb. Less than a few hundred metres down the road she started ranting. 'You girls are silly. Don't you know what you're doing getting into the cars of strangers? You're putting your lives in danger.'

In the rear-view mirror, I had seen her eyes bulging, her forehead creasing. She muttered to herself, heightening her agitation. Olivia and I were tight-lipped, not game to say a word. Our driver slammed on the brakes, pulled over at the top of a steep hill. Without taking her eyes off the road, she shouted, 'I refuse to contribute to your delinquency any more. Get out.' Then drove off, leaving us stranded a long way out of town. Unable to catch another ride, we walked the rest of the way, causing us to be more than an hour late for work.

The safety tips had not included anything about the personal dangers of hitchhiking. I was never alerted to the stories about serial killers who had often found their young victims by offering them a ride. Travelling with another can lessen the risk but the huge empty stretches between outback towns in Australia significantly added to the danger. Of course, I was never out of harm's way when entrusting my life to a stranger by jumping into their car. However, I preferred the comforting words of a friend who assured me the statistics revealed that the risks of being involved in a car accident when hitching, were far greater than those of running into evil.

At the beginning of October 1972, I was still living in Tully. Dad was getting jumpy at my intimations about hitchhiking the overland trail across Southeast Asia then on to Kathmandu in Nepal with Jack and Casey. I thought he would have been excited about our plans to travel. Instead, when I shared them, the line had gone silent. Remembering the cold winters in Sydney, I wondered if it was his asthma until he said, 'We're terribly worried about you Evvy.'

On another telephone call when Dad was not home, I spoke to Mum who revealed she had been so worried about me she had been crying at work. Upon hearing those words, I was speechless. She filled the silence by telling me Dad had been to hospital that weekend after a particularly severe asthma attack brought on by the cold weather. I cringed at my selfishness at enjoying the warm northern conditions whilst forgetting the harsh winters in the western suburbs of Sydney. Mum continued. 'Your father's gone grey. He's so worried he's also having trouble working.'

'I'm fine. What's Dad worried about?'

Hearing about my father's frailty had left a lump in my throat. On my next call, he was home. We chatted for a while. My assurances that I was okay did not appease him. He stuttered, 'If you don't want to come home.'

His voice cracked mid-sentence. 'Would you consider staying with your sister in Melbourne?'

Dad's words punched me in the stomach. My reasons for leaving home had been to go out into the world to search for who I was meant to be, not to reject my home, hurt my family. Yet now I felt certain I had deeply wounded the person whom I loved the most. The mere thought that anyone in my family would believe that I did not want to be with them made my heart heavy – like something or someone had died. To lighten the mood, I tried to make a joke about 'just having some fun' but my words sounded hollow as they echoed down the line. I closed my eyes, took a deep breath, and told Dad I would think about his suggestion.

The strain I had heard in Dad's voice haunted me for days. I wondered if the fun activities of the past months had been at too high a cost. I worried that one day Dad might not recover from one of his bad attacks. I told Jack what my parents had suggested about Melbourne. I was not dismissing the plan to hitchhike through Asia with him, but right now, I needed to go home. A week later, the three of us were on the road, heading back to Sydney.

The day of our departure began as putrid and muggy, following downpours throughout the night. Steam rose from the hot asphalt as we made our way onto the highway on the outskirts of Mackay to continue our journey after alighting from our first ride. The next section terrified me because I knew we would be travelling along the isolated inland stretch of the notorious Sarina to Marlborough highway. There would be no service stations for the next few hundred kilometres. Referred to by locals as the Horror Stretch, it had initially earned its name in response to the harsh terrain. Over time, the tag came to reflect the highway's notoriety as the scene for numerous disappearances and grisly murders. Many of the victims were hitchhikers, both male and female. Some had been shot, strangled, or stabbed. The police were yet to solve many of the cases.

Casey screamed with joy when a Falcon, Holden, or Toyota sedan, I was never one for cars, pulled over with a lone driver. Soaked to the bone, including our backpacks and everything inside them, I was thankful for Jack's suggestion that we pack up our belongings for mailing to our parents' homes. A balding, forty-something-year-old poked his head out of the window. The starchy, long-sleeved white shirt he wore made me think he worked in an office. He confirmed those suspicions when he said, 'I'm going to our Rocky office on business. But I'm stopping overnight in Marlborough if you're interested.' We were not willing to pay for a hotel room so I wondered what we would do for the night.

Jack got in the front seat. Casey held the back door open for me. A waft of citrus smelling hair cream, just like Dad's, seeped out. My sticky wet clothes made squeaking noises as I slid across the leather seats. I felt clammy and uncomfortable. The car became steamy. But there was no way I was removing my jacket. I wriggled to scratch at the feeling of things crawling on my neck. They turned out to be water droplets from my wet hair.

Despite the insides of my mouth feeling parched from the uncertainty of being in a stranger's car on such an inhospitable road, instinct reminded me of the importance of being assertive, not showing fear, and above all, to keep talking. All three of us were aware of the hitchhiking rules, so maintained an animated and effusive conversation. At one point, we were talking so much, I wondered if the driver would find us annoying enough to throw out of his car. I stared out of the window, smiling at the serenity of the cane fields. I had loved the sight of them since my first glimpse on the bus trip to Tully. I reminisced about the treacly smell that had radiated throughout the little river town at crushing time, reminding me of our family eating pancakes on rainy Sundays.

The stranger's car passed the scrubby floodplains which did not offer the same warm memories as the cane fields. Large sections of the road were unsealed. When there was no oncoming traffic, the car drove on the bitumen, but as soon as another vehicle approached, it swerved to one side, two wheels on the bitumen and two wheels off.

Our driver said he worked for the council. They had booked him into a motel in Marlborough for the night. He seemed harmless. 'If you're still around in the morning. I'll drive you to Rockhampton.' That night, the three of us slept in a park across the road from the motel, along with some other young hitchhikers whom we had met that afternoon at a milk bar in town. At daylight we were standing outside the stranger's car. He let us out in Rockhampton. I wondered if the ride from our safe council worker had saved us from harm. Or if he was really a serial killer who did not think he could tackle the three of us at once.

Various short rides carried us further south without incident, the last one dropping us off in the town of Gosford. Within minutes, a pale blue sedan pulled over. When the driver stuck his head out to say, 'Where you headed?', I saw that he wore a pale blue zippered jumpsuit, like those I had seen racing drivers wear at the Bathurst races.

'Sydney, mate,' Jack said.

'Get in kids, I'm going all the way.'

'Yesss.' The three of us exclaimed in unison.

Exhausted from the arduous two-day trip and eager to get to my parents before nightfall, we jumped in without haste, Jack in the front, Casey and me in the back. The car smelled of stale cigarettes and body odour. I coughed to clear my throat. The driver must have caught my look of apprehension because he shot a smirk at me in the rear-view mirror. His hawklike eyes scared me. I looked away. He pulled away from the kerb and quickly turned onto the freeway.

Sounding to me like he was boasting, he said, 'I'm on my way back from a race in Newcastle.'

Adhering to our rule to keep talking, Jack responded feigning interest and talking about where we had come from. I wondered what the driver was doing when he leaned forward to fumble around the floor with one arm stretching under his seat, like he was searching for something he had dropped. When I saw the shotgun, I reached for the door handle but stopped, mindful that jumping out would likely kill me because of the speed he was travelling. Seeing the shock on Jack's face, the driver let out a sickening chortle.

'I carry this for protection. In case people I pick up try something.'

The sight of the gun changed everything. I shelved the talking-rule, imagining Jack and Casey had done the same. The silence sounded ominous. Only the driver spoke, or Jack with short replies. In the back seat, Casey and I sat frozen, certain in the shared knowledge that we would not be continuing this ride. The three of us would attempt a safe escape when the driver stopped for fuel or food. The possibility of the three of us jumping out of the moving car at the same time seemed remote but not impossible. My morbid thoughts went into overdrive, pondering whether passengers in passing cars would recognise a silent scream for help.

Finally, our gun-toting driver pulled into a petrol station. He became agitated when all three of us hopped out of the car at the same time before he had switched off the engine.

'Where're youse goin?'

'We've changed our minds mate,' Jack said. 'We're not going to Sydney just yet.' His words sounding implausible the minute they left his lips. Casey and I looked away to hide the expressions on our guilt-ridden faces. Jack continued, each word becoming more anaemic as they tumbled out. 'We're gonna hang around here for a while.'

I turned around in time to catch our driver rubbing an eye, tugging at the collar of his driving suit, looking down at his dusty shoes. He raised his head to stare at us. His one-sided smirk almost reaching the corner of his eye. 'That's bullshit. Yuz reckon yuz are stopping on a concrete island in the middle a nowhere for a coffee? Yuz said yuz were goin all the way to Sydney. And that's where I'm taking yuz.'

The three of us continued towards the roadside café, Jack shaking his head from side to side to reinforce our decision not to get back in his car. With our backs still turned, we heard him grab the petrol pump. From the safety of the café, we watched him pay at the cashier, then swagger towards his car, looking over his shoulder towards us before screeching away.

Delaying our departure in such an isolated place proved to be a challenge. We hung around for half an hour before picking up our backpacks and making for the highway, eager to resume the trip. Within minutes our former driver pulled up in front of us. He had doubled back and been waiting a little way up the road.

'Get in the car,' he screamed from his window.

We stayed calm, declining his offer with a smile, careful not to upset this crazy man. But he continued to insist until Jack screamed wildly, 'We're not getting back in your car, mate. If you don't leave us alone, we're gonna go back to the café and call the police.' At this threat, he became irate and drove off revving his car with fury, leaving a cloud of petrol fumes in our faces.

It took three different rides to reach the western suburbs of Sydney. Casey had left us halfway for another address. Jack and I were in luck, when the last ride dropped us one street away from my parent's house. It felt odd knocking on the front door. The times I had been forced to do so after one of my late-night returns came to mind. This was different. The thought that I no longer lived here seemed strange.

The front verandah and steps looked like Dad had refreshed them. The forest green shone brand new. A pang of guilt punched me in the belly so hard I had to take a deep breath to stop the tears at the sight of the garden. Both Mum and Dad had spent endless Sundays transforming it from a plot of gravel, sand, silt, and clay. The flourishing shrubs of velvety blood-red geraniums, which Dad had planted for Mum, evoked a memory of the time I had watched her cup one of them in her hands. The furry leaves had made my teeth go funny when I touched them, but she had seemed enchanted.

Inside, Mum hugged me tightly, until my neck hurt. Dad left the room a few times, his eyes bloodshot on his return. They welcomed Jack with tea and sandwiches. They were attentive about our stories of Queensland, but I could tell they were both distracted.

'Your sister sent this for you,' Mum said breaking the awkwardness by handing me an unsealed envelope. A peek inside revealed a small wad of twenty-dollar bills. 'She wants you to buy an airline ticket to Melbourne. To move in with her. We think it's a good idea. You can get a job down there. And stop hitchhiking.'

There was no need for a drawn-out conversation or argument. It was obvious the concern I was causing Mum and Dad left me no choice but to shelve my plans to hitchhike through Asia. At least for the moment. The cash was sufficient for one airline ticket because no one had counted on me travelling with Jack. We could have bought two bus tickets. Instead, the next morning, the two of us were standing across the road from the famous water tower on the Hume Highway in Greenacre, thumbing down a semitrailer.

Our hitchhiking experiences had taught us that a ride in a long-haul truck was often one of the safest. And the driver was usually going all the way to the next town. When the truck pulled over a few metres from us, we sprinted towards it, buoyed by our good fortune.

The cabin was so high, Jack had to help me up. I sat in the middle, he by the door. The driver seemed to be a nice enough guy, again an assumption made by both of us in minutes. He said he was the father of a teenage girl and how horrified he would be if he ever found out that she was hitchhiking. He laboured the point about why the two of us were 'doing something so dangerous.' Then, he took his eyes off the road for a moment, turned towards me and asked, 'Are your parents aware that you are jumping into the trucks of strangers?'

The driver's remarks, together with the familiarity of the area where I had spent my teenage years, brought Dad's face to mind. For a long period, only LeRoy had known about my hitchhiking because he had been doing the same. Until Dad had overheard the two of us discussing our rides after my return from the south coast. He had clenched his jaw so hard I thought it would break. 'Are you mad? he had shrieked. 'You're a girl. They'll rape you. Murder you. I forbid you from doing it. Do you hear me?' I had promised to stop. Yet here I was, sitting in semitrailer cabin.

The sign welcoming us to Yagoona, a suburb no more than five minutes down the highway, came into view. Gripping the steering wheel, knuckles turning white, reminding me of our pastor whenever he had delivered one of his hellfire sermons, our driver stepped up his remonstrations, his fury swelling like a monster wave. I rolled my eyes. This was not the first time Jack or I had been admonished by a well-meaning driver. We both suspected how it could end. Assuring the driver that no one had forced me, hitchhiking had been my choice, he performed as expected. Striking his steering wheel with a gavel-like hand, he pulled over to the kerb where he ordered us out. 'There's a station across the road. You can easily catch a train to Melbourne.' We were fortunate to get a ride with the driver of another semi, who drove us all the way to the centre of Melbourne.

19

The Tango

The hands on the starburst-shaped clock on the wall, said I was early for my four o'clock job interview, by fifteen minutes. It was Monday, 23 October 1972. I did not know anything about the job other than it was for an office receptionist. Glynis had found it advertised in the newspaper. She had left work early to drive me to the city to ensure I was on time.

'You know this meeting was originally set up for last week,' she said. It was the first time the two of us had been alone since yesterday when Jack and I had landed on her doorstep in the upmarket Melbourne suburb of South Yarra, 'Looking like a couple of hippies.' she had said. 'I sent you the money so you'd be on time, wouldn't hitchhike. You're killing Mum and Dad with worry.'

Trapped together inside her car, I did not say anything. I took a deep breath, sighed, rechecked the newspaper cut-out for the address of the building, then stepped out as soon as the car stopped. A crisp spring breeze hit my face, tangled my hair. My steps pounded the footpath, heavy with uncertainty, plus the added weight of the anvil now attached to them.

It felt good to be in a luxurious office again. The ash wood furniture, slinky panelling, and a mind-melting watercolour hanging on the wall, were contemporary, alive, modern. The scent of new leather unleashed a cascade of memories from my job at the law firm in Sydney. I sat transfixed at the sight of the receptionist answering incoming calls on the switchboard. Images flashed through my mind of when I had done the same, wearing my zany stars and stripes outfit, Go-Go boots, maxi dresses, and miniskirts.

The flashback prompted me to scratch the skin above my knees where the elastic from my cornflower-blue woollen socks had left a welt. For the interview, I had paired them with a black and white smock dress and blue suede platform heels. They were some of the tokens which Mum had kept safe since my exodus from Sydney to Tully. Reminders of the decision I had made to leave a well-paying job that I loved when Jack had bounded back into my life with a Greyhound ticket. If not for that last check-in telephone call with Mum and Dad, I might have been bouncing around on a psychedelic bus on the road to Kathmandu in Nepal, dressed in my white calico dress with the hand-painted field mushrooms across the front, the gothic-style sleeves sweeping the floor. Thanks to my feelings of guilt, those plans had been put on hold. And after hearing Glynis lay down the rules to me, loud enough for all to hear, 'He can't stay. There's no room in the apartment,' Jack, who had come to Melbourne to keep me company, was hitching his way across to Adelaide alone.

He had left in the early hours of that morning. 'I'll stay with a friend,' he had said, promising to return in two weeks. 'If things are okay, I'll get a job. We can rent a unit together. Or we'll leave Melbourne. Go back to Sydney.'

My mind muddled with the uncertainty of the situation. More than a year had passed since leaving home. It was no longer the Swinging Sixties as people were now referring to the era during which I had drank, bathed, but fortunately not drowned in the fountain of my own youth. Now, it seemed

I had survived them simply to find myself living with my sister, waiting to be interviewed for a job I had not applied for, in a city I had not intended to visit, in a country I wanted to leave. Yet, it was nothing compared to how much my life was about to change.

'Beverley?' the sophisticated voice asked.

Within a heartbeat, butterflies swarmed in my stomach. The gulp of cold air I breathed in came out warm. I felt its gossamer veil tickle the bare skin of my arms. It calmed the fluttering but gave me goose bumps. The room swirled with his scent. Was it cinnamon, sandalwood, patchouli, or musk? He was handsome, charismatic. Like an actor from a romance movie: George Peppard from Breakfast at Tiffany's, Ryan O'Neal from Love Story. I stood to meet him. His eyes were the colour of the Greek sea I had not yet seen. His shirt matched them. His tie swirled paisley teardrops. His brown leather shoes were shiny, though homely. His broad smile revealed dimples. We shook hands awkwardly. His touch felt warm, familiar, like someone I had met before. He took a step forward. I paused, then took one back.

That's how our dance began.

Back at Glynis' apartment, I headed for the bathroom.

'Where are you going?' she yelled through the locked door.

'Out to dinner,' I yelled back.

'Who with?'

'The guy that interviewed me.'

'Are you crazy?'

Mind your own business, I wanted to say, forgetting what it was like to have someone question me. Glynis and I had not seen each other since I had left home to move to the south coast, around the same time she had moved to Melbourne. Although the law considered me an adult when I turned eighteen a few months earlier, I had been working and making my own decisions for almost three years. The two of us had never discussed boyfriends. Nor had I depended on her for emotional support since the Bad Moon Rising incident.

'Nope, it's just dinner,' I said. It was going to be a long two weeks before Jack got back.

I reflected on how Alan and I had struck a chord in the interview, chuckling together at my response to his question about typing speeds. 'I don't like typing,' I had said, screwing up my nose as if I had smelt something bad. 'In fact, I hate it. My sister arranged this interview. So, if there's a lot of typing maybe this job isn't for me.'

His response had been to throw his arms up in the air. 'You know what, I've had enough for today.' Then he had leaned across the desk to whisper, 'Would you like to have dinner with me tonight, Beverley?'

The buzz of the intercom brought me flying back to the moment. I needed to answer it before Glynis. I was unsure of what she might say and not ready to make introductions yet.

'I'll come down,' I said.

Too impatient to wait for the lift, I took the stairs, making me breathless by the time I reached the double glass doors at the entrance. Through them I saw that Alan was wearing the same clothes from the interview. His blue, chambray shirt a reminder of my earlier attraction. We exchanged pleasantries as he led me towards a dark green sports car parked out the front.

He opened the door to usher me in. Our arms brushed against each other. A quiver shot through mine. Just as it had when we shook hands at the interview. I slid into the leather seat, the charge spreading through my body. The car oozed his scent. I bit my bottom lip. I wanted to kiss him so much it hurt. When he got in the car, he smiled across at me. I took it as a sign that he felt the same way.

'We're heading to a French restaurant in Toorak,' he said. 'It's just a few minutes away. It's one of my favourites. I know the owner.'

Alan asked most of the questions, repeating some of the ones from the interview. 'Is this your first time in Melbourne? Where do your parents live?' Though I did learn he had been divorced and had two children.

We parked in front of the restaurant. He jumped out; walked around to open my door. We stood opposite each other. What's happening? Why am I swooning like a schoolgirl? Jack had left just a few hours ago. He was coming back for me. We were going to hitchhike across Asia. Alan grabbed my hand, cutting short my ruminations. We walked to the front door where a man greeted us. 'We'll have a drink first,' Alan said in response. Weaving around the tables and chairs with me in tow, he cupped his mouth with his free hand to whisper in my ear, 'He's the owner.' My skin tingled when his lips touched my hair.

Pulling up a barstool for me he said, 'Mind if I suggest something to drink?'

I nodded. I only knew about Tequila.

'Two Southern Comfort Sours. Make them with egg whites please.'

He turned towards me. 'It's the popular way to drink them these days.'

The frothy, cloudy cocktails arrived in small bowl-shaped glasses. I smacked my lips together at the syrupy sweetness. I liked the feeling of being with someone who took charge. Our conversation unfolded without effort. In between eating dinner and taking sips of more cocktails, we shared information about ourselves the way new acquaintances do. He was thirty-six years old. Born in the suburbs of Melbourne, he had trained on the job as an electronics technician.

'Working at a bench wasn't for me,' he said. 'So, I became a consultant.'

'I've never met one of those.'

'I consult to both the client and the supplier. They're both my customers. Whoever hires me, pays. Now I provide advice mostly on import and export of technical products. A company will pay me to go and find a particular type of product. Sometimes they want me to find them new customers. That's where the travel comes in. It's taken me all over the world.'

'So how come you're interviewing receptionists and secretaries?'

'It's not my company. I'm setting up the Australian office for a client in England.'

The drinks had made me tipsy. I did not really care what this man said. I had fallen under his spell. When it was time for me to tell my story, he formed a steeple with his hands. With his index fingers pressing against his lips, he stared at me from across the table. My story about hanging out at rock concerts and rallies in parks, following the music scene in England and America, living in a garage with a concrete water tank for a shower, dancing in the cane fields on the communal farm in Tully, sounded banal as the words left my lips. Except for my plans to hitchhike across Asia to Kathmandu with a friend. That caused him to lower his hands, widen his eyes, and shake his head from side to side.

'How could you do such a thing? Won't you be scared?'

I did not have the courage to say, not half as terrified as I feel sitting opposite you. Instead, I talked about some of my recent hitchhiking experiences and how I had been driven by a feeling of freedom. Now he nodded. I could not fathom the connection I felt towards this man. Even our age difference had not fazed me. But I did wonder about how he knew nothing about the revolutionary music that had been guiding my decisions for the past five years. It seemed to have passed him by.

'I've been lured by the charm of Mandarin love songs instead,' he said. 'Do you know any?'

'No.' *But listening to you makes my insides vibrate.*

'I once had a Chinese girlfriend who lived in Hong Kong. She introduced me to the music. I've been around the world a few times. I love Europe, but I'm captivated by Asia. I'm going to Singapore again soon.'

I, who had never travelled outside of Australia since my family's arrival, knew nothing of the magic of Asia other than from my mother's stories. Alan's fondness for Asia took me by surprise.

'I was born in Singapore,' I said.

'Oh really. Have you been back?'

'No. But my mother went there a couple of years ago. It was her first trip home since we immigrated in 1956.'

'Oh really? What did she think of it after all that time?'

'She had a wonderful time seeing her mother and all her brothers and sisters. She said something about the Australian dollar being worth a lot more there. I remember her coming home with heaps of gifts including an electric rice cooker.'

'Yes, the exchange rate is still pretty high.'

'Mum was mostly happy to eat all the food she had been dreaming about for over a decade.'

'I eat a lot of Asian food. Mostly Chinese.'

'Mum cooks Malaysian and Nonya style dishes. We're Eurasian.'

'Half English, half Asian?'

'Yes. You're the first person I've met who knows that.'

'Do you cook with Ve-Tsin? Eat shiitake mushrooms?'

I had done neither. Alan knew a lot about Asian ingredients. I swivelled around, pretending to be looking at other people in the restaurant. I did not want him to see my face or read my thoughts. Did he know that when he smiled only the left side of his mouth curled? And his eyes scrunched up, nearly closing, but not enough to prevent the electric sparkles of Aegean blue piercing through.

'What? You don't have a passport?' he said, shaking his head from side to side at my admission. I would have found out when Jack and I formalised our travel plans but at that moment, realising I was still on my mother's passport, made me feel naïve, like a child.

I noticed a gleam in his eyes when he said, 'We'll have to fix that.'

I recalled the snap decisions I had made over the last few years. The jobs I had left. The decision to move to the coast. Tully. Perhaps he was as impulsive as me.

He winked, patting his jacket pocket. 'You should carry it with you all the time. You never know where you might end up after a long lunch. I'm licenced to fly small planes. Only in Australia though. I started a small airline years ago. Just a single plane flying businessmen around. It wasn't very successful. But I'd like to give it another try one day.'

Tell me. Show me. Let's go!

Then, as if he had read my mind, he leaned across the table. Facing me straight on and staring into my eyes he said, 'Let's go together. Marry me.'

His words did not sound like a question. I giggled them away. In response, he leaned further across the table, took hold of both my hands then whispered, 'I mean it. We should get married. Go on the adventure together.'

Though his words did not sound like I had imagined a proposal of marriage they did seem genuine. My tummy had not stopped fluttering since meeting this man. All my actions over the past few years had been spur-of-the moment wafting between doing the right thing by Dad and following my own path. The past few years since leaving school had been akin to a lifetime. I had moved five times. Now here I was unexpectedly in Melbourne having shelved plans to go freewheeling around Asia to placate Dad. My future had seemed so fuzzy.

'Why not,' I said. 'I'm not doing anything for the next 10 years.'

My response to the marriage proposal from a man whom I had met that afternoon had tumbled out of my mouth without too much thought before being carried along by an intense feeling of connection. Intercepting any doubts, the same feeling convinced me that fate had orchestrated my trip to Melbourne, my attendance at the job interview, meeting this stranger. Alan's response to my acceptance seemed far more sensitive than mine. His blue eyes, gleaming in the light of the candle on our table, had fixed onto mine.

'I think I'm going to fall in love with you,' he said. His softly spoken words, having seemingly travelled all the way from his heart to mine. He had clung onto my hands for what seemed like an eternity. Until, reluctantly letting go of one, he signalled the waiter for the bill, whilst blurting out an agenda for us. I nodded, not knowing what to say. I was flabbergasted by his potency. It made me feel alive, energised.

Top of his list of things 'we must do straight away' was breaking the news to his mother. I felt moved at such a warm and loving thing to do. During the drive to the northern suburbs, I learned of their close relationship. Born out of wedlock in an era which had forced many mothers to give up their children to adoption, she had refused to do so despite pressure from family to sign the papers. His willingness to reveal such intimate details was touching, endearing.

It was close to eleven o'clock when he knocked on his mother's door. Certain the lack of response meant she would be staying at his sisters in the next street, we drove there. Like it had been fated, I met them both, propped up against the bedhead, sheets stretched up to their necks like a pair of baby birds bobbing over the rim of a nest. I sat on the end of the bed as the two of them chirped well wishes through beaming smiles at our startling news.

'Where, when?' Alan's sister Pam asked.

I had not thought that far ahead.

'Only the best will do,' Alan said. 'Saint John's at Toorak. If we can get in.'

Looking at me he said, 'It's one of the best churches in Melbourne.'

We kissed goodnight at the entrance to Glynis's apartment block. It was electric. I did not want to let go of his warmth. 'Call me at the recruiter's office tomorrow,' he said. 'I'll be there about ten.' The moment he was out of sight, I missed him more than anyone I had ever known. His scent lingered on me, leaving me still wondering if it was cinnamon, sandalwood, patchouli, or musk.

I slid into the bed alongside Glynis, feigning sleep which I continued to do the next morning while she showered, had coffee, then left for work. I had no plans to tell her my news yet. I did not want to hear anyone else's opinion. Alan and I had agreed to tell her later that night. The sound of the door closing was my cue to get out of bed, jump in the shower, wash my hair, paint my long black Twiggy lines. I dressed in a pair of jeans then pulled on my cherry red kurta. Before I knew it, the electric clock glared ten.

Instead of switching my call through to Alan, the consultant, who had introduced us the day before, came on the line. When she said, 'All contact must go through me,' I hung up, annoyed. The feeling of dread was so great in the pit of my stomach, it rose to join the lump of anger that swelled in my throat. It percolated all the way through to the tips of my fingers, which redialled the office number with such fervour that Glynis's telephone almost flew off the kitchen wall.

'Hello,' said the voice I recognised.

Was it fate, kismet, or destiny that connected us? Or simply the circuit between the internal and external chords on the PBX plug switchboard still being connected. Knowing manual switchboards as I did, I guessed that my second call had gone straight through to the open extension on which Alan had been dialling out, bypassing the telephonist.

Choked by a rush of butterflies at the sound of his voice, I plucked up the courage to whisper, 'It's me.'

'I'm in a meeting,' he said without emotion, which left me feeling cold. 'I can't talk right now. I'm almost finished here. I'll come over.'

'Okay,' I said. The butterflies now morphing into swarming bees. Without a soul with whom to share my news, feelings of joy, or concerns, I had spent a lonely morning in the apartment. I had erased all school friends when not one had contacted me after the expulsion. It had been my choice to leave behind new friends from my time at Levi's when I left the company. Some friends from Sydney had simply disappeared. I would have called my good friend Louise. She was the one person with whom I could have discussed what I was planning. But we had lost contact since her move to America.

I was not ready to discuss my plans with Glynis without Alan. She would say I was crazy. I had made a promise never to ask my mother's advice on anything after being left at the school gate alone. I could have called Dad, but I did not want to talk to anyone who might dissuade me from my decision. At that moment, my only friend in the world was Jack. But he would already have arrived in Adelaide, and I had no way of contacting him.

Myriad questions floated in my head, revisiting the whirlwind of the night before. I questioned whether I had dreamt about meeting Alan, drunk too many cocktails, misunderstood the proposal or my acceptance, and our plans to marry as soon as we could. If it had really happened, I thought anxiously about how he might feel about it this morning. I wondered if the music had influenced me once again. Everyone knew about the high-profile weddings of the rock stars including John Lennon, Paul McCartney, George Harrison, Ringo Starr, Mick Jagger, and many more. John Lennon's chart-topping song about his wedding to Yoko Ono came to mind. The one I wished I had written my name against on the infamous Top 40 chart.

I felt certain my decision to marry a stranger was far less dangerous in comparison to my exploits over the past few years. Like leaving good jobs on a whim, hitchhiking up and down the coast, tripping on LSD in cane fields with vermin and wild animals around me, scaring my parents out of their minds with plans to hitchhike through Asia.

I flopped onto Glynis's bed, reeling with confusion. Since arriving at her apartment in response to Mum and Dad's pleas, and without Jack for support, a feeling of loneliness had washed over me. I felt hollow inside. I did not belong here. I was in the way, invading her exciting new life in Melbourne. The minutes ticked by. I got on and off the bed, lost count of the number of times I checked my hair and makeup, went to the toilet, made coffee I did not drink.

Despite expecting it, I jumped with shock at the sound of the intercom, an hour after hanging up the phone. Every nerve in my body burnt like it was on fire when I buzzed Alan in. I heard him bound up the steps. Then he was standing in front of me, holding out a bunch of flowers. The sparks had not diminished. I was infatuated, dizzy in love, struck by a thunderbolt.

The first thing he wanted to talk about was the coincidence of my phone call getting through. 'When you called, I was in the middle of discussing you. Remember the consultant in the interview with us yesterday?'

'Yeah. I do.'

'Well, she's the owner of the business. She wasn't happy about me taking you to dinner. Said it was highly inappropriate. When you called, she told the operator to connect you to her instead of me. But when she left the office, I picked up the handset to dial out and there you were. It was weird. Did you call back?'

'I did. And I thought it was weird too but that's what can happen with those plug boards. The circuit was still connected and bypassed the operator.'

During the hours I had spent pacing the apartment, Alan had been having similar thoughts to mine. Wondering if I might have changed my mind in the light of day. And if he would ever see me again. His words made me feel giddy. *Don't sound too eager, like a schoolgirl.* I wanted him to hold me so much my body ached. He must have read my mind. Was I so transparent? He put his arms around me. We kissed passionately but we did not make love. I wondered why. Instead, we talked, agreeing fate had brought us together, re-affirming our decision from the night before. We were getting married. It was simply down to where and when.

'I've got the number for Saint John's,' he said. 'Let's call together.'

We cradled the receiver between our ears as a pucker sounding man, who had introduced himself as Vicar Maddick, chuckled, 'Well dears, weddings at Saint John's are usually booked twelve months in advance.' Could it have been the eerily hollow silence echoing down the line that prompted the fatherly sounding reply. 'Better come in next week to start arranging things. Let's say Monday morning. Ten o'clock?'

The confirmed appointment never took place. Alan was still at the apartment when the vicar telephoned back within the hour with words that would change our lives forever. 'Short notice,' he said. 'And I'm flabbergasted at the pure happenstance. But there's been a cancellation for this Saturday. The booking is yours. If you want it.'

There was no time to ponder what tragedy might have transpired to cause a couple to cancel their nuptials at such short notice. We simply believed it to be destiny. 'We'll take it,' we said in unison. 'What do we do next?'

The vicar chuckled, 'Better come in this afternoon. Say three o'clock?'

Alan had been right. Saint John's was a magical place. Significantly more ornate than the unpretentious Adventist churches. Much time had passed since I had been in one, but I felt a renewed sense of faith in God in this holy place. The vicar welcomed us into the vestry. He matched how I had imagined him, fatherly, kind, radiating warmth. He invited us to sit on wooden chairs opposite him, forming a circle, then proceeded to ask questions about how we had met, why we wanted to get married 'all of a sudden', and whether either of us was a baptised member of a Christian church.

We had both agreed not to reveal that we had just met. In case the vicar refused to marry us. I watched Alan as his hands rose to his mouth to form the steeple I had already recognised as one of his traits. 'We've been in a relationship for six months,' he lied.'

I sensed the vicar may have been suspicious when he smiled at Alan's response. Could he demand evidence of our relationship. He turned towards me. 'Have you thought about the age difference between the two of you?' Might he suspect I'm pregnant.

'I was baptised into the Adventist church,' I blurted out, ignoring his last question, but shuddering at the realisation that three years had passed since the event. Alan proclaimed that although his family did not attend church on a regular basis, they were Anglican who attended services for Easter and Christmas. The age question was left hanging.

Content with our answers, and I suspected eager to fill the empty space on the upcoming Saturday, now just four days away, the vicar slowly lifted his hand, lay it on his chest, then leaned into our circle. 'Marriage laws require seven days' notice.' Then through a smile and a nod of his head, 'However, we ministers have the power to waive those rules. Which I am prepared to do for you both.'

My sigh of relief was quickly followed by a feeling of guilt. Would God bless our union despite the lie. The vicar's questions moved to what kind of service we would like him to perform. Alan's response was to pull out his cheque book. 'How much for a traditional service with all the trimmings?' Until then, the question of money had not entered my head. Regardless of where I ended up living, I hoped to be working soon.

Glynis arrived home from work, soon after our visit with the vicar, to find Alan and I perched atop her kitchen bench drinking coffee. Perhaps it was his conservative appearance that subdued her reaction to our news. She did not seem overly interested or surprised until we told her we had come from a meeting with the Vicar of Saint John's of Toorak where we had discussed wedding plans. She was tired. I could tell from the twist of her lips, the flick of her head, that our news did not impress her, though she seemed reluctant to say anything in front of the stranger.

No doubt it would have been different if I had announced my intention to marry Jack, or someone dressed in a kurta, headband, and moccasins. All the same, I was thankful not to have broken the news to her without Alan's support. Because when I began dialling Mum and Dad, I heard her say to him, 'They won't be surprised.'

Dad sounded happier to hear from me than he had on my many calls from phone boxes on the road over recent months. I guessed my being with Glynis had allowed him to breathe a little easier. Her prediction had been correct. He was not surprised by my news, but he was excited. He sounded the same as he did whenever he had been told something incredulous. Like the American's landing on the moon, sharing the story of the Japanese landing in Malaya, or the first time he flew on an aeroplane when he took my brothers to Perth.

At first, I suspected he was not sure I was being serious. Until I heard him yell out to Mum, 'She's getting married,' and Mum responding, 'What?' After some garbled conversation with Dad, she yelled, 'I've just got home from work Evvy. I'm pleased you're in Melbourne with your sister. I love you very much my darling girl. I'm cooking dinner. I'll talk to you later.'

When Dad was certain I was not joking, his questions toppled down the line, one after the other: 'Is this what you want? Has Glynis met him? What's his name?'

'He's here now, Dad. I'll put him on. His name is Alan.'

I thrust the receiver into Alan's hand, happy to relieve myself of any further explanations. I was not surprised to hear the conviviality that came from the conversation as Alan explained about the cancellation at the church, how we would be organising everything for the wedding and the reception, and how all they had to do was 'turn up.' However, I held my breath when I heard Alan say, 'I suppose I should ask for your permission to marry Beverley.'

We did not need permission because I had already turned eighteen, but I guessed Dad's response had been favourable when Alan said, 'Nice to talk to you Wilbur. See you and Margaret on Saturday. Beverley will give you the details.'

I grabbed a few clothes. I was staying at the hotel next door to Alan's apartment from now. We had a lot to do before Saturday. That evening we addressed the one hundred invitations we had bought from a newsagent near Saint Johns. I was learning that one of the personality traits of my husband-to-be was his ability to think big. 'I believe in starting at the top and working down, rather than the other way around,' he said. 'I'll call the manager of the hotel tomorrow morning. It's probably the only place in Melbourne that could pull off a wedding reception by Saturday.'

Shooting ducks in a side show alley circus was how Alan and I tackled what had to be done. Each task had been effortless, enjoyable. Which made me wonder what people did during the year leading up to a grand marriage ceremony like the one we were planning.

When the bridal boutique opened its double wooden doors onto Collins Street at nine o'clock on Wednesday morning, I was waiting outside. The Southern Belle style gown, made of white satin and enveloped in a fine layer of voile fitted perfectly. Intricate embroidery scalloped the hem, the bell-shaped sleeves, and the high neckline. The dress was the first one I tried on. I opted for a floppy white hat instead of a veil, in keeping with the fashion trend of the time. One side of the enormous brim flopped over my right eye. Summery silk flowers of red, green, and white encircled the crown. A flyaway train flowed from the hat to the ground.

For my two bridesmaids, I chose a flowing, gossamer-light dress with mauve floral pattern and similar floppy hats to mine but with flowers to match the dresses. Glynis and Veronica were to try them on that afternoon. Veronica was the eighteen-year-old who had landed the receptionist job for which I had applied. She had been delighted to accept my request to be one of my bridesmaids. I did not know anyone else in Melbourne. Within less than an hour of entering the boutique, the assistant was helping me into a taxi with two enormous white boxes, containing my complete wedding outfit except for shoes, paid for with a signed cheque Alan had given me that morning. I was on my way to meet him at the jewellery store he had chosen.

Our eyes landed on the same ring at the same time. 'Something for this era and her personality,' Alan had suggested to the jeweller before my arrival.

The daisy-shaped setting had a central round diamond surrounded by a cluster of smaller diamonds in the shape of petals. Wearing my dazzling new ring, we set off to deliver some of the wedding invitations in person. That evening the Vicar rang to say he had received numerous telephone calls asking if our wedding was 'for real'.

Whilst I had been at the bridal boutique, Alan had organised our wedding reception in a single phone call. Upon his return from Asia, he had moved into the luxurious Chateau Commodore Hotel on Lonsdale Street, where I was now staying, and where he had rented a suite before moving into the new apartment tower next door. The concept of the apartments having access to the hotel's twenty-four-hour services had been a first in Australia. When asked if the hotel could host a wedding reception for somewhere between seventy and one hundred guests on the coming Saturday, the manager had jumped at the opportunity. It would provide publicity for the hotel's new venue which had opened a few weeks earlier to coincide with the release of the box office hit of the Australian movie, The Adventures of Barry McKenzie. It was a coup to land the prestigious setting which was most certainly the only place that could have pulled off a large function at such short notice. Though the movie became a hugely popular satire with both Australian and British audiences, I cringed at the name of our reception venue, which was the movie's namesake, Bazza's Bar.

On Friday morning Alan and I were boasting to each other about our achievements when a phone call came through from the caterers. The words, 'when can we expect the wedding cake,' sent me into a spin. It was one of the ducks in the gallery still quacking. When a friend of Alan's called Ric, referred me to a baker next door to his office in Carlton, I wasted no time in catching a taxi there. Only to be told, in a similar tone to the vicar, 'My dear, a traditional wedding cake, fed with brandy, covered in marzipan, and decorated with fondant icing, can take anywhere between three and six months to make.'

A chocolate sponge would have sufficed until the baker suggested I consider the three 'spares' he had left over in his cold-room. There was one catch. Though all three were iced, each was a different shape. There was a rectangle, a square and a circle. With no time to be pedantic I arranged to have them decorated into a three-tier cake and delivered to the reception venue by Saturday.

My feet had barely touched the ground from the preparations when, on a splendid sunny afternoon in late October, I stood at the portal of St. John's. Dad and I looped arms and commenced the slow walk down the 23-metre central aisle, returning smiles and nods to the sea of mostly unrecognisable faces comprising Alan's friends and family, some of whom I had met fleetingly in the preceding days when we had delivered our invitations. The trimmings included a professional organist, an attendant, a bell ringer, flower arrangements at the front of the church, documentation, and lodging of forms.

Mum and Dad had arrived on a flight from Sydney that morning. Dad looked dashing in a hired tuxedo. Mum was resplendent in an olive-green velvet gown. Glynis and Veronica were angelic in their gossamer dresses. Closer and closer Dad and I inched towards the splendour of the two magnificent stained-glass windows, towering over the alter. When we reached it, Dad let go. I paused, then took a step forward, to stand beside the man I had met five days earlier. 'I will,' I said, hoping he would be the missing puzzle piece in my life.

After the ceremony, we posed for photographs under a deep-rooted tree in the courtyard. It was spring. The birds tweeted. White and red flowers speckled the courtyard. It rained confetti. Starry-eyed, arms coiled, Alan introduced me to the guests whom we had invited by telephone.

We left for the reception in a limousine, oblivious to the pandemonium that was taking place outside the reception venue. Our wedding day had coincided with the controversy surrounding the first Australia tour of bluesy British rocker Joe Cocker. As a devoted fan, I had been following what the press had labelled his 'comeback to the stage tour' after a two-year drug and booze-fuelled hiatus. Adelaide police had arrested Cocker and members of his entourage for possession of marijuana. Upon release, the band flew to Melbourne and were guests at the Chateau Commodore.

Despite drug charges, resisting arrest, and a deportation order hanging over his head, Cocker refused to leave the country until he had performed the remaining two concerts on Friday and Saturday in Melbourne. The episode turned into a political scandal, causing a public outcry from his fans in Australia. In response, Victorian police dropped all charges and granted permission for him and his group to perform the concerts.

Cocker was on the way to his final concert on Saturday afternoon as our wedding car approached the entrance to the hotel. I came face to face with him when I stepped out of the car. He paused to offer his congratulations, shook Alan's hand, planted a kiss on my cheek, then jumped into a waiting limousine for the concert venue. That night he performed two sell-out events and by the next morning he was on his way back to America. The brush with Joe Cocker was going to have to sustain the connection to my past life for a while. Despite the compelling ceremony, during which the two of us became a couple, legally bound by Church and State, the fact remained that we were strangers who had met less than a week earlier.

We did not consummate the marriage on our wedding night. Despite being attracted to each other and spending every waking hour together in the few days leading up to the ceremony, there remained an awkwardness on both sides towards taking the kissing and cuddling to the next stage. I had learnt that Alan was different from many of the men I had met. He was not a big drinker, nor was he simply seeking sexual pleasure. Which is perhaps why I happily agreed to his suggestion that we invite his friend Ric, the man who had referred me to the life-saving cake maker in Carlton, and his wife Joy, to join us in our suite for a coffee after all the guests had left the reception. We chatted for over an hour about our future, which mostly included travelling to Asia.

The consummation happened unexpectedly about a week later after we found ourselves a little tipsy after a dinner at Alan's favourite restaurant in Melbourne's Chinatown in Little Bourke Street. Alan had broken the ice by kissing me in the street whilst holding the car door open for me to slide in, repeating the romantic gesture outside the door to our apartment.

Neither of us had articulated any sort of expectations other than the thrill of experiencing life with the person with whom we had become wildly infatuated. If the same rockets that blasted us into fated, magical love, were going to jettison us at some point, it never crossed my mind what life, post lift-off, might be like. I forged on, full speed on the buzz of the moment. No drugs. I no longer felt like I needed them.

19.1

My brain started stumbling and stuttering, over what to say or do, upon hearing the words, 'We're leaving for Singapore in a few weeks.' I wanted to jump up and down on the spot, flail my arms in the air and scream. However, only one word escaped from my mouth. To which Alan responded, 'Yes. Really. But I can't book the tickets until you get your passport.'

The rush of adrenaline gave me a welcome burst of energy. Because, in the weeks since the excitement of our lightning romance and grand wedding ceremony, I had been slipping into the doldrums. Apart from Glynis, whom we saw often, I had no friends in Melbourne. I also had no prospect of finding any whilst I did not have a job. It was difficult to telephone Mum and Dad during the week because of their work and busy evenings with my brothers but we did talk every now and then.

I had been feeling down since learning of Jack's return to Melbourne, exactly two weeks after leaving, as promised. 'He buzzed the intercom quite late,' Glynis said. 'I'd just got home from work. I told him you were married. But when he didn't respond, I thought he'd fainted, or something. So, I invited him in. He ran up the stairs instead of taking the lift. I got the feeling he didn't believe me because he asked me what had really happened. He was very concerned about you. Wanted to know if you were safe.'

Despite knowing the day would arrive, Glynis's telephone call left me feeling disoriented. She had all but thrown him out into the cold after our arrival. I imagined her matter-of-fact way of telling him what had happened. And over the intercom, no less. News of Jack's return triggered a series of flashbacks, leading me down a path of emotional memories. I had no explanation for what I had done. Nor why I had left Glynis to break the news to him. I knew I could not explain my actions to Jack when I did not fully understand them myself. I felt too embarrassed to face him. He would think I was stupid, reckless. I imagined I would be wondering about these things forever.

Glynis had put herself out to help me get to Melbourne. I recalled the day I had arrived at her apartment with Jack. How I had felt like a stray dog. Like I did not belong. She had begun a new and exciting life, had influential friends, a terrific job, a chic apartment, and a car. I had nothing. I was like the urchin baby sister, come to borrow her things again. I had started realising how everything she had done over the years had been to help me. However, I felt wretched about what I had done to Jack. I speculated on whether I would ever see him again.

Although it felt good to be living in the heart of the city, some of my boredom was due to there not being much to do in a fully furnished apartment with hotel services at our fingertips. Alan said he loved having access to room service, concierge help, reception staff, and restaurants. I had also found it convenient, but it contributed to there being less for me to do. Some mornings I walked with Alan to a nearby coffee shop for breakfast before he went on to a meeting. Most days we met for lunch. Every night we dined at a restaurant.

It was obvious to me that Alan had spent a lot of money on our whirlwind romance, and he was still spending. Yet, money seemed to be a taboo subject. I knew nothing about his finances. After the wedding I was none the wiser. His reluctance to involve me made me feel ignorant. I wanted to know more about him. When I suggested getting a job because I had no money or income, Alan continued to insist I did not need to work. Instead, he gave me his cheque book with half a dozen or so signed cheques like the one he had given me for the bridal boutique. I had never had a cheque book until then. They were as good as cash in the 1970s. The gesture was well meaning but made me feel awkward. I had been independent since leaving school three years earlier and been living away from my parents' home for more than a year. Some days, after our coffee, I would walk around the boutiques and department stores, but I did not feel comfortable spending Alan's money on myself. So, when he suggested I might like to cook dinner instead of us going to a restaurant, I pushed aside the shiver of nervousness creeping up the back of my neck and took on the challenge.

Tournedos Chasseur laden with slices of foie gras and mushrooms. Tournedos Rossini covered in a rich tomato-based wine sauce. The spectacular images jumped out of the pages of the colourful cookbook we had received as one of our wedding presents. I raced to the city butcher who did not bat an eyelid at my request for four pieces of two-inch-thick slabs of eye fillet steak. That night I made the Chasseur version. The next night I made the Rossini. Soon I could prepare both dishes to perfection, so I made them often, content to use my cache of signed cheques solely on food.

On my fourth trip, the butcher who now knew me well, took me by surprise when he walked out from behind the counter and stood in front of me. Hands on hips, head slightly bent to one side, he said through lips that smiled in tune with his wrinkled brow, 'Can't you cook anything else love?'

His rising intonation of the word 'love' made me feel childlike. Tossing my head back defensively, I explained that I had recently married. To which he responded, 'Then you'll send your new hubby broke love' before proceeding to give me a lesson on some of the less expensive cuts of meat. 'Round steak, lamb chops, mince love.'

It must have been serendipity that the news about flying to Singapore coincided with using my last cheque at the butcher shop. I wasted no time in telephoning the British embassy to find out what I had to do to obtain a passport. Being told 'it could take anywhere up to six months' left me with such an uncomfortably dry throat that the silence prompted the female officer to ask if I was 'still on the line'. The delay had provided the seconds I needed to find the words to respond. 'Yes, but I've just got married and we're leaving in two weeks.' The slight quiver in my voice seemed sufficient to elicit her pity. 'You should contact the Australian Embassy. If you qualify, they'll issue you a passport within a week.'

Although Alan and I received a warm welcome at the passport office, I was shocked to learn that despite having lived in the country for over sixteen years, the authorities did not consider me to be Australian. A sudden feeling of hollowness gripped me. The empty feeling continued until Alan's voice broke the silence.

'So, what does she have to do?'

'Well, she must apply for citizenship first. After that's granted, she can apply for a passport.'

'Can we do both at the same time?'

'I don't see why not.'

And so, I completed both applications on the spot. For a time, I struggled with feelings of disloyalty at how easily I had let go of my British passport. Until the telephone call came from the embassy a few days later, advising me that my citizenship certificate and my first passport were awaiting collection. Alan was my hero. Like dancers learning a new routine, we were starting to move in sync, one step at a time.

Alan's energy had fuelled my own. Since the proposal, I had been carried along by his vigour, my euphoria. I had begun living a new life, in another world. We both had been acting on one impulse after the other. Now, my stomach fluttered at the daringness of what I had done. I drew in a deep breath, feeling light-headed at the thought of being on a new and unknown path. It was too late to look back. We were leaving for Singapore in a week. I smiled at the memory of the joy I had seen on Dad's face at the wedding. I resolved to live a life unmarked by regret.

20

Flying Home

The Merpati flight from Darwin, bound for Jakarta, the capital of Indonesia, generally carried locals returning home or hippies preparing to trek through Asia. Passengers were required to clear customs and immigration at the first entry point into the country, which for this airline was one of the small islands surrounding the mainland. Alan and I stood out because compared to the other passengers, we were both more formally dressed. He wore one of his pale blue chambray shirts with a tie. I wore the yellow dress and high heels he had bought me. I was thankful I was not travelling in one of my kurtas or tie dyes.

Cleared to enter Indonesia, the two of us waited in a transit lounge, no bigger than a small bedroom, with the remaining passengers for our connecting flight to Jakarta. When an official of some sort sauntered towards us, Alan leaned over to whisper, 'Here's trouble.' I suspected Alan's concern was related to the attempted coup d'etat in the country which had taken place a few years early. The uprising had resulted in violent reprisals with reports saying the military had killed up to a million people in the aftermath. The Australian press had widely covered the unrest, bloodshed, and political upheaval. I was scared to be in a country where a military dictator had taken control to instil his authoritarian New Order.

The large man approaching was dressed in a brash, over embellished military uniform, with enough stripes for me to assume he must have been a General or some other high-ranking officer. 'Salamat Datang,' he said as he sat down on the empty seat beside me, causing a knot to start rising in my stomach. It was a kind of early warning system which I had mastered during my hitchhiking days. I reminded myself to stay calm and friendly. Wondering how Jack and I would have fared on the overland trip to Kathmandu.

The smell of burning cloves wafting from his unfiltered crackling kretek added to the dark and dangerous persona I was sure he wished to project. Holding the homemade looking cigarette between his thumb and forefinger, he inhaled deeply then blew out a steady stream of smoke that made me feel nauseous and dizzy. The swap from one hand to the other was deliberate and before I knew it, his cigarette-free hand stretched out in front of me.

Through a creepy smile, he said, 'Ma'am, may I see your passport?' I handed it across trying to seem relaxed despite feeling wary of his motives. Instead of opening it he leaned across me to motion for Alan's which he thumbed through, as if without interest, before closing it. Mine seemed to be of more interest. Still so new, it reflected the overhead lights. He held it up to my face as he looked at the photo, which back then boasted a beaming smile.

'Are you a model in Australia?' he asked. The question seemed out of order, but I knew it was better to answer rather than risk irritating him.

'Yes. I've done some modelling.'

He talked about the weather in Jakarta, mentioned a few other insignificant things. Then, through the same smile that had made me cringe earlier, asked why we were going to Jakarta.

'We're on our way to Singapore,' Alan said.

He did not acknowledge Alan's response. Instead, looking at me he said, 'I see you were born in Singapore. Is this your first trip back home?'

'Yes. It is,' I said with a smile.

Without an explanation of why he had approached us, he handed back our passports, stood up and said a simple, 'Salamat,' before walking off. I watched him go. I was not game to move for a while, scared he might return. My unease continued until we re-boarded the plane, and it was in the air. It was obvious he had singled us out, but for no apparent reason other than we were the only passengers that did not look like hippies. We both suspected he had hoped to uncover something irregular in our passports, perhaps so he could demand money. Or worse still, arrest us.

We arrived in Jakarta at nightfall. Everything felt dark, desperate, and dangerous. From the young men in orange overalls who carted off our bags without permission as they shouted out different prices to take them to a taxi, to the dark teak wood that lined the walls of our hotel. I was happy to be flying out the next morning, even if it was on another Merpati flight.

20.1

My window seat provided a view of Singapore which only my mum and I had seen. Everywhere, the symbols of a country's move towards transformation. Tentacles of cranes tangled beneath us, flaunting the triumph of the country's first container terminal. White public apartment towers reached for the heavens. As our plane descended, the reddish terracotta roof tiles of the colonial buildings in the town centre became more defined. Haphazard shanties sprawled around them.

The grinding sound of landing gear, vibrating beneath my feet, signalled that we were about to touch down at Paya Lebar International Airport. My tummy somersaulted with the excitement of finally being able to visit the country where I was born, the Singapore of my dreams. More than a few of those somersaults turned into bundles of knots, as the plane taxied towards the terminal. The experience with the General in Indonesia had heightened my apprehension about arriving in a foreign country.

When the aircraft door opened, the cold air evaporated, and a musty smell seeped into the cabin. It resembled the steamy redolence that lingered whenever Dad used to hose down our concrete footpaths at the height of a Sydney summer. I lightly smacked my tongue against the roof of my mouth, remembering the taste that had followed.

'It's the first rain smell of the Northeast Monsoon,' said the glamorous air hostess. 'There's a thunderstorm coming.'

At the top of the stairs, a wall of dank, steamy heat slammed into me, taking my breath away. By the time I had reached the bottom step, beads of perspiration had begun to collect across my brow. As we crossed the blistering tarmac, they trickled down the sides of my temples. The humidity frizzed my hair. To my delight the modern terminal was air-conditioned. Allowing me to forget, for a moment, how close we were to the equator.

At the immigration screening gate, an unsmiling official extended his hand for my passport. Comparing me to the photo, he said, in a sort of staccato English that was more rhetorical than a question, 'You wish a tourist visa to enter Singapore?' It felt weird needing permission to enter my birth country as a tourist. I was curious as to whether all immigrants felt this way on their first trip home. Thump-thud, a metal stamp granting me a three-month tourist visa, interrupted my reflections.

Outside the terminal, a beaming Chinese man bowed as he opened the door to usher us into a black and yellow taxi. Hurrying around to the front, he climbed into the driver's seat and squinted at us through the rear-view mirror. 'Me Henry. Oberoi Hotel not far. Maybe tenfifteen minutes.'

Though every window had been wound down, no breeze entered our suffocating sauna box. I was thankful that the hotel Alan had booked by telephone from Indonesia was 'not far' according to Henry. The sights, sounds, and smells aroused my curiosity. I strained to link each one to a story of Mum's. Barely a moment passed without Henry providing a running commentary, in his heavily broken English, dropping most of the auxiliary verbs, articles, and pronouns. Just as Portuguese Granny had.

'They hawkers,' he said when the taxi slowed past a busy marketplace. 'Chinese sell vegetable. Indian sell radio, curry powder, spice. Malay sell hot, spicy food.'

'They seem to be mostly Chinese,' I whispered to Alan.

'Yes,' Henry said overhearing me. 'Most Indian living in Chulia Kampong. Malay in Joo Chiat. Must go see.'

Like many people in Australia, I had imagined all Chinese people looked alike. Now, even from the taxi, I could see that the features of the hawkers were very different. Some had shiny golden tans, some were dark brown, others had faces as white as my mum's. Most of the men and women wore the same off-white sloppy tops, hanging over faded black pants, which did not reach their ankles.

We passed another market, selling live chickens and ducks from a mishmash of crates piled haphazardly on makeshift stalls. Each stall appeared to be hanging precariously from the awnings of two-storey, stone terraces. 'They call shophouse,' said Henry. 'Shop on ground floor. People live upstairs.'

He had not long finished his sentence when two boys, who looked about fourteen years old, came running out of one of the shops. Both were bare-chested and dressed only in striped pyjama pants, like the ones my brothers wore to bed, and each carried two steaming-hot bowls of something.

'What are those boys carrying?' I asked. 'And why are they wearing pyjama pants?'

'They take mee soup to offices,' Henry said in a serious tone. 'They very poor. Work hard. If not bring hot, boss no pay. Very hot inside. No air-con you know.'

The *mee soup boys*, as Henry said they were called, looked so young. I felt guilty at having asked the question. I thought about my life in Australia. Despite dropping out of school at fifteen, it had been a carefree one. I had worked in plush, air-conditioned offices, in well-paying jobs; left those jobs to live in beach towns; hitchhiked around parts of the country; bought expensive clothes, shoes, and makeup; and enjoyed a glamorous wedding. Now I was travelling overseas at the age of eighteen.

The markets looked harsh. Not at all like the relaxed pace of the market in Cairns or those I had frequented in the beachside suburbs of Sydney. Strolling through them for hours on end on lazy Saturday and Sunday mornings, I had soaked up the ambiance, been entertained by buskers and fortune-tellers, chatted with the hippies, often buying one of their hand-made trinkets. Here, life seemed serious. The working conditions tough. Portuguese Granny's stern face came to mind.

The sudden transition from shanty town to opulence, took me by sur-prise, when our taxi drove into a grand entrance. Oberoi Imperial Hotel, the sign said as we pulled up under a concrete awning. Once again, as if reading my thoughts, Henry said, 'This one come last year. Many big buildings out of city now. Big boom. This one modern. Got coffee house, three restaurants, Chinese, Indian, American. Also, sky lounge and swimming pool. Famous now. King of Tonga stay in presidential suite. Ha ha ha,' he laughed. 'They make special bed. He giant.'

Henry changed the subject by nodding towards two young men dressed in exotic uniforms, complete with lacy shirts, gold braid, and turbans. 'Bellboy take bag now.'

Alan paid Henry with our fresh new Singapore dollar bills. He had exchanged our Australian ones for more than double from the Indian man called a 'money changer' at the airport. 'These guys give the best rates,' Alan had said, handing me half of the notes. 'Far better than the banks.'

'Thank you for the commentary, Henry,' I said leaning forward to tap him on the shoulder.

'Most welcome,' he replied through the same beaming smile he had flashed at the airport. After thanking Alan with excessive nodding, he jumped out of his seat to direct the turbaned bellboys. One of them opened my door with a smile, reminding me of a toothpaste advertisement and greeting me with another of the hundreds of welcomes I was about to hear. The other removed our suitcases from Henry's trunk.

I was not sure if it had been the pressure from the steaming heat outside that had pushed us into the lobby or if we had been forced inside by the arctic-like suction. Either way, we were both grateful for the relief. Though I had serious questions about how long I could withstand this type of cold stinging my skin.

Despite the two or three giant chandeliers that sparkled overhead in the high ceilings, the dark teak panelling ensured the grand lobby had a similar spooky, half-light glow, to the hotel in Jakarta. Lavish furniture, upholstered in purple, scarlet, and gold, adorned the room. Ornate tiles covered the floors as far as I could see.

The faint smell of cinnamon and cloves seeping throughout reminded me of the kretek cigarettes some of the passengers had smoked on the

Merpati flight. Though I liked both those spices, the cigarettes, which according to Alan had been named for the crackling sound of burning cloves they made when inhaled, irritated my nose and made me feel sick in the stomach.

'Welcome to the Oberoi Imperial, Sir, Ma'am. You had a pleasant flight? Passports please.' The young woman at reception spoke in an accent that sounded a lot like Mum's. The desk clerks were mostly female who were dressed in a variety of outfits denoting the different races of Singapore. Some wore Chinese style satin jackets and pants. Others, dresses in gold or red, with ornate knot buttons. The Indian staff spoke excellent English with varying accents, but the Chinese staff struggled to articulate some of their words.

The young lady attending to us looked Eurasian, like me. Would it be rude to ask? After examining our passports, she put them aside. 'Passports must stay in the hotel safe.' It surprised me to learn that even the locals in Singapore had to produce their passport to stay overnight in a hotel. The law had been introduced to discourage prostitution.

'Wow. This room is beautiful,' I said, pulling aside the heavy curtains to see the view. From our room at the front of the hotel, we could see the older parts of the city and the grand fountain in the park across the road. 'It's like a furnace outside. But it's freezing in here. First thing I'm going to do is buy a cardigan.'

'I'm here!' I squealed down the receiver when I rang home to announce we had arrived safely. Dad sounded breathless after rattling off the questions I assumed he had been preparing for my call. 'Did you have a good flight? Was the airport crowded? Is it boiling hot? Are you safe?'

I responded with a giggle. 'Yes. Yes. Yes. And yes, Dad.' Better not tell him about Indonesia. Allowing him to catch his breath, I filled in the blanks about the taxi trip, Henry the driver, the Oberoi, and how I needed to buy a cardigan.

Dad began rattling off the names of 'must see' places. 'You both must see Great World, New World and Happy World. They're amusement parks that people go to at night. Oh, the food is delicious there. They've got cinemas, musical shows, and restaurants. They're magical places. My brothers and I used to go there.'

I picked up the sigh in his last line. Was he remembering bygone days spent here as a young man? If he had been worried about me, he was hiding it well. Dad confused me. Throughout my childhood he had decried my desire to return to my birthplace, imploring me to forget about the past. Now he was bubbling with enthusiasm that I was here, beseeching me not to miss the fun landmarks of his youth. He had been thrilled ever since my announcement that we were flying to Singapore. Perhaps he had put his fears about Asia aside.

Dad had been different since the wedding. No doubt it was because he no longer had to worry about me. The thought that he had handed over his responsibility to someone else stirred up a complex blend of emotions in me. I was excited about no longer being considered a child and having the independence to navigate my life with Alan. However, feelings of guilt lingered at the thought of leaving my parents and siblings behind. Freedom seemed to be a bitter sweet triumph.

It felt as if Dad had read my thoughts when he said, 'I'm glad you're there with Alan.'

Mum butted in, 'They used to have taxi dancers at those World places.'

'They don't know what those are, Honey.'

Mum ignored Dad and carried on. 'That's what they called the girls who danced with the men for a fee. Your father used to go there before he met me. The men bought dance coupons for a dollar a dance.'

'No. It was one dollar for three dances,' Dad piped in. His laughter crackled down the line. 'I don't even know if they're still open. But you should look for them.'

Mum gave me a list of must-search-for foods: 'Satay. Kway Teow. Nonya cake. Durian.' Her voice brimmed with excitement. 'Oh, by the way. I called my brothers and sisters to let them know you were coming.'

I felt certain that everything in my life had aligned now that I had returned home.

Up in the Sky Lounge, the female guests were dressed glamorously for the evening. I heard many different accents, a mix of East and West. Most of the easterners looked Eurasian, like me. A handful wore the feminine, body-hugging cheongsam. Their slinky silk and satin dresses in vibrant shades of emerald greens and fiery reds dazzled. I felt the tiniest sense of belonging when I told Alan I knew that the style had its origins in China, which explained the ornate embroidery depicting birds, swans, and flowers. Displaying its trademark high collar and slits up each leg, some reaching as high as the woman's thigh, I remembered that Mum's wedding dress had been fashioned in the style of a cheongsam, without the slits.

The men were also a mix of European and Asian. The Europeans favoured the lightweight safari-style suits in beige or sky blue. The Asians mostly wore starched shirts with ties and black or brown trousers. From the number I had seen in Indonesia and now in Singapore, I guessed the safari suit had become a sort of uniform for westerners in Asia. Though so much seemed foreign, there was a touch of familiarity amongst the faces, the voices and even the aromas. It was as if a time capsule had been unlocked.

We did not leave the hotel that night as we were both exhausted after the flight. Instead, after a few pink coloured gin drinks, which the waiter said was a mix unique to Singapore, we went back to the room and ordered room service. Alan immediately started telephoning people in Australia. I did not take any notice of whom he had called, but despite the late hour, I overheard him talking business and money.

At dawn, the telephone rang. Mum's calls to alert her family members that the first one of her children to return to Singapore was on her way with her new husband, had an immediate effect. Offers to dine flooded in. 'Must come for lunch, *lah*.' Each one spoke in a sing-song style which I learnt was the colloquial Singaporean patois, mostly English, but interspersed with a mix of Malay, various dialects of Chinese, and Indian words. They all sounded like Mum.

We accepted their invitations and experienced the generosity of close relatives. Some lived in houses called bungalows which were houses built of stone by the British during the colonial era. I recalled Mum's story about the one our family had lived in before emigrating. Most lived in flats in the concrete towers we had seen from the air. The flats were modern but small. Multi racial food courts had been built at the bottom of each complex to compensate for compact kitchens in the flats.

One aunty invited us to her family's charming bungalow for dinner. We arrived in the early afternoon, sat on rattan lounges on a veranda that wrapped around the house, sipping cold black coffee and beer. At sunset, we moved inside. Aunty had done the cooking herself in the expansive outdoor kitchen. Built from stone, like the bungalow, it was set away from the residence to keep the heat and cooking smells away from the house. A memory flashed of our home on Laksa Sundays.

'The kitchy girls cannot cook our food,' grumbled Aunty, as the young maid who worked in the kitchen carried in the pots and pans from outside. 'I don't always cook,' she added. 'Some days the kitchy girl collects food from one of the hawker stalls nearby. We can buy all types of food here.

Indian, Malay, Chinese, Thai, and European. We don't need to cook at all. But I like to cook my special dishes.'

She threw back her head and laughed at my stories of Mum's endless search for authentic Asian food and ingredients in Australia. Over dinner, I enjoyed much laughter and chatter with my aunty and her children, the cousins I had longed to meet.

On the days we were not visiting a relative, the cluttered streets beckoned. No matter what time of day, the mélange of aromas, sights, and sounds perpetuated. Alan and I explored the mystery of Singapore together, as if on the honeymoon we had not yet taken. We held hands in the sultry, syrupy air that enveloped us. Ate lunch in shophouses or hawker centres that sold delicacies in shapes and sizes my eyes had never encountered. Sat at outdoor tables to eat exotic looking seafood dishes that had been whipped up by a swarthy man, on a trolley no bigger than an ice-cream cart in Australia.

We learnt that eating out, rather than at home, had been part of Singapore's culture, dating back to the creation of the port city in the early 1800s. In response to the demands of migrants, like my father's family, who had flocked to the booming freeport, the island city had developed into a culinary melting pot, which had changed little in over a century.

We took Henry's advice and visited the various ethnic districts throughout the city. One day, the taxi from the hotel set us down on Serangoon Road in the Chulia Kampong district where many from the Indian community lived or gathered. We found ourselves amongst several Hindu temples, some built in the early 19th century. Each left us staggered by its intricate design. On one, hundreds of tiny colourful statues and images, representing various deities, covered the exterior. It was mandatory to leave our shoes at the front entrance before entering. I gingerly placed my wedged heels alongside the pile of others, expecting them not to be there when we exited. Inside, the temple was dark and dimly lit. Rather basic we thought, compared to its ornate exterior. Incense and dust filled the stone rooms making them stuffy and claustrophobic. I dropped my chin to my chest when I saw my shoes where I had left them, hoping no one had read my mind.

Just as we had seen in the Chinese districts, white-stone, two storey shophouses lined the streets. Except that in the Indian areas, the buildings boasted bright yellow, orange, and red garlands on the awnings. In some I saw pyramids of scarlet coloured chilli powder, golden turmeric, cinnamon quills, and myriad other spices. Others sold brilliant emerald or ruby stones set in yellowy-gold rings, bangles, or chains from overcrowded glass cabinets. Cluttered rows of transistor radios, cameras, and other electrical goods looked down from dusty shelves above.

Demonstrating the religious complexity of the multi-cultural population of Singapore, we were surprised to discover a Chinese Buddhist temple, a Muslim Mosque, and a Methodist Church contained in the Indian district, all within walking distance of each other. For lunch that day, we ate Indian style, with our fingers, gathering up mouthfuls of pungent yellow curry made from a giant fish head and served on a freshly picked banana leaf.

One evening, in response to our request 'where can we eat the best satay', the concierge at the hotel organised a taxi to take us to the Satay Club in down town Singapore. It was not a club as the name suggested but rather an open-air food centre across the road from the famous Raffles Hotel and close to the mouth of the Singapore River. The hawkers predominantly sold beef satay from the shelter of covered hawker stalls. When we arrived, just before sunset, crowds had already begun gathering around the numerous stalls to watch the meat being grilled over hot charcoals. Not wanting to miss out, we hovered with other patrons over the cooks, unafraid to brave the immense heat emanating from the barbecue style cooktop. The long, thin, rectangular shape looked more like a portable piano keyboard that had been filled with glowing red embers, than the brick one, topped with a wire rack, which Dad had built at home.

Our satay man appeared to have an endless supply of bamboo sticks. In expectation of the crowds, hundreds had been threaded with paper-thin slices of beef. With a deft flick of both wrists in unison, he turned each one over with lightning speed. The aroma of smoking, sizzling, mouth-watering, charcoaled meat engulfed us. Once cooked, he served us half a dozen sticks at a time, accompanied by a pot of heavenly sweet and savoury peanut sauce. We need not have worried about missing out. We learnt from our fellow satay lovers that the stalls operated until the early hours of the morning.

Over several days, the taxies servicing the hotel took us to various kampongs. One of the drivers explained that the kampongs, which is the Malay word for villages, had blossomed in conjunction with Malaysian migration to Singapore. The influx had arrived in anticipation of economic growth through manufacturing and export following Singapore's independence. Another driver praised the work Lee Kuan Yew's government had done to instil tolerance in Singapore's multicultural communities since its election. And how the development plans for each kampong included a design to attract tourists.

Dad had told us about Lee Kuan Yew's campaign for independence for Singapore. Fearing that those plans would one day require us to surrender our British passports, Dad and his family had chosen instead to give up their Singaporean status to emigrate to Australia before the ambitious politician became Prime Minister.

'He's a dictator,' Dad had said of Mr Lee.

Mum had not agreed. She often spoke highly of the new Prime Minister's bold plans to build new housing estates. I smiled at the memory of seeing Mum's nose scrunched up as she said, 'He's getting rid of the smelly sewers, the slums, and the sampans.'

Many considered Mr Lee to be one of the most forward-thinking political leaders of all time. Determined to save Singapore from being relegated to Third World status like its Asian cousins, his new government had commenced numerous development initiatives. The modernisation projects included building Hawker Centres, at breakneck speed, to control hygiene as well as public order. And introducing air conditioning systems to combat the limitation of working hours in the tropics.

'Where are you planning to go tonight?' the hotel concierge asked as we stepped up to his desk to book a taxi.

'Fatty's,' Alan said with gusto. 'I was there a year ago. I believe it's become a bit of a cult.'

'Yes,' said the concierge. 'And I believe Mr Fatty got his nickname from Australian soldiers,' he giggled. 'It's got the best Chinese food in Singapore. Night time is the best time to go. The whole place comes alive.'

Like many of them, the Chinese taxi driver that night had been talkative. I had felt embarrassed at the sight of his face in the rear-view mirror when, with eyes halfway up his forehead, he had said, 'Aah, you want to see Ladyboys in Bugis Street?' Alan had told me about the street which was around the corner from Fatty's. Renowned for its transvestites, it had become a phenomenon, making it one of Singapore's most notable and profitable destinations for foreign visitors. 'You see them there every night,' the driver had continued. 'After Fatty, you go Bugis Street. See Ladyboys.' Our driver had giggled uncontrollably as we stepped into the bustling night market, shouting to hear each other above the resounding din from crowds of people eating, talking, and laughing around tables set up in the street.

The signwriting over the entrance to the shophouse said Wing Seong Restaurant. However, the modern neon sign hanging from the top floor said Fatty's Restaurant, in honour of its owner. The waiter seating us pointed out a short, pudgy, Chinese man with a shiny, shaved head, wearing a white T-shirt which expanded over his protruding belly.

We sat close to the shophouse entrance, surrounded by a clothesline of dead animals. Bright orange mud crabs, whole squid that had been coloured turmeric yellow, crispy slabs of roast pork, fish of all shapes and sizes, and a dozen or so limp, boiled chickens with their feet still attached, staring at us from an eye that had been pierced with a large metal hook. We ordered shark fin soup, mud crab, noodles, rice, and a large bowl of chopped red chillies marinated in vinegar and sugar.

We watched the jolly Fatty doing the rounds with the westerners surrounding us. The man himself delivered some of our dishes, stopped to talk when he heard Alan's Aussie accent. 'Aah. Many Qantas pilots come here,' he said in good English. 'Australians come since war.'

After finishing our meal of the tastiest Chinese food I had ever eaten, we hailed a taxi to ask if he would take us the short distance to Bugis Street, in response to my telling Alan I did not feel safe walking there. The driver agreed for double the rate. I was glad we had not walked. I found Bugis Street a bit frightening. Alan said he felt the same. The sight reminded me a little of the seedy aspects of Kings Cross. Drunken men, most of them westerners, propositioning beautiful young Ladyboys, who were men, hoping to turn themselves into women through a camouflage of silk cheongsams, high heels, jewellery, cakey foundation, fire-engine red lipstick, and rouge. We did not stay long.

Each day, we ventured to a different eating place as suggested by the hotel concierge or the taxi drivers. One day we sweated over steaming bowls of mee soup flavoured with a chicken gizzard, served in an open-air restaurant by bare-chested Chinese boys wearing the same type of striped pyjama-pants I had seen on our drive from the airport. When I saw Mee Goreng advertised, I felt compelled to order it despite not being hungry. I could not wait to mail a postcard to Dad telling him how the 'locals slur the two words together faster than at the Malaya Restaurant in Sydney'. I knew it would either bring a smile to his face, or he would twist one corner of his lips in annoyance.

An elderly Chinese woman approached our table whilst Alan was laughing at my attempts to eat the mee with chopsticks.

'You born what year?' she said brusquely.

'1954,' I replied.

'Where?'

'Singapore.'

She leaned closer to stare into my eyes. 'You look like pre-war Eurasian,' she said. 'Born Year of Horse. In Chinese culture, horse brave, strong, talented.' She put out a wrinkled brown hand into which I deposited a coin.

It was common knowledge that the Asian component of many Eurasians from my parent's pre-war era came from the South and South-East regions. Areas where the Spice Traders had left their mark, along with their genes. And like me, the European component was mostly from the Dutch and English.

The Portuguese were also European, but the people of Singapore seemed to class them differently, which might explain why Mum's birth certificate described her race as both Portuguese and Eurasian. During the post-war decades following my family's emigration from Singapore, the racial mix amongst Eurasians had gained a greater Chinese element.

I had expected to be recognised as Singaporean because of the way I looked. However, as far as the locals were concerned, I was not one of them. I neither understood, nor spoke Malay, which was officially the national language of Singapore. Apart from the old Chinese lady, everyone we met was either surprised or disinterested when I said I was born in Singapore.

Food appeared to be the main attraction in Singapore. Even amongst my relatives, it dominated our conversations. At the end of each day one of the aunts would either call into the hotel or telephone to ask, 'What did you eat today? Where?' If I said it was not good, she would say, '*Aiyoh*, don't go to that place. No good *lah*.' If I said it had been delicious, she would scream, 'Shiok *lah*'. Which I learnt meant 'great'. The lah just seemed to be added on to the end of everything. For something good it was a short sharp *lah*. For something bad it was drawn out with a crescendo at the end, *laaaah*.

When a cousin offered to take me to the traders in the shopping alleys to shop for bargains in clothes, shoes, and makeup, I was excited. However, although I was a slim dress size 8, I was now 170 centimetres tall. And, as my mother had often reminded me, I had inherited the large breasts of my Dutch Burger grandmother. These factors combined made it difficult to find clothes or shoes to fit. Everything was tiny, intended for the smaller locals I guessed. And the Indian section only sold saris and kurtas. Realising that I was not going to be able to buy anything from the traders, we headed for Robinsons department store, a popular haunt for the European community because of the goods they imported from England.

The brand-new store had opened in Orchard Road, a few weeks before our arrival, following the massive fire that had destroyed their landmark building in Raffles Place barely three weeks earlier. I bought a silk, safari-style pantsuit in navy blue, with a matching belt and teamed it with a neckerchief in swirling paisley pastels and a pair of red leather cork wedges. I also bought a pair of flat sandals. Back at the hotel, I was not surprised to see Alan dressed in a pale blue safari suit.

Our sightseeing adventures revealed that not all the government's ambitious plans to transform the entrepôt into a modern metropolis had left their drawing boards. Not all the villagers had been dragged from their shanties kicking and screaming into the futuristic apartment blocks. Dilapidated shophouses still lined the streets of the commercial district. Boat Quay still teamed with the same flat-bottomed sampans and sea-going twakows that had crowded the harbour when my family sailed away in 1956.

In a matter of years, they would undoubtedly disappear. I was certain that destiny had brought me to my birth country now, so that I could feel its spirit, smell its soul, witness its rawness before the dazzle of the glass towers concealed them forever. However, now that I had witnessed them, the disparaging words I had heard repeated about Singapore over the years from Dad, floated back at the sight that was the mire of the sampan area. Whole families lived on tiny boats. The smell of rotting wet garbage and fish drying in the open air, choked us. The children wore rags. The sights were overwhelming. We did not stay long before catching a taxi back to the Oberoi. I stared out of the window wondering about my feelings for this country. Whether I really belonged here. Whether it was still my country. And how the aroma of exotic fruits had turned to rotting garbage in a matter of weeks.

As the days progressed, Dad's comments about Asia being 'third world' crept into my thoughts more often. Most of my life I had dreamt about my connection to Singapore. Now, despite waking at first light and falling asleep each night, to the smells that sizzled from the same equatorial frying pan from which Mum's stories had emanated, my relationship was not the same as I had dreamt it would be.

I realised the connection I had fantasised about was not mine to enjoy. It was my mother's. The experiences I had tried to replicate were hers. Mine were of climbing mulberry trees in a parched vacant lot in the western suburbs of Sydney. Walking the long dusty streets to school with my siblings. Eating a hamburger at a milk bar on Saturday night. Hitchhiking along long stretches of country roads. Dressing like a hippie to prance around the Domain, listening to the radicals speak. Meeting long haired blond surfers on Manly beach at the height of summer.

I had not seen one man sporting long hair since our arrival. The news back home had covered the controversy about the ban on long hair for men in Singapore, a style considered the norm in the West. The reality of the law had not hit home until I saw the posters for myself, stuck on walls outside shops, banks, government buildings, and marketplaces, warning men that it was against the law to wear their hair in a style that either fell across the forehead, touched the eyebrows, covered the ears, or hung over an ordinary shirt collar. Those who did not comply would be 'attended to last, or not at all'.

I wondered what sort of country could tell people how to wear their hair. It reminded me of school. I was outraged to learn that as far as the Singapore government was concerned, men with long hairstyles, were seen as untidy and deviant, potentially disrupting social order. The intention was to thwart any incursion from the hippie subculture gaining popularity. Prime Minister, Lee Kuan Yew had made it clear that the government saw long hair as negative and detrimental to the country's development.

The law had described almost everyone I knew in Australia, including my brothers who had tried in desperation to keep their hairstyles in the face of private school rules. The consequences of defying the long-hair ban in Singapore varied from receiving a fine, being forced to cut it short, or having it cut by police. Civil servants who did not comply were fined or fired.

Long-haired male tourists attempting to enter Singapore were made to visit the barber shop at the airport or leave the country. Those who refused to have their hair cut were barred from re-entering for months, even if they had complied after leaving.

The year before we arrived, the pop-rock band called the Bee Gees had been granted permission to play for a pre-arranged concert, without cutting their hair. However, they were made to leave the country immediately after the event. Some bands were offered visas if they complied. Many preferred to remove Singapore from their tour destinations. My roots were in this country, but now I had arrived, I was unsure about a future here.

20.2

Rain had just fallen, when we arrived in the small town of Johor Bahru in Malaysia, where my father had once lived and worked as a building contractor. After three weeks in Singapore, an aunty had suggested we take the short trip. 'Malaysia is just across the causeway you know. Many people travel between the two cities each day for all sorts of reasons like work, see doctors, and sightseeing. And there is plenty of cheap shopping. Go to Woodlands. Can catch a bus or taxi from there. Only takes half an hour.'

We decided on one of the black and yellow taxis lined up at the terminal rather than a bus. Our driver entertained us with bursts of information about the city's history. 'Malays are mostly Muslim…The railway has been connected between Woodlands and Johor since 1920…The Japanese occupied the State of Johor during the war…The Malay anti colonial struggle started there because they wanted to protect their religion of Islam, their language, and their sultans…After the formation of Malaysia in 1963, Johor Bahru was granted city status.'

Our driver was of Indian origin. As he had been born in India, the locals referred to him as Indian-Indian. Unlike those who were born in Singapore to Indian parents, who were simply called Indian or Singaporean-Indian. After the short but informative trip, he set us down in the centre of the city, close to the smelly Sungei Segget River which proved to be an assault on our senses. Earthy, after-rain smells of mud, soil, grass, insects, mustiness, and open drains melded with the aromas of coconut husks, over ripe bananas, mangos, and other pungent tropical fruits from the nearby markets.

The break-neck building works and frenetic clean-up campaigns of Singapore, had not yet interfered with the old-world atmosphere across the border. Here the loudest sounds came from the revving of motorcycles and bus exhausts. Most women wore head scarves that showed their faces, some in full hijab which also covered their hair, ears, and neck. They were friendly. When they smiled at us, their beautiful brown eyes lit up. Their placid natures charmed us. They seemed soft, compared to the Singaporeans. A lump caught in my throat at the sound of faint music playing. Like someone was magically piping it throughout the land.

Our historian taxi driver had not given us any sightseeing tips, but he did warn us that the humidity would reach a sticky 100%. Unsure of what to see first, we began walking the streets. We passed administrative buildings which had been constructed in the British style, Buddhist and Hindu Temples, and Mosques, as we had seen over the previous few weeks. Our wanderings led us back to the markets by the river which cut through the centre of the city. It was hard to believe the locals, when they assured us that it had once flowed with clean water, before being polluted from unregulated industry and sewage.

Alan seemed to relish being in the thick of the crowds and chaos of the pasar pagi, as the Malays called the market, striking up conversations, in broken English, with the merchants. They were mostly men, who called out to us to buy their wares, a mix of household items, haberdashery, and bric-a-brac. I bought a headscarf from one, hoping to thwart the stares I had been receiving from some of the men. The sage green and pink coloured flowers swirled on luxurious silk. The seller said it came from Darul Iman which we learnt was the Muslim name for a State on the east coast called Trengganu. It was the first Malay State to receive Islam around 1300 A.D.

Despite the pelting heat of the midday sun, we continued through to a wet market, hop scotching all the way to avoid the smelly water, animal blood, and rubbish. The hawkers in the pasar pagi were in the throes of packing up their fresh fruits, vegetables, live fish, chickens, and recently laid eggs. The hubbub from people eating and talking drew us further along the river to the cooked food section. In the same manner as we had seen in Singapore, a sort of organised chaos reigned amongst the outpouring of intoxicating sights, sounds, and smells. All around us, the cacophony from spices hissed in sizzling oil. Countless wicker baskets overflowed with mounds of freshly pounded rempahs, the Malay word for a spice paste, crimson-coloured dried chillies, ikan bilis which were the tiny, dried, white fish we called anchovies in the West, and fresh herbs and vegetables – all waiting to be transformed into a host of mouth-watering delights, at our request.

My rumbling belly reminded me that my family ate lunch around eleven o'clock on weekends, so I knew we were late, according to Asian standards. We made our way to the Hainan Chicken Rice vendor. The popular dish was one of Dad's favourites. Alan said it was his as well, after being introduced to it by the Chinese girlfriend he had mentioned before. I went with him to ensure he collected the essential sides of sambal chilli, soya sauce, and the ginger and spring onion sauce mixed with sesame oil.

We both watched the hawker man chop into a side of chicken with a dangerous looking cleaver. Saliva gathered in my cheeks as I watched him pile it atop the mound of steaming rice which I knew had been cooked in the chicken stock. A bundle of pandan leaves had been stuffed into the cavity of the chicken. When the aroma reached me, it stirred memories of home, and Dad. He loved the food of the East, had grown up eating it. It was sad how he now criticised Asia so much.

I left Alan slurping away at his soup to search for the Laksa stall. The sight of the prepared bowls of white rice noodle, topped with paper thin slices of cucumber, the seeds removed the same way Mum had prepared them at home, and the long thin, forest green coloured laksa leaves on top, once again transported me to the Sunday lunches at home in Greenacre. After eating it at our home, Portuguese Granny had crowned our mum the Laksa Queen. 'Laksa leaves are essential for the Singapore version.' Mum had said to Glynis and me. Though she had no choice but to make it without them for many years in Australia. Until the *boat people* from Vietnam brought the plant with them. I had been with her the day she beamed with joy at finding some in an Asian grocery shop in Sydney's Chinatown, under the name Vietnamese mint.

Alan cut short my reminiscing when he suggested we pay a local taxi to drive us around the shoreline. A great idea given our limited time. The area was largely undeveloped and resembled much of the parts of Singapore that had not yet been touched. We drove around Istana Bukit Serene, the grand palace of the Sultan of Johor. Facing the Straits of Johor, it had a splendid view of Singapore, which had once been a possession of the Sultanate.

Our Chinese taxi driver seemed happy to tell us about the Sultan who had welcomed the Japanese during the invasion. 'Before war, Sultan Ibrahim had Japanese friend. He descendant of warrior family. General Yamashita bring that man to Johor Bahru. Japanese make him important politician in Malaya. Ibrahim allow Japanese officers to use palace to plan for Singapore invasion. They have bird's eye view of Australian Army and Navy across the Strait.'

The disclosure was not new to me, but it was nonetheless shocking to hear. Some of those Australians could have been the fathers or grandfathers of people I knew. In the silence of the car, I recalled my mum's stories about how some Malaysians and Indians had sided with the enemy, believing in their promise of a New Order in East Asia, which would unite Asians against the West. Towards the end of the occupation, those who had turned against the Allies had realised that the ideology promoted by the Japanese had been nothing more than propaganda to ensure cooperation. The sight of a man pushing a food cart advertising an ice dessert, provided an opportunity to break the solemn mood.

'Oh look, he's making Ice Kachang', I screamed with joy. 'It's one of the things on my list from Mum.'

Our driver pulled up. We jumped out to watch the hawker scrape ice from a huge block, form it into a ball with his bare hands, then drizzle red and green syrups over it, transforming it into a delicious dessert. I remembered Mum's story about the Ice Kachang Man from her childhood. How he would place the perfectly rounded ice ball into her open hands, leaving her no choice but to lick it ferociously before it melted and ran down her arms in the tropical heat. Here, ours was served in a plastic bowl with a plastic spoon.

Back in the town centre, the weight of the early afternoon heat became unbearable. We had to squint through air so opaque, I could have sliced it with a knife, just like I had seen a hawker slice pale-green honeydew melon earlier in the day at the pasar pagi. Without warning, the delightful fragrances from the hawker food, collided with the fumes that drifted from putrid open drains, like rotten egg gas from a school science experiment.

The people around us seemed unperturbed by the new heights the smells and heat had reached, continuing their daily routines as if nothing had changed.

I covered my mouth with my new headscarf, forcing myself to take shallow breaths to avoid the gas from the sewers. But the overpowering vapours engulfed me, leaving me feeling drained and dizzy. I could feel my body slumping where I stood. I could take no more. A pang of homesickness for Australia and my family shot through me. I was no longer certain of how I felt about coming home.

Much of my connection to these lands had come from my parents' stories. Now everything felt foreign. I wondered if the connection with Asia, which I had dreamt of all my life, had disappeared. Perhaps it had never existed. And this was nothing more than the place where I was born. If that was so, I wondered where my real connections might lie. And if I could ever live in a country like this. Maybe Dad was correct about forgetting about the past.

The dilemma of whether I was Eastern or Western had churned inside me since childhood. Here in Asia, it had erupted. I was both. I was neither. I cowered by the side of the road feeling overwhelmed by the confounding confusion and the stabbing pain in my heart, at the dichotomy of being both connected and disconnected, at the same time, to my birth country and Asia.

Seeing something had distressed me, Alan interrupted my soulful feelings. 'Do you want to find an airconditioned place for a while?'

I nodded.

'Okay, we'll look for a hotel until the taxi time.'

We entered the first modern looking hotel we came across. Instead of air conditioning, massive teak fans whirred overhead. The lobby café felt cool, pleasant, and more comfortable than the icy cold hotels in Singapore.

We sat on luxurious lounge chairs as we scanned the afternoon tea menu. Seeing several types of kueh listed, prompted me to tell Alan about my mother's childhood stories of the rainbow coloured kueh. But we had eaten too much at the hawker centre. And the fumes had put me off food. This 'must-try' of Mum's would have to wait. Instead, we decided on iced coffee, made the Asian way, without milk. We had enjoyed this drink in Singapore made by a man at a kopi tiam, which was a sort of coffee shop cum eatery. Kopi is the Malay word for coffee. Tiam is Hokkien for shop. The drink is served in a milkshake type glass filled with crushed ice, cold black coffee, and gula melaka.

The sweltering conditions outside had not bothered Alan as much as me. He had happily struck up conversations with the locals as we wandered through the streets, in and out of temples and shops. I recalled our first conversations about his love for Asia. The feelings of belonging. The constant desire to return. Even his admission at how entranced he had become upon hearing his first ever Mandarin love song. He did not know from where the longing had come but admitted that here in Johor Bahru he had heard the mystical music in the streets.

I had blood ties to Asia. And I had also been intrigued by the music. But my feelings were not as strong as his. There was still much to learn about my new husband. My life had been a whirlwind since meeting him at the job interview. I had abandoned Jack within a day of arriving in Melbourne, married Alan in less than a week, left Australia a little more than a month later. Now, I was in my birth country unravelling childhood stories and matching faces to relatives who a few weeks earlier had been little more than names on Christmas cards.

The interlude from the street sounds, the retching odours, and the food, gave me a chance to think more about my roots in Asia. 'Come find me,' the ghosts of yesteryear had whispered since early childhood. Here in the lands where their souls rested, their voices reverberated with every tick, tick, tick of the overhead fans.

Dad's story of escape from Singapore came to mind. I remembered that his father and brother were buried there. He had never said much about his brother other than the sad story of his having been left behind during the Japanese invasion. 'The authorities couldn't get his paperwork in order,' Dad had said. Separating the family for something so trivial seemed outrageous to me. I made a mental note to search for their graves; learn more about my uncle's death. Perhaps this was the reason Dad had condemned Asia so much.

Under British rule, Malaya had become one of the most profitable territories of the Empire, being the world's largest producer of tin and rubber. I guessed it was the reason my maternal great grandfather, Frederick Ware, had travelled here from England at the end of the nineteenth century. I knew of the legend that he had been the first stationmaster in the colonial capital of Taiping. But, unlike my paternal family who lauded their European blood, nobody on the maternal side seemed interested in this Englishman.

Like many of the Europeans, Frederick had boarded a steamer heading for the far reaches of the empire to become a Colonial Railwayman. The wanderlust inside me had soared, at the very thought of being related to a man who had risked his life on a dangerous sea voyage to a mysterious land, not knowing if he would ever return. Frederick had married a local woman called Mary in this country where I had heard the piped music playing. I wondered how they had fared amongst the colonial cronyism where interracial unions were frowned upon. Even more so on the coffee-coloured children those unions had produced. Coping with smelly open drains and unbearable heat since arriving had been a struggle for me. I wondered how Frederick had coped almost a century ago.

Life in the tropics would have been precarious for a European during an era when a person could fall ill one day – be dead the next. I wondered if that could have happened to Frederick. Some of the members of Mum's family believed it to be true. I had sensed their indifference about my efforts to learn more about the past and my great grandfather and whether he had in fact returned to England as Mum believed. If Frederick had died in Malaya, it was going to take me more than a day trip to search for his grave.

Our driver collected us at the pre-arranged time of four o'clock. It had been a long and dreary day. Our interlude in Malaya had brought back memories of childhood stories. Some of them flashed past as we made our way back to Singapore. Bombs raining over Taiping a few weeks before Mum turned twelve years old. Grandpa Ware being arrested and taken to the notorious Death Railway. Dad, and his family's miraculous escape before the fall of Singapore. The Allies blowing up the very causeway we had just crossed over, to slow down the enemy's advance into the heart of Singapore city. The Australian soldiers who had defended the shoreline in vain, against an enemy being aided by some of the locals. So many memories. None of them mine.

20.3

Our weeks in Singapore dragged on. By the beginning of the third month on the island, I was bored. There was only so much eating and shopping I could do. Alan still did not want me to get a job, but I rang the embassy anyway to enquire about my ability to work. Learning that Singapore did not hand out work visas easily, not even to those who had been born in the country, forced me to rethink the possibility of making it my home.

Whilst I had been spending time with my aunts and cousins, exploring eating houses and shopping, Alan had been making telephone calls to local companies, seeking out consulting assignments. He had impressed me with his ability to network with past contacts and uncover new ones in his search for an opportunity that would allow us to stay longer in Singapore, but nothing had been forthcoming. Unperturbed, he had scheduled a meeting with a prospect for a potential assignment with a shipping company. Rather than wasting the day in the hotel, I had accepted an invitation from a cousin for a luxurious High Tea at the Hilton Hotel. As we would both be in town at the same time, Alan suggested we meet at the Hilton's taxi rank to travel back to the Oberoi together.

In the taxi I noticed him shifting in his seat, checking his watch, and looking out the window, whilst attempting to make small talk about my tea date. He had a habit of shutting me out when something was bothering him which often left me in the dark about his plans. However, because I felt such a connection to him, I was certain I could hear the cogs turning in his turbo-charged brain. He had continued to oversee our daily decisions. I was okay with that because I had no plans of my own. I was being carried along in his slipstream, searching for somewhere to belong. At times, I felt like I was back in my hitchhiking days where learning on the job had been a mix of fight-or-flight. Except now, I had no desire to do either because I was in love. Like hitchhiking, learning about my new husband in real-time was thrilling. Though today I sensed something was up.

Back in the hotel room, I watched Alan roll up his sleeves before bending over to search inside the refrigerator. He grabbed the glass he liked to store in the freezer, filled it with ice from the tray, which crackled as he poured gin over it from one of the miniature bottles supplied in the room, then topped it up with tonic water. Drink in hand, he walked towards the curtains, holding them apart to stare out as if he was looking at something whilst taking a sip of his drink. When he turned around, his tongue was balancing on his upper lip before dropping to lick across his bottom one. I opened my mouth to speak but before I could say anything, his words pierced the silence of the room.

'We're almost out of money.'

I did not respond because I did not know what to say.

'I had hoped to pick up some consulting work here.'

I decided to wait before asking questions. So, he continued, revealing the reasons why he was upset. 'I transferred money to the account I'd opened here at the Hong Kong Shanghai Bank. But I was expecting more to come from some of the work I did in Melbourne. Now that client is saying I left before doing a complete handover so he's not paying the second half of the contract. He's short changed me. There's nothing more to come from him.'

My first reaction was one of relief that Alan had chosen to confide in me. When he added that he had been calling into the bank in between meeting prospective customers, it answered one of my queries about why he had gone to the city so often. Finally, some disclosure which made me feel like we could survive anything as long as we were honest with each other.

'How much were you expecting?' I asked boldly.

'Ten thousand dollars.'

We spent a quiet night in the hotel. Neither of us felt like living it up. It surprised me that the situation had not fazed me as much as it might have others. Like it would have Glynis who, upon learning our news about flying to Singapore so soon after the wedding, had accused me of behaving like a puppet on a string since meeting Alan. Maybe she had a point. I had not had much control over my life these past months. But then I remembered how I had been making decisions on the fly since the age of fifteen, following my instincts, meandering through life, swerving around the occasional rocks, avoiding a few boulders. Marrying a stranger after being hit by a thunderbolt had simply been another of those impulsive decisions. Except that now I was in a foreign country, thousands of miles away from my family, and with practically no money. Somehow, I had plunged from the relative safety of the slipstream into a whirlpool of worry.

In the morning, I showered, dressed, put on my makeup, then sat in one of the roomy armchairs with my feet tucked under my legs. Alan was at the small table by the window offering words of reassurance in between sips of coffee. I barely heard him. I was too busy thinking. The lack of money was concerning, but it paled against not knowing what was going on in his head. I had learnt to decipher some of his mannerisms, but I wondered if I would ever know them all.

He steepled his hands, fingers touching his lips which I was learning was one of the gestures he used to block out distractions. It made him look serious. His brain was churning, thinking, planning. Something was coming. It occurred to me that I had contributed to setting Alan's life on a new trajectory. He now had responsibility for me, had to include me in his plans. His voice pierced my reveries. 'This is just a setback you know. Remember, it was always our plan to go to England one day.'

From a situation which others might have seen as dire, Alan seemed energised. I liked that about him. It was early days. I was still learning about his quirks. Although I did wonder about his naivety in leaving the contract in Melbourne early and expecting the company to pay him in full. However, it reassured me that he believed he had done the right thing by them. It also made me feel less gullible about the faith and trust I had placed in him. Regardless, I needed him so much it hurt. And he needed to be needed by me. Two needy people. We were perfect for each other. So, I had not expected what came next.

'I've decided to go to England,' he said, sliding his chair away from the table. His eyes fixing on mine, he continued. 'I've been paying the hotel every week, so the bill will only be for a few days. There's enough money to buy one-way tickets. Just means we'll have to start from scratch, get jobs.' When I failed to respond, he added, 'But it might be better if you go home first. You can always join me later.'

An avalanche of thoughts exploded in my head, tumbling over each other as if racing for clarity at the utterance of both the word home and the option of not going with him. I had mixed feelings about the prospect of returning to Australia. Even more so alone. A hundred tiny daggers stabbed my heart at the realisation that he had contemplated going without me. After all, I had said, 'I wasn't doing anything for the next ten years.' I hoped my commitment for a decade had not ended in a matter of months. However, his last comment sure sounded like a goodbye.

Not enough time had passed to judge Alan. However, the realisation that he was responsible for my being in a foreign country with little money, brought the face of the scary Indonesian General to mind, forcing me to consider whether I should continue this journey or return to Australia. I was certain the room felt stuffier than usual. Perhaps the cleaners had switched off the air-conditioning. Why else would I feel like I could not breathe. The new situation evoked memories from the past when I had been forced to decide on a path with little or no time to think about the consequences. I mulled over some of the choices I had made, reflecting on whether they had always been for the best.

My thoughts moved quickly to how I would tell Mum and Dad I had made a mistake. That I would be returning to Australia, alone. They would feel I had let them down. Though I refused to regret any of my past decisions, my heart felt heavy at the concern I had caused them over the past few years. Despite my antics they had always been there for me, had never let me down. They had continued to support my decisions regardless of the outlandish things I had done. Like the time they had driven to the south coast to rescue me after someone had stolen my wallet. And Mum's reassurance of Dad's anger at the principal, the school, and his church for their treatment of me. Without committing to having made any errors, I did wonder if I had overestimated my ability to make important life decisions over the past few years.

Despite Dad's urging throughout my childhood to forget about the past and leave Asia behind, I had not been able to do so. My never-ending desire to return to Singapore had distressed him but he had let me find my own way. I was thankful he had not tried to stop Alan and me. Instead, he had simply replaced his directives about Asia with earnest advice about 'must see' places from his positive memories.

The opportunity to experience life in my birth country and the visit to Malaysia had made me realise that neither country was where I belonged. The voyage had opened my eyes to Dad's reasons for moving his family to Australia. He had been driven by a desire to protect us, keep us safe. What did I know of war, loss, exodus, being stateless? Dad and the members of his family had suffered all those experiences which had caused the loss of their father, brother, and sister, the family home and belongings, and the fracture of his family. In contrast, I had grown up in the safety of Australia with my siblings around me. We had Dad to thank for that.

I had walked along the same waterfront from which the lifesaving ship carrying Dad's family to safety had departed days before the invasion of Singapore. Imagining his anguish, I had cringed with guilt at the thought of how much he had sacrificed to protect his children from experiencing similar horrors. Since I had left home he had softened his approach towards the subject. I felt thankful that he had stopped urging me not to return to my birthplace. By doing so, I had realised for myself that it was not where my future lay.

Dad had been relieved that my first trip to Asia would be with my new husband, an older, conservative man, rather than hitchhiking to Kathmandu with a couple of young Americans. But Alan was as erratic as me which was now contributing to my feeling flustered over the less-than-ideal situation. It was as if someone had tied a blindfold on me, then spun me around a few times. I felt dizzy at the thought of having to make another life-changing decision in the dark.

And what of God and me? Donovan had encouraged me to keep the faith right up until our breakup. Soon after, I had moved to the south coast. Out of the reach of the congregation and Dad, I had stopped attending church, questioning whether God had deserted me during the expulsion. Being away from home seemed to be the catalyst for Dad to stop pressing me to resume my attendance. I hoped he had realised that I was still very much a Christian but that I had a different path to follow from my missionary namesake.

The memory of his reaction to my news about getting married flashed through my mind. I had expected him to be disappointed upon learning the wedding service would be held in an Anglican Church. 'There's nothing to forgive, Evvy,' he had said in response to my apology. Instead, he had literally whistled with delight down the telephone line, 'Evvy, I only ever wanted you to be happy.' I smiled at the memory of the look of joy on his face as he led me down the aisle at Saint John's.

I had not deserted God. I had never stopped praying. Like whenever Dad was sick or those times when I had found myself in a dangerous situation. I giggled out aloud at the memory of my fervent prayers on the day I had contemplated jumping out of a moving car. And like Dad, I thanked

God for every meal. However, the trauma, loss, and illness, which Dad had suffered over his lifetime, had never reached me. So, whilst I understood his need for the sanctuary offered by a religion with such strong doctrines, belonging to it had caused me to feel like I was bound up in a straitjacket. And after experiencing the conflict in our home over different religions, I wanted to make my own decisions. The messages I had heard from the turbulent social revolution during my teenage years had provided the impetus to explore my own values, beliefs, passions, and purpose in life.

I did not believe that the God I knew would punish me for deserting a particular denomination. But I did wonder if He had continued to hear my prayers. He had been keeping me safe, so I guessed He was still there for me. I needed Him to hear me now because, compared to the fog that had engulfed me in the shower after being expelled from school, this felt like a waterfall. The sense of white-water thundering over me was drowning out my ability to think clearly. If I made the wrong decision, about whether I should go to England or return to Australia, I might be plunged into an abyss. At that moment, I needed someone with whom to consult. Someone who could help me work through the pros and cons. Alan had gone downstairs to pay the bill. I felt alone. As I had on so many occasions during my teenage years.

'Dear God,' I whispered as I picked up the handset and dialled our home number in Sydney. 'What should I do?' I drew in a deep breath when Dad answered.

20.4

The sneaky shard of sunlight piercing my eyes delivered a welcome break from a night of turbulent thoughts. I had hardly slept. Dragging aside the heavy curtains, I opened the windows. Over in the older part of the city,

I saw people in rags crowded around their fragile shanties — the dregs of which the government could not rid itself fast enough. The stench of rotting seafood and sewage flooded my nostrils, smelling a lot worse than when we had arrived. Neither of us had a desire to venture into the streets. We stayed in the hotel for the day before catching a taxi to the airport where we boarded a British Caledonian flight to London. Weeks remained on our visas.

One of the flight attendants begged me to tell her where I had bought my silk pantsuit so she could 'pop in' on her next stopover. When I said Robinsons, a lump caught in my throat. Another swooned at my engagement ring, oohing and aahing when we explained why we had both chosen the daisy design. Casting my mind back to the day we had bought it, I smiled and chatted to them happily, wondering how long I would be considered a young newlywed. When they moved on, Alan leaned across to whisper, 'I've been thinking. It's the dead of winter in England. We'll need coats. We might have to use your engagement ring to get some cash when we get there.'

My heart missed a beat as those words tumbled from his lips. Speechless from the rush of confusing emotions, my head touched the back of the seat. I turned to look outside hoping to disguise the crystals I felt forming in my eyes. Silly me, because against the darkness of the night the porthole had become a mirror. Sensing my upset, Alan grabbed hold of my hand. 'Don't worry,' he said. 'We'll buy it back with our first pay packets.'

I was certain Mum and Dad had believed their worrying about me was over. What new heartache might I cause them, I wondered. But they were both experienced in the ups and downs of life; knew it was not a fairytale. My thoughts shifted to the shocking news they had delivered on my last telephone call when I rang to tell them I would not be returning to Australia.

'Not just yet,' I had said, to avoid sounding like it was forever.

When Dad went quiet on the line, I had thought it was because of my announcement. Until he started, 'We have some news too. It's not very good news Evvy.'

I had held my breath.

'Donovan died.'

'What?' was all I could manage to say.

'He died earlier in the week, but we didn't know how to tell you.'

'But how?'

'It was from his illness. We don't know all the details. We're going to the funeral on Sunday. Your mother and I are going to church to pray for his soul this Sabbath.'

'Mum's going with you?'

'Yes. Mum has been coming to church with me for a while.'

Donovan's death had left me feeling utterly bereft. Though Singapore had returned some of the pieces of my heart left behind at the age of two, my time there had been filled with conflicting emotions, which had included the challenge of navigating a new relationship, and now the death of my first love. 'I wasn't sure if I was doing the right thing including you in my uncertain future,' Alan had said over our final Singapore sling in the roof-top bar. 'That's the only reason I suggested you might want to go back to Australia.'

My response had been to make a joke about looking forward to leaving the icy hotel air conditioning. It was all I could do to conceal my pang of guilt at having contemplated not going to England with him, albeit for a millisecond. The moment I had realised I was more afraid of losing him than leaving him, I knew I would be on the plane. We belonged together.

Any doubts I had about my future paled against the feeling of need that consumed me. I did not want to live without him.

Whilst Alan raved at the excitement of arriving in London, my thoughts drifted to the things I had left unresolved in Singapore and Malaysia. I had barely scratched the surface of this island of sampans and safari suits. There were many stories from the past waiting to be unpacked. I needed time to explore my mixed feelings about the land where I was born, where my family had roots dating back to the rajahs, the riots, and colonialism. But for now, I was glad to be leaving.

Despite the feelings of not belonging in Mum's Malaya, I reasoned how fortunate I had been to have visited the Singapore of my childhood dreams. I was meant to come. Though I had learnt that just like Dad, no one here seemed interested in the past. I had hoped to find some common ground between the old and the new amongst the members of Mum's family but like everyone else I had met in Singapore they were rapidly moving into the future. 'Better left buried,' they had said about the past. 'That's the old Singapore. Mr Lee is building a new one.'

I was yet to see many of the places Mum had talked about during my childhood. I hoped to make it back before Mr Lee pulled them down to make way for more multi-storey housing, shopping malls, and modern food courts. Nor had I paid my respects at the gravesites of relatives buried in Singapore's cemeteries. I prayed the land starved city-state would not exhume them one day to pave the way for a new township.

When the captain announced we would be flying into strong headwinds at Gatwick Airport, which he said was about thirty miles south of Central London, I buckled my seatbelt in preparation for the disarming jolt on the tarmac. Our touchdown turned out to be much smoother than it had been in Singapore.

The high-altitude clouds evaporated before my eyes, revealing a drizzly, foggy winter morning. Despite the gloominess outside, a sudden feeling of elation washed over me. I became excited at the thought of being in the same city as some of my favourite music groups like the Beatles and the Rolling Stones. I could visit Carnaby Street to see the mod fashions. Most of all, I felt elated at being in a country where I had permission to work for at least two years. Our situation had released me from my dependency on Alan. We were now on the same footing.

The opportunity to earn my own money would allow me to contribute to the decisions affecting my future. But I knew nothing of that future. I did not know that my expectations of London would come true or how I would feel more at home there than either Singapore or Australia. I did not know that after a month temping as a receptionist for the largest international secretarial agency in the world, the founder and owner would offer me the opportunity to train as a Recruitment Consultant which would be the start of a lifetime career.

There were many things I did not foresee. Like how Alan and I would remain in London for four years. How after consulting to a small British airline for a period, he would fulfil his desire to once again run a charter airline specifically for business executives. Because of its success, we would begin spending our weekends between a motor cruiser moored at Southampton and flying to Europe. The airline would introduce us to social circles which included magnates, royals, and everyone in between. Those experiences would enhance the knack I had gleaned from my humble hitchhiking days to quickly assess people and situations. I did not know that one day that skill would lead to a successful career in executive recruitment and evaluation and eventually the creation of my own management consultancy.

Taxiing towards the terminal seemed to go on forever. I recalled what Alan had said about London being so big that Gatwick was one of three airports servicing it. My thoughts drifted to Dad. I knew for certain I would never become the missionary he had hoped I might. Also, that despite continuing my strong faith in God and Christianity, I had no desire to return to a church of any denomination. And although I was quite sure I would never again see anyone from my teenage years, I still wondered where life had taken Jack. But how could I know that he would complete the overland trail through Asia, return to live in America, and we would reconnect when he and his wife travelled to Australia for a holiday, fifty years after the last time I saw him in Melbourne.

With daylight now backing the aircraft porthole, I had to squint to see the mirror image of the woman staring back at me. It was hard to recognise myself without those thick black lines running from the edges of my bottom eyelids to the tops of my cheeks. Despite wondering if all my experiences up until now had been pre-ordained, I did not have the ability to divine the future. So, I did not know that despite our successes in London, our planes along with hundreds of others would be grounded when starved of fuel during the Middle East oil crisis, setting our lives on a new trajectory. Or, that a few years later I would be delivering our first child back in Sydney; five years after that our second.

Oblivious to what the future might have in store for me; I took one final look at my reflection. I smiled at how well the neckerchief I wore matched the paisley tie on the man sitting next to me. It was 1973. I was eighteen years old. Together, we were about to plunge into "the most exciting city in the world".

Author's Note and Acknowledgements

The decision to pursue creative writing began after my retirement from the corporate world. Researching the lives of my ancestors launched the idea of writing a memoir about the childhood dilemma of escaping preordained fates to make one's own choices, even if those choices defied expectations or traditions. Numerous life events delayed the completion of this project, including births, deaths, marriages, health issues and cyclones, in addition to requiring a dramatic shift from a business writing style to a creative one.

My first short stories centred around the often-humorous events of my siblings and me growing up as immigrants in Australia. At the invitation of ABC radio, I enjoyed reading some of those during their afternoon broadcasts and I thank them for the opportunity. Thank you also to Queensland Writers Centre for the expertise and encouragement they provide to new writers and for choosing a short story of mine for an annual print anthology edition. My writing buddies at Ruff Writers deserve a warm mention for their endless advice and editing help.

I will be eternally grateful to my parents and siblings, without whom my life would have been empty and there would be no stories to share.

Both parents never wavered from supporting their children, no matter the circumstances. They both lived longer than expected: Dad to the age of eighty and Mum to ninety-four. I was extra privileged to live near Mum for the last years of her life. We became remarkably close, spending endless hours gossiping and laughing together. For my siblings, the bonds developed during childhood remain strong to this day; having shared the closeness of a large family, never being without a playmate, and knowing throughout the years there was always someone to lend an ear.

Thank you to all the people who encouraged me to write this memoir then harangued me until I finished it. You know who you are. Thank you to Alan Watt, Founder and Creative Director of AlanWatt.com for encouraging me to stop wandering in the desert of self-doubt and confusion about how to get my story on the page, by teaching me the process of marrying the wildness of my imagination to the rigor of structure. Thank you to my publisher Ark House Press for their vision and belief in this project with a special thank you to the design team for their guidance, support, and contributions to the book's cover, graphics, and layout.

www.ingramcontent.com/pod-product-compliance
Lightning Source LLC
Chambersburg PA
CBHW021217090426
42740CB00006B/258